The sixth report 1996 - 1997

social attitudes

in Northern Ireland

The sixth report 1996 - 1997

social attitudes

in Northern Ireland

Edited by

LIZANNE DOWDS

PAULA DEVINE

RICHARD BREEN

APPLETREE PRESS

First published by
The Appletree Press Ltd
19-21 Alfred Street
Belfast BT2 8DL
1997

Index compiled by Helen Litton.

A catalogue record for this book is available from the British Library.

ISBN 0-86281-637-8

Printed in Ireland

Contents

The Contributors

Richard Breen
Professor of Sociology and Director of the Centre for Social Research, The Queen's University of Belfast

Iain Bryson
Research Associate, Centre for Social Research, The Queen's University of Belfast

Paula Devine
Research Fellow, Centre for Social Research, The Queen's University of Belfast

Lizanne Dowds
Research Fellow, Centre for Social Research, The Queen's University of Belfast

Mary Duffy
Research student, Nuffield College, Oxford

Geoffrey Evans
Research Fellow, Nuffield College, Oxford

Tony Gallagher
Reader in Education, The Queen's University of Belfast

Bernadette C. Hayes
Reader, Department of Sociology and Social Policy, The Queen's University of Belfast

Norma Heaton
Lecturer in Human Resource Management, University of Ulster

Edgar F. Jardine
Chief Executive, Northern Ireland Statistics and Research Agency

Ian McAllister
Professor, Department of Government, University of Manchester

Alan McClelland
Survey Manager, Central Survey Unit, Northern Ireland Statistics and Research Agency

Marina Monteith
Research Officer, Centre for Child Care Research

John Pinkerton
Senior Research Fellow, Centre for Child Care Research

Gillian Robinson
Lecturer, Department of Social Administration and Policy, University of Ulster

Rick Wilford
Senior Lecturer in Politics, The Queen's University of Belfast

Introduction

Lizanne Dowds, Paula Devine and Richard Breen

Seven years and six published volumes after its inception, the Northern Ireland Social Attitudes Survey (NISA) has by now established itself as the major attitudinal time-series in Northern Ireland. As a measure of how we see ourselves, our beliefs and the development of our social values, the survey provides us with a unique record of Northern Ireland in the last part of the 20th century. That the survey has achieved its major aim is not in doubt - all that remains now is to disseminate the results as widely as possible and allow the greatest possible access to the data. This, the sixth volume, continues the tradition whereby academics provide a 'snapshot' of our attitudes, beliefs and values on a diverse range of social issues; what we *hope* it will also encourage is for students, journalists, lobbyists, pressure groups, government and schoolchildren to delve further into what is a unique resource for all of us. If we want to learn anything about social attitudes in Northern Ireland, this is the place to start.

The survey is constructed with a 'modular' format, so that although some 'core' modules (such as the one on community relations) are asked every year, other modules are only included every two or three years as thought necessary. Appendix 2 gives details of what has been included each year since 1989 and provides a rough guide for those wishing to use the data. Copies of the survey datasets are available from the Data Archive at the University of Essex.

Because of its link with its sister survey 'British Social Attitudes', NISA routinely provides comparative as well as time-series data. All the modules that are included in NISA in any one year (with the exception of the community relations questions) are also asked in Great Britain. As usual, many of the authors in this volume have drawn comparisons with Britain to assess how far we, in Northern Ireland, have a unique view on certain social issues. The scope for comparison is further extended by the

inclusion of a module that is fielded simultaneously in over 20 countries across four continents. This is done under the auspices of the International Social Survey Programme (ISSP). In 1994 it dealt with changing gender roles, in 1995 it covered beliefs about national identity and in 1996 it explored the role of government. The ISSP data is probably the most under-used aspect of NISA, though those who have explored attitudes in Northern Ireland compared with say, those in the United States and the Republic of Ireland have certainly unearthed some intriguing results.

Acknowledgements

That the survey exists at all is thanks to the efforts of Social and Community Planning Research (SCPR), who agreed to extend the British Social Attitudes survey to Northern Ireland and who have largely directed operations ever since. The Central Community Relations Unit (CCRU) and the Nuffield Foundation provided the initial financial support, soon joined by all the government departments in Northern Ireland. The survey owes a particular debt of gratitude to CCRU for its unswerving support over the last seven years. The survey fieldwork is carried out by the Central Survey Unit within the Northern Ireland Statistics and Research Agency (NISRA), though final responsibility for the form and content of the survey rests with SCPR, who also undertake the necessary coding and data preparation. The Economic and Social Research Institute (ESRI) in Dublin were kind enough to supply some ISSP data from the Republic of Ireland for inclusion in this volume, and we are very grateful to them.

At the Centre for Social Research, Lois McCammond did a superb job converting draft chapters into camera-ready copy format, though the responsibility for any errors that were overlooked must remain with the editors. We would also like to thank the authors who produced their drafts in the face of unreasonable deadlines and cheerfully tolerated our interference with their texts. Finally we would like to thank the people of Northern Ireland who took part in the survey and without whose help we would have no data to analyse.

1

Attitudes to Education in Britain and Northern Ireland

Tony Gallagher

Introduction

There is a popular myth among educators that most parents prefer to send their boys to mixed-sex schools and their girls to single-sex schools (Smithers and Robinson, 1995). This is explained as being due to the supposed civilising effect of mixed-sex schools on boys, and the educational benefits for girls of single-sex schools. That this is a myth, however, is revealed by the results of the 1995 Northern Ireland Social Attitudes (NISA) survey. Almost three quarters of our respondents say that they would advise an 11-year-old boy or girl to go to a mixed-sex school. Educational advantage is the reason put forward by the minority who prefer single-sex schooling, for either sex. However, the majority who prefer mixed-sex schools say this is because boys and girls should learn to mix together. Interestingly, this pattern among Northern Ireland respondents mirrors almost exactly the pattern found among respondents in Britain, despite the fact that Northern Ireland has a much higher extent of single-sex schooling.

Previous reports on the Northern Ireland survey have included one chapter on attitudes to educational issues (Osborne, 1995). Osborne examined views in Northern Ireland on a range of issues, including selective and comprehensive schools, nursery schools and higher education. The present chapter differs in that it compares attitudes to educational issues in Northern Ireland and Britain. The most recent report on education in the British survey can be found in Halsey and Lievesley (1994). The

discussion in this chapter is organised around two main themes. The first, and main, part of the chapter looks at views on primary and secondary schools, not least because this part of the school system has undergone a series of radical reforms and changes since the latter part of the 1980s (DENI, 1996). Our survey provides an opportunity to examine views on some aspects of these reforms. The second main area examined in the chapter concerns attitudes to higher education. There has been a marked increase in participation rates in higher education, with more young people now attending university than at any time in the past. Two issues in particular have arisen from this situation. Firstly, how is the expansion of higher education to be paid for? Should the state continue to pay fees and maintenance grants to students, as in the past, or is there a case for increasing the personal cost of higher education, perhaps through a loans system? Secondly, given that the conversion of the old polytechnic colleges into 'new' universities has at least doubled the number of institutions from which eligible young people have to choose, is there a case for more public information on higher education in order to inform choice? We begin by looking at attitudes to primary and secondary education.

Primary and Secondary Schools
One way of comparing attitudes to education in Northern Ireland and Britain is to compare the priorities attached to education in both areas. A number of questions in our survey addressed this issue. The first question asked people to identify, from a list, which *two* areas of education should receive priority for extra government spending. Table 1 illustrates the responses, firstly in terms of our respondents' highest priority, and then for the wider range of measures identified as either the first or second priority.

A number of interesting differences emerge even at this early stage. We can see that while the main priority area for our Northern Ireland respondents is less able pupils with special needs, the main priority for the British respondents is for extra spending on secondary and grammar schools. A further difference lies in the slightly higher proportion of British respondents who placed nursery and pre-school children as their

main priority. This is interesting because of the relatively lesser provision of nursery places in Northern Ireland generally.

Table 1

Views on priorities for extra spending on education (%)

First priority for extra government spending on education...

	Northern Ireland	Great Britain
...nursery or pre-school children	15	21
...primary school children	18	18
...secondary and grammar school children	20	32
...less able children with special needs	31	19
...students at colleges and universities	14	9

First or second priority for extra government spending on education...

	Northern Ireland	Great Britain
...nursery or pre-school children	29	31
...primary school children	40	43
...secondary and grammar school children	44	52
...less able children with special needs	56	45
...students at colleges and universities	28	24

Table 1 also shows the proportions who mentioned a category as either their first or their second priority. At this level of response there are fewer differences between our two samples. For both sets of respondents the three main priority areas concern primary, secondary and grammar pupils, and less able pupils with special needs. Smaller proportions in both cases identified nursery and pre-school children, or students at university or college, within their first two priorities for extra spending.

In practice, of course, recent years have seen a wave of reform measures all promoted by the government with the objective of improving the effectiveness of schools. These measures contain a diversity of elements, but essentially they embody the application of market principles to education. The reforms changed past practice which was claimed to have placed too much power in the hands of educational providers, that is, schools and local authorities, and too little power in the hands of educational consumers, that is, parents and pupils. The reform measures attempt to reverse this power relationship by giving parents more freedom in choosing schools for their children and by informing this choice through the provision of more information on school performance. A further dimension of the reforms is to devolve more administrative and financial responsibility to schools, and away from local authorities, in order that schools can orient their activity to compete for pupils in the educational market.

What do our respondents feel about these issues? We asked a series of questions about measures to improve education in schools. Separate questions were asked for primary schools, and secondary and grammar schools. Table 2 shows what our respondents felt would improve the education of children in primary schools.

Table 2
What would improve the education of children in primary schools...(%)

First or second most useful measure	Northern Ireland	Great Britain
...more information on individual schools	3	2
...more links between parents and schools	23	20
...more resources for buildings, books and equipment	38	46
...better quality teachers	22	29
...smaller class sizes	68	57
...more emphasis on exams and tests	7	5
...more emphasis on developing the child's skills and interests	37	37

The most striking result here is that a majority of respondents in Northern Ireland and Britain feel that smaller class sizes would be the first or second measure best designed to improve the education of primary school children. Indeed, when we focus on the measure placed as first priority for school improvement we find that over twice as many identified smaller class sizes as compared with any other item on the list. This has been an issue of some debate in Britain, with some arguing that smaller class sizes would help to improve education, particularly in the early years of primary school, while others, including the Office for the Inspection of Schools and the government, have argued that the quality of teaching is more important than class size. The National Commission for Education (1993) argued the case for smaller class sizes in primary schools, at least in part on the intuitive basis that smaller classes must make it easier for teachers to teach. The evidence of our survey suggests that most people agree with this.

Thereafter, about two in five say that extra spending on education should go towards more resources for schools, a little over a third suggest that it should be spent on placing more emphasis on developing the child's skills and interests and about a quarter say that better quality teachers, or more links between parents and schools, would best improve the education of primary school children. Given the thrust of government reforms of education, with their emphasis on outputs and information, it is perhaps equally striking that such a small minority of our respondents, in both surveys, opt for more emphasis on examinations and qualifications, or for more information on individual schools.

In Table 3 we turn to our respondents' views on the measures which they feel would best improve the education of children in grammar and secondary schools. Here we find less consensus than was the case for judgements on primary schools, with four measures being mentioned by between a third and two fifths of the sample. These included more resources for buildings, books and equipment, more training and preparation for jobs, smaller class sizes and more emphasis on developing children's skills and interests. Despite the fact that, among these, no single measure commands a much higher level of support than any other, it is

noteworthy still that no great sympathy seems to exist for options directly related to education reform measures. Thus, while more say there should be greater emphasis on examinations and tests in grammar and secondary schools than for primary schools, this is still less than three in twenty of our respondents. Furthermore, only a very small minority say that more information on individual schools would help to improve the education of children.

Table 3
Which do you think would be the most useful for improving the education of children in secondary and grammar schools...(%)

First or second most useful measure	Northern Ireland	Great Britain
...more information on individual schools	4	2
...more links between parents and schools	17	10
...more resources for buildings, books and equipment	40	38
...better quality teachers	20	29
...smaller class sizes	34	35
...more emphasis on examinations and tests	13	15
...more emphasis on developing child's skills and interests	36	30
...more training and preparation for jobs	33	36

The main conclusion we might draw from this part of our survey evidence is that few appear to be convinced of the efficacy of some of the main strategic approaches adopted for education reform over recent years. Indeed, the most common factor across the options chosen by our respondents in both surveys and for both parts of the education system, is the perceived need for more resources to be directed into schools. In view of some of the points to be discussed below it is perhaps noteworthy that our respondents in Britain were slightly more likely than those in Northern Ireland to choose better quality teachers as the most useful measure to improve education.

If there appears to be a general consensus in the British and Northern Irish surveys in regard to what needs to be done in education, does the same consensus exist when respondents are asked about the point and purpose of education? A series of questions addressed this issue.

Table 4

If you were advising a 16-year-old about their future would you say they should...(%)

	Northern Ireland	Great Britain
...stay in full-time education to get GCE 'A' levels	63	53
...study full-time to get vocational qualifications	12	12
...leave school and get training through a job	6	12
...varies/depends on the person	18	22

We first asked how our respondents would advise a 16-year-old. As we can see from Table 4 hardly anyone on our survey would advise a young person to leave school to seek training through employment. Only a small proportion say that they would advise a young person to study full-time for vocational qualifications, while over half our sample in Britain, and almost two thirds of our sample in Northern Ireland, would advise a young person to stay in full-time education to work towards GCE 'A' levels. This pattern may reflect a broader perception in the United Kingdom that GCE 'A' levels represent the 'gold standard' of the education system. This is despite the views of some educationalists that a more broadly based qualification, such as Scottish Highers or the Baccalaureate, would be preferable to the specialisation involved in 'A' levels. More generally the results may also reflect the relatively lower status accorded to vocational qualifications in the UK, a situation which has been described as contributing to the UK's poorer competitiveness internationally (Prais and Wagner, 1995) and which has prompted discussions on ways of strengthening the standing of vocational education.

The lower standing of vocational qualifications, in comparison with GCE 'A' levels, is even more striking when we consider the responses to

Table 5

In the long run what do you think gives people more opportunities and choice in life?...(%)

	Northern Ireland	Great Britain
...having good practical skills and training	35	43
...having good academic results	41	32
...mixture/depends	24	25

our next question, as can be seen from Table 5. This time we asked our respondents whether they felt that practical skills and training or good academic results gave people more opportunities and choice in life. The most striking feature here is that neither of these two options predominates over the other, in terms of respondents' choices. Not surprisingly, responses here are linked to the previous question. The minority who would advise a young person to stay in full-time education to take vocational rather than academic qualifications, or to leave school and get training through employment, was also more likely to point to good practical skills and training as useful for life, rather than good academic qualifications.

There is a difference between our two samples in that the highest proportion of our respondents in Northern Ireland chose good academic results, whereas the highest proportion of respondents on the British survey chose good practical skills and training. The privileging of the academic was noted in the previous NISA report on education (Osborne, 1985). Osborne identified a religious difference in his Northern Ireland sample in that Catholics were somewhat more likely than Protestants to highlight the importance of academic values. Osborne suggested this might arise from a perception that discrimination may have limited job opportunities for Catholics in the past and hence academic qualifications may have provided one way of overcoming this barrier. Our comparison between responses in

Northern Ireland and Great Britain allows for the examination of another possibility, that is, that schools and the education system generally are held in higher regard in Northern Ireland than in Britain.

We explored this by asking our respondents two sets of questions. The first set of questions asked for their views on how well schools prepared children for jobs, taught them basic skills and brought out their natural abilities. The second set of questions asked for our respondents' views on how better or worse schools were now, in comparison with ten years ago, covering a range of issues. Table 6 shows us the pattern of responses to the first set of questions and highlights different perceptions of schools on either side of the Irish Sea. While over four in five in Northern Ireland say that schools teach basic skills well, this is so for only three in five in Britain. Even more striking is the difference in response to the other two questions. A majority in Northern Ireland say that schools do a good job in preparing young people for work and in bringing out their natural abilities, whereas in the British sample a majority say that schools do not do these objectives well.

Table 6
How well do you think state secondary and grammar schools...(%)

	Northern Ireland		Great Britain	
	well	not well	well	not well
...prepare young people for work	62	36	40	56
...teach young people basic skills such as reading, writing and maths	84	15	60	36
...bring out young people's natural abilities	56	43	42	54

Turning to the next set of questions, where we asked our respondents to compare schools nowadays with ten years ago, we find a similar pattern emerging, as we can see from Table 7. Thus, whereas two thirds of our Northern Ireland respondents say that school leavers are better qualified now in comparison with ten years ago, this is so for less than two in five

respondents in Britain. Indeed, over a quarter of the British respondents, but only a little over a tenth of Northern Ireland respondents, say that school leavers have lower qualifications than ten years ago. The pattern is confirmed also in the responses to our question on perceptions of the standard of teaching. Here we find that while four in ten people in Britain feel that the standard of teaching is worse now than ten years ago, nearly four in ten in Northern Ireland think that the standard of teaching is better. Indeed, while twice as many respondents in Northern Ireland as in Britain

Table 7

Opinion of state secondary and grammar schools, compared with ten years ago...(%)

	Northern Ireland	Great Britain
School leavers are better qualified	67	38
About the same	20	30
School leavers are worse qualified	13	28
Teachers are better paid	57	42
About the same	27	31
Teachers are worse paid	15	23
Classroom behaviour is better	6	4
About the same	13	16
Classroom behaviour is worse	79	76
The standard of teaching is better	37	18
About the same	40	38
The standard of teaching is worse	22	40

say that the standard of teaching now is better, twice as many in Britain as in Northern Ireland say the standard of teaching is worse now than ten years ago. Although it perhaps does not tell us directly about the perceived status of teachers, we can see from Table 7 that more of our Northern Ireland respondents than our British ones felt that teachers are better paid now than in the past.

The one area where there is widespread agreement between our two samples lies in their perceptions of classroom behaviour: over three quarters of both groups say that classroom behaviour is worse now than ten years ago. The most striking aspect of responses to this question, however, is that while it might be interpreted as part of a more general malaise evident in perceptions of schools and education in Britain, this is clearly not the case in Northern Ireland. Here a perception that classroom behaviour is worse now than ten years ago is held *despite* the more general perception that schools are doing better for young people. Indeed this difference in perception of the general state of education is the most striking conclusion to emerge from this first part of our analysis of the NISA and BSA surveys. What is even more intriguing is that these alternate judgements exist despite the fact that the aggregate level of performance of schools in different parts of the United Kingdom, as measured by examination results, is not that different.

This can be seen from Table 8 which shows data on the National Foundation Targets for education and training. Furthermore, international

Table 8

National Foundation Targets for education and training

	1993	1994	1995
Proportion of young people with NVQ level 2 or equivalent			
England	61	64	64
Wales	58	61	56
Scotland	70	70	70
Northern Ireland	63	67	69
Proportion of young people with NVQ level 3 or equivalent			
England	37	40	44
Wales	32	39	39
Scotland	49	50	51
Northern Ireland	34	40	37

Source: DFEE (1996): Table 32

comparisons suggest that all parts of the United Kingdom are performing at a lower level than many other OECD countries. For example, it has been shown that the proportion of 16-year-olds reaching the equivalent of GCSE qualifications at grades A-C in a range of subjects including mathematics, the national language and one science is 27 per cent in England and 22 per cent in Northern Ireland. By contrast, the proportion of 16-year-olds achieving this basket of qualifications is 62 per cent in Germany, 66 per cent in France and 50 per cent in Japan (NIEC, 1995).

So for this part of our analysis, while the survey evidence suggests a generally positive perception of schools in Northern Ireland, it suggests a generally more negative perception of schools in Britain. However, these perceptions do not appear to be explained by the actual performance of the schools in both places. It may be that the more traditional structure of grammar and secondary schools in Northern Ireland inspires more confidence than the range of comprehensive systems operating in most parts of Britain, despite their similar aggregate performance levels (although see Benn and Chitty, 1996). Alternatively, it may be that education has been more of a 'political football' in Britain: if all the main political parties appear to talk constantly about ways of improving education and dealing with 'failing schools', then perhaps this fuels a public perception that all is not well in the system, despite the statistical evidence of steadily improving examinations results. By contrast, the same rhetoric of failure is much less evident in Northern Ireland and, in any case, local politicians generally concern themselves with matters other than the educational. This different climate, allied with similar patterns of examination statistics, may have produced a more positive public judgement on the schools system.

Attitudes to Higher Education

As we noted above, there has been in recent years a marked increase in the number of young people going to university. We asked our sample whether they felt the current level of participation in higher education was too high, too low or about right. In the Northern Ireland and British samples about a half say that the current level of participation is about right, while a very slightly smaller proportion say that the number of young

people going to university should actually be increased. Only a very small minority in both cases suggest that the number going to university should be decreased.

If it is clear that our sample see the expansion of higher education as worthwhile, what do they see as the main point of a university education? We explored this by asking two questions. Firstly, we asked what qualities they felt universities *should* develop in young people, and secondly, we asked what qualities they felt universities *did* develop. In both cases we asked our respondents to identify the two most important qualities from an offered list. The answers to these questions are illustrated in Table 9.

Table 9

The qualities universities should develop in their students and the qualities they do develop by region...(%)

	qualities universities should develop		qualities universities do develop	
	NI	GB	NI	GB
...skills and knowledge for a good job	60	58	42	44
...knowledge to equip them for life in general	55	52	28	17
...self-confidence	30	28	30	32
...how to live with people from different backgrounds	18	9	19	23
...readiness to challenge ideas	8	12	29	28
...ability to speak and write clearly	8	16	20	18

The responses show that our respondents rated utilitarian considerations as the most important quality that should be, and in fact is, developed by universities in their students. This would appear to confirm qualitative evidence found by Gallagher et al. (1996) in a study of the views of parents of 'A' level pupils in Northern Ireland on higher education. While many of the parents interviewed for the study recognised the social benefits to be derived from a university education, by far the most important reason they

gave for going to university was the employment opportunities it created. However, a university degree was seen not so much to provide a labour market advantage, but as an essential if young people wanted to obtain worthwhile jobs.

In the present survey our respondents accord a significant place also to personal social skills. Interestingly, only a minority of our respondents in both places mention critical reasoning as an important quality to be developed at university. There is something of a mismatch between the aspiration and the perceived reality, in that there is clearly a greater consensus on what ought to be done, as opposed to what is actually done, within the universities. It is particularly interesting to note that a higher proportion of our respondents say that universities do develop critical qualities in their students than say they should do this. Also, for the British sample, far more say that universities do encourage people to learn to live with others from different backgrounds than say this is what universities should be doing. On this last point it is also worth noting that this particular quality is rated as being a little more important by our Northern Ireland respondents than by our British respondents.

We next asked our respondents a series of questions to explore their assessment of the value of a university education. As with their views on primary and secondary schools discussed above, we asked our respondents whether they felt universities were doing better, worse or about the same as ten years ago on a number of dimensions. The responses are shown on Table 10.

In a number of interesting ways a comparison of the judgements offered by our respondents in Northern Ireland and Britain mirror the pattern that was found above for judgements on primary and secondary schools. Specifically, while the clear majority of our respondents say that the standard of qualifications of students leaving university and the standard of teaching within universities is the same or better than ten years ago, our respondents in Northern Ireland offer a generally more positive judgement on both criteria. However, this positive picture exists despite agreement from both groups that the job prospects of students are very much worse now than was the case ten years ago. There is no evidence from these

surveys to suggest that responsibility for the poorer job prospects seen to be facing graduates is perceived as the fault of the universities.

Table 10

In comparison with ten years ago, in universities and colleges...(%)

	Northern Ireland	Great Britain
...the qualifications of students leaving are		
better	54	34
about the same	38	49
worse	6	13
...the standard of teaching is		
better	42	25
about the same	48	56
worse	8	14
...the job prospects of students are		
better	15	8
about the same	29	24
worse	70	72

We have seen above that a key feature of the reform of schools was the greater provision of information to prospective parents and their children on school performance. In a similar vein, more information has been published in recent years on the performance measures of universities. We asked our respondents whether they felt it was essential, important or not important to have information on three different areas. A common pattern of response emerged from both our samples. About three in five felt that it was important to have access to the three types of information we identified, but there was a difference in emphasis that reflected both the utilitarian priority and the employment concern identified above. Thus, while only about one in ten say that it is essential to have information on the number of students receiving first class degrees, and about one in six

say it is essential to know the number of students who complete their degrees, a little over one in four say it is essential to have information on the number of students getting jobs when they complete their studies.

The final area we asked about concerned money. Specifically, the expansion of higher education has raised questions about who should pay the costs. Traditionally the United Kingdom has had a comparatively generous system of support such that students accepted for university places do not have to pay fees for their courses and have had access to means-tested grants. In recent years the personal cost of higher education has increased as the grant element of student income has been effectively frozen and a student loan element is increasing in importance. The current aim is that student income will be split equally between grant and loan elements. Notwithstanding these existing arrangements, financial cut-backs on the universities provoked the Committee of Vice-Chancellors and Principals (CVCP) to threaten levying top-up fees to students. Although the political parties in Britain appear to be a little reluctant to lay out detailed plans for the payment of fees and loan arrangements prior to the general election, there seems to be little doubt that the personal cost of higher education will continue to rise in the future.

We asked our sample three questions related to student finance. Firstly, we asked whether students should continue to get their course fees paid by their local education and library board (or local education authority in Britain), or should they contribute something towards the cost of fees. We find that only 24 per cent in Britain and 15 per cent in Northern Ireland say that students should contribute towards the cost of their fees. The second question dealt with student loans. While many students are now taking out loans, which they must repay when they start working, we asked whether our respondents felt, generally speaking, that students should or should not be expected to take out loans. The pattern of response is almost identical to that above in that only 26 per cent in Britain and 18 per cent in Northern Ireland say that students should be expected to take out loans. By contrast, almost two thirds of the British respondents and three quarters of the Northern Ireland respondents say that students should not be expected to take out loans.

The third and final question in this section asked about the provision of student grants to cover living expenses. Hardly any of our respondents, in both groups, say that students should not receive grants. However, there is a slight difference in emphasis between our two samples. Most of the respondents in both groups say that *some* students should get grants, but a somewhat higher proportion of the Northern Ireland (41 per cent) than the British (30 per cent) sample say that *all* students should get a grant to cover living expenses.

The general conclusion is, however, clear. A solid majority of the respondents in both samples say that some or all students should get grants, they should not have to take out loans and they should not have to contribute towards the cost of their fees. The conundrum, however, is that, as we saw at the beginning of this chapter, our respondents also place students in universities and colleges as the lowest priority for extra spending on education.

Conclusions

This chapter compares attitudes in Britain and Northern Ireland to a range of education issues. The first section of the chapter examines issues related to primary and secondary education, while the second looks at views on a range of issues related to higher education. In the first part of our discussion perhaps the most interesting theme to emerge is the generally more positive light in which the schools system is held in Northern Ireland, as compared with views in Britain. Not only is this evident in a number of direct questions, but it can be seen also in our respondents' identified priorities for education spending: respondents in Britain see a need for extra resources to be spent on primary and secondary school pupils, while respondents in Northern Ireland identify pupils with special educational needs as the main priority. This difference in perception does not appear to be explained by different levels of educational performance in Britain and Northern Ireland. It may be that the more traditional system of grammar and secondary schools in Northern Ireland inspires more public confidence, or alternatively it may simply reflect the greater extent to which educational standards are a focus for intense political debate in Britain.

Regardless of the reasons for different perceptions of schools, there is a consensus among respondents in Britain and Northern Ireland on future needs. Our survey shows little support for the type of measures that have played a key strategic role in educational reforms in recent years. By contrast, most respondents to our survey say that more resources would provide the best means of promoting school improvement.

Higher education has undergone significant changes in recent years and we examine views on some of these changes in the second part of our chapter. On these issues there is a wider level of agreement between respondents in Britain and Northern Ireland. We find that most respondents agree with the increase in the number of student places in higher education and feel that universities generally are doing reasonably well for their students. However, there is a strongly held view that the job prospects for graduates are worse now than in the past. The importance attached to this can be seen also in the strongly utilitarian view that emerges with regard to what people feel universities ought to offer their students.

The expansion in university places in the United Kingdom has been accompanied by changes to the arrangements for student income, with a reduction in the level of grant, an increase in the proportion of student income derived from loans and the possibility of students being asked to contribute towards the cost of their course fees. Our respondents are clearly opposed to those changes: the consensus emerging from the survey is that students should not have to contribute to the cost of course fees, should not be obliged to take out student loans and should be entitled to student grants. The difficulty, however, is that despite these aspirations, our respondents do not place the needs of students in universities and colleges as a high priority for additional spending when set alongside other educational needs.

References

BENN, C. and CHITTY, C. 1996. *Thirty Years On,* London, David Fulton.
DENI. 1996. *Strategic plan for education 1996-2000,* Bangor, Department for Education in Northern Ireland.

DFEE. 1996. *Education statistics for the United Kingdom, 1995,* London, HMSO.

GALLAGHER, A. M., CORMACK, R. J. and OSBORNE, R. D. 1996. *Attitudes to higher education,* Report No.1 from the Centre for Research on Higher Education, Northern Ireland, The Queen's University of Belfast/ University of Ulster.

HALSEY, A. H. and LIEVESLEY, D. 1994. 'Education: reaction to reform', in R. Jowell, J. Curtice, L. Brook, and D. Ahrendt (eds.) *British Social Attitudes: the 11th Report,* Aldershot, Dartmouth.

NATIONAL COMMISSION FOR EDUCATION. 1993. *Learning to succeed: a radical look at education today and a strategy for the future,* London, Heinemann.

NIEC. 1995. *Reforming the education system in Northern Ireland,* Belfast, Northern Ireland Economic Council.

OSBORNE, R.D. 1995. 'Social attitudes in Northern Ireland: education', in R. Breen, P. Devine and G. Robinson (eds.), *Social Attitudes in Northern Ireland: the Fourth Report,* Belfast, Appletree Press.

PRAIS, S.J. and WAGNER, K. 1995. 'Schooling standards in England and Germany: some summary comparical bearing on economic perform- ance', in D. Phillips (ed.), *Education in Germany: tradition and reform in historical context,* London, Routledge.

SMITHERS, A. and ROBINSON, P. 1995. *Co-educational and single-sex schooling,* Manchester, Centre for Employment Research, University of Manchester.

2

Attitudes to the Welfare System

Rick Wilford

Introduction

Between 1993 and 1995 the debate about the affordability of welfare spending accelerated. One effect of this debate was the burgeoning interest throughout Europe in the model of provision common among the 'tigers of the east', implying a readiness among policy makers to contemplate a shift towards a 'Japanised' or 'liberal' welfare regime (Jones, 1993). Such regimes are characterised by a heavy reliance on the market for education and health care; the cultural expectation that families will themselves cater for the needs of their elderly and infirm relatives; and a correspondingly low set of expectations about the state's role in supplying social protection for its citizens. Commonly, such regimes provide merely a residual system of support, especially for those who occupy a tenuous and peripheral role in the economy.

In the UK, the drift towards 'liberal' welfarism, or what Peter Lilley, the Secretary of State for Social Services, has described as the 'welfare society', is a token of the mounting fluidity in the pattern of social protection. Reform of the NHS, the stricter criteria applied to forms of income support and the development of 'care in the community' exemplify the continuing changes that have been wrought in the welfare state. These and other changes, together with the open rehearsal of alternative models, have contributed to uncertainty about the future of state welfare provision.

The 1995 Northern Ireland Social Attitudes (NISA) survey was undertaken during the first full year of the cessation of violence. While

few were complacent and some were gloomy, there did appear to be a glimmer of light at the end of the tunnel encouraging a mood of cautious optimism. In the event, following the bomb at Canary Wharf on 9 February 1996, the Jeremiahs rather than the Panglossians seemed to have their views justified. Yet, though fragile, the peace did inspire a 'feel-warm' factor that, among other things, rested on a set of attitudes concerning state welfare provision that previous surveys showed were both widely shared and strongly supported.

Although the third NISA survey revealed some evidence that 'the traditional conception of welfare citizenship [was] beginning to fray', the weight of cross-community opinion in Northern Ireland supported universalism as a leading principle of social provision, especially in relation to the NHS and education (Wilford, 1995: 15). Moreover, despite the fact that most people were worried more about a rise in prices than losing their jobs, the existence of a collective consciousness was apparent from the preference given to the reduction of unemployment rather than the reduction of inflation (Wilford, 1995). Thus, while among policy makers and watchers there was a mood of flux about the direction in which the welfare state was moving, within the general population the attachment to its underlying values was robust.

The current report provides the opportunity to assess whether that attachment has been sustained during a period notable for the absence of chronic political violence. In particular, the 1995 survey provides much information about the reception accorded to the effects of the reforms of the NHS, which has consistently emerged as the jewel in the crown of the UK's welfare system.

Getting and Spending

The relationship between the acquisition of public finance and its allocation to public services – what some style as the getting and spending equation (Pliatzsky, 1984; 1985) – lies at the heart of political debate. The demonstrable failure by successive Conservative Governments to both alleviate the burden of taxation and reduce public spending has not diminished its ambition to achieve these objectives. To date, as successive

NISA surveys have disclosed, this goal has run against the grain of public opinion. Is that still the case?

As Table 1 shows, attitudes in Northern Ireland towards the third option have moderated since 1993 and occupy an intermediate position between the opinions expressed in the two earlier surveys. While the gap between the *status quo* and the third option narrowed between 1993 and 1995, there

Table 1

Suppose the Government had to choose between the three options on this card. Which do you think it should choose? (%)

	1990		1993		1995	
	NI	GB	NI	GB	NI	GB
Reduce taxes and spend less on health education and social benefits.	6	3	5	4	7	5
Keep taxes and spending on these services at the same level as now.	42	37	33	29	38	31
Increase taxes and spend more on health, education and social benefits.	46	54	59	63	52	61

Table 2

Support for both increased taxation and welfare spending (%)

	1990	1993	1995
Social Class			
I	68	65	60
II	47	65	49
III (Non-manual)	52	57	52
III (Manual)	43	63	50
IV	41	51	57
V	52	60	53

is still a majority in favour of higher taxation and spending, although the level of support it secures continues to lag behind that in Britain.

The recent decline in overall support for increased taxation and spending as Table 2 indicates is, with one exception, reflected across all social classes. The growing burden of taxation between 1993 and the current survey do appear to have exerted a toll on attitudes: public opinion in 1995 is generally more like that in 1990 than in 1993. However, attitudes do diverge on both a religious and a partisan basis, as Table 3 demonstrates.

Table 3
Religious affiliation and attitudes to welfare spending (%)

	Catholic			Protestant		
	1990	1993	1995	1990	1993	1995
Reduce taxes and spending	6	5	5	7	4	8
Keep both the same as now	40	30	33	44	37	41
Increase taxes and spending	49	61	59	44	56	48

While successive NISA surveys reveal that Catholics have always been more disposed than Protestants to an increase in both taxes and welfare spending, the attitude gap between them on the third option is now at its widest at 11 percentage points. Protestant opinion, though not exactly split as it was in 1990, is much more divided between the second and third alternatives. This differential between the two religious communities is clearly reflected among party identifiers, as Table 4 shows.

Endorsement of increased taxation and welfare expenditure is lowest among unionist supporters and highest within the nationalist electorates, with Alliance identifiers occupying the median position. Unionist opinion is clearly sharply divided whereas SDLP and Sinn Fein voters favour the tax and spend option by a significant margin. Since 1990, the trend among nationalist voters has been for support to strengthen in favour of increased taxation and spending, whereas the unionist electorates have displayed a trendless fluctuation. The sharpest change in opinion has occurred among Alliance supporters. In both 1990 and 1993, they accorded the

Table 4

Party identity and attitudes to tax and spend options (%)

	Reduce taxes and spending	Keep the same as now	Increase taxes and spending
Ulster Unionist Party	8	48	43
Democratic Unionist Party	11	43	45
Alliance Party of Northern Ireland	6	33	59
Social Democratic and Labour Party	4	32	63
Sinn Fein	3	34	63

highest level of support (at 65 per cent and 75 per cent, respectively) to the third option, compounding the current pattern of diversity among electorates. After the convergence among partisans in 1993 in favour of increased taxation and welfare spending, Northern Ireland's voting blocs now exhibit a marked divergence of opinion, with unionist identifiers apparently succumbing to the Government's efforts to achieve financial rectitude in public finances.

Spending Priorities
As in previous years the NISA survey includes a range of questions designed to establish the preferred areas of government spending. Given the narrow overall majority in favour of both increased taxation and welfare expenditure (see Table 1), further results indicate the favoured beneficiaries of extra public spending. In previous surveys, health and education have dominated the public's wish list for increased expenditure and, as Table 5 indicates, this remains the case.

In both Northern Ireland and Great Britain, the health and education services retain pride of place as the preferred recipients of extra government spending. In fact, the level of support in Northern Ireland for

the NHS is at its highest since the NISA surveys began in 1989. Despite

Table 5

First priorities for extra government spending (%)

	Northern Ireland		Great Britain	
	1993	1995	1993	1995
Health	51	58	45	49
Education	16	23	27	32
Social Security	9	6	5	4
Housing	7	5	9	5
Roads	6	3	2	*
Help for Industry	7	3	6	4
Public Transportation	1	1	1	2
Overseas Aid	*	*	*	0
Police/Prisons	2	*	4	3
Defence	2	*	1	*

*Note: * indicates less than one per cent*

increases in real terms in health spending since 1979, the public continues to display an unsated appetite for this area of welfare expenditure. In Britain, though first order support for health spending is at a lower level, 77 per cent of the population rank it as either their first or second priority for extra resources, compared to 81 per cent in Northern Ireland. Moreover virtually two-thirds of the British population (65 per cent) and 60 per cent in the province opt for education as either their first or second choice for increased spending.

The lion's share preferred for these two services has the effect of dwarfing support for increases in expenditure on other spending programmes. All show a noticeable decline since 1993 which in some cases, notably help for industry, is noteworthy. Buoyed by the ceasefires, Northern Ireland appeared in 1995 to be on the verge of a period of

sustained economic regeneration. The two fora on the economy, one in Belfast presided over by John Major and the other in Washington DC hosted by President Clinton, seemed to herald a phase of increased investment in the economic infrastructure. Indeed in July the Government, in response to the Northern Ireland Affairs Select Committee's report on job creation (HMSO, 1995a), stated its agreement with the Committee that 'permanent ceasefires' could unlock enormous potential for employment in the province and 'attach[ed] great importance to helping the private sector ... to grasp the economic growth opportunities ahead' (HMSO, 1995b). The slippage of public support for government expenditure on industry may then rest on the changing belief that in the future private investment holds the key to increased prosperity and employment, despite the fact that Northern Ireland relies heavily on the public sector for jobs and incomes.

The fall in support for extra resources for the police and prisons seems more consistent with the mood of guarded optimism created by the ceasefires. Both informed and public opinion turned towards the prospective reform of the RUC, including a reduction in its establishment, and efforts to reduce the prison population, each of which would result in lower programmes of public spending. Similarly, the decline in support for housing expenditure may in part be explained by Northern Ireland's being spared the ravages of the collapse of the housing market which was occurring in Britain. Indeed, the fact that housing expenditure also slipped down the agenda of British public opinion does itself appear rather at odds with the upsurge in repossessions and the phenomenon of negative equity that was materialising there. That said, it may be plausible to contend that people do not perceive a link between any increase in the stock of public housing and the vagaries of the housing market. Nevertheless, in the context of a bleak property market, the finding that there was a concurrent growth of support for health and education spending is even more noteworthy.

The primacy of the health and education sectors demonstrates the durability of at least two of Beveridge's ambitions: the eradication of the 'giant evils' of 'disease' and 'ignorance'. The priority given to extra health spending is common to all partisans, although SDLP and Sinn Fein identifiers emerge as the strongest supporters of the NHS: 66 and 69 per

cent, respectively, accord it primary importance, compared to 61 per cent of UUP voters, 60 per cent of DUP voters and 54 per cent of Alliance supporters. The latter, at 30 per cent, are those most disposed to rank education as their first priority for increased spending, followed by UUP (24 per cent), SDLP (20 per cent), DUP (19 per cent) and Sinn Fein identifiers (13 per cent). The three remaining evils – 'squalor' (housing expenditure), 'want' (poverty) and 'idleness' (unemployment) – seem to have shrunk in stature as preferred targets of government expenditure.

Social Benefits

Extra spending on social security benefits emerges as a poor third in the priorities of Northern Ireland respondents. However, such benefits encompass a wide range of recipient groups and the survey indicates which are prioritised by the public. As Table 6 shows, the general population continues to harbour a clear preference for the retired as the most deserving of the candidates for extra social expenditure. Both the rank order of these

Table 6
Which of these social benefits would be your highest priority for extra social spending? (%)

	1989	1990	1993	1995
Retirement pension	43	39	40	41
Disability benefits	25	22	22	27
Unemployment benefits	14	13	16	14
Child benefits	12	19	15	13
Single parent benefits	6	7	7	5

priorities and their respective levels of support have remained remarkably uniform over the period, reflecting a stable set of attitudes. Catholics and Protestants share the above ranking, although currently the former accord pensions a lower level of support (35 per cent) than the latter (45 per cent). Catholics are also significantly more likely to endorse extra spending on both child benefits (17 per cent) and unemployment benefits (18 per cent) than Protestants (10 per cent and 11 per cent respectively), perhaps

reflecting both larger family size and a higher incidence of unemployment. Where the religious communities converge are in relation to disability and single parent benefits. Among Catholics the former secures the support of one in four (26 per cent) and the latter just five per cent for increased spending, figures that are almost exactly matched by Protestants, 28 per cent of whom favour more spending on the disabled and five per cent on single parent benefits.

Starker differences, as Table 7 shows, are apparent among party identifiers.   During a year in which several Government Ministers

Table 7

Social benefit priorities of party identifiers (%)					
	UUP	**DUP**	**APNI**	**SDLP**	**SF**
Retirement pension	50	41	52	32	18
Disability benefits	30	29	31	24	18
Unemployment benefits	6	17	7	22	38
Child benefit	9	12	6	17	13
Single parent benefits	3	2	3	4	13

expressed openly their reluctance to dip into the public purse to reward what they regarded as irresponsible, even promiscuous, behaviour by young unmarried mothers, it is perhaps unsurprising in the morally conservative climate of Northern Ireland that single parents languish at the foot of the benefit league table. By contrast, pensioners continue to enjoy most favoured status, especially among unionists who, as Protestants, have an older age structure than Catholics. SDLP and Sinn Fein voters are, on the other hand, significantly more likely to support extra spending on the unemployed, perhaps reflecting their position in the labour market, while the disabled emerge as the second priority among all party identifiers, albeit at varying levels of support. Indeed, since 1993 the proportions of partisans favouring the disabled as the first priority for extra spending has, with the exception of SDLP voters, increased.

Further items throw more light on these rather simple wish-lists. A more closely focused question (see Table 8) invited respondents to specify the scale of increase they favoured for each of a number of social benefits. To lend realism to their views, respondents were advised that any increase in spending was likely to mean an increase in the taxes they would have to pay, while any decrease would make a reduction in their tax bill more likely.

Table 8
Preferred levels of spending on social benefits (%)

	Much More	More	Same as Now	Less	Much Less
Pensions	26	51	18	2	*
Disability	22	53	21	*	0
Unemployment	9	31	37	12	4
Benefits for working parents on low incomes	18	57	21	*	0
Single parent	9	31	41	10	5

Note: * indicates less than one per cent.

These results suggest a readiness within the population to support those regarded as the deserving poor – pensioners, the disabled and the working poor with children – even at the cost of increased taxes. However, there is significantly less support available for the unemployed and single parents who are perceived as much less deserving cases, despite the fact that the incidence of poverty is pronounced within single parent families, especially those that are female-headed. However, this broad pattern is heavily structured by religion. Catholics are twice as likely (56 per cent) to favour increased spending on single parent benefit than Protestants (28 per cent) and are much more reluctant to endorse a reduction in this benefit (six per cent) than Protestants (20 per cent). Similarly, more than half of Catholics (56 per cent), compared to less than one-third of Protestants (31 per cent), are prepared to shoulder a heavier tax burden in order to spend more on the unemployed, whereas 22 per cent of the latter and just eight per cent of

Catholics favour a reduction in their tax bills at the expense of benefits for the unemployed.

Protestants also adopt less supportive attitudes to the working poor with children. While 85 per cent of Catholics express a willingness to pay more in tax to increase their benefits, this view is shared by 68 per cent of Protestants. If preparedness to bear a (notional) loss of disposable income to support the less well-off is a measure of collective sentiment, Catholics in Northern Ireland emerge as more richly endowed with such feelings. They are also more disposed to increase spending on the elderly (81 per cent) and the disabled (82 per cent) than Protestants (79 per cent and 70 per cent, respectively), even though it would entail a hike in taxation.

As Table 9 indicates, the religious division is mirrored among party identifiers. Though electorates tend to converge in favour of pensioners

Table 9
Willingness of partisans to pay more in tax to aid benefit dependants (%)

	UUP	DUP	APNI	SDLP	SF
Pensioners	78	73	85	78	73
Disabled	71	73	77	83	73
Unemployed	24	30	37	61	71
Benefits for working parents on low incomes	64	66	79	87	83
Single parents	23	21	53	57	44

and the disabled, they clearly diverge in relation to single parents and, most significantly, the unemployed. Moreover, while the employed poor with children might be hypothesised to strike a chord among stereotypically industrious and thrifty unionists who subscribe to the Protestant work ethic, they in fact also elicit more redistributive attitudes among nationalists.

Evaluating Benefits and Beneficiaries
Underpinning respondents' priorities for extra spending on social benefits lie opinions about both the various beneficiaries of income maintenance programmes and the adequacy of benefit levels.

In relation to unemployment benefit just over half the population (51 per cent) believe that 'benefit levels for the unemployed are too low and cause hardship', whereas 30 per cent agree that their 'benefit levels are too high and discourage the unemployed from finding jobs'. (The remainder either agree with neither proposition or adopt a variety of other opinions.) Catholics, reflecting their greater preparedness to pay more tax to assist the jobless, are significantly more likely to agree with the first of these statements. Two-thirds of them (66 per cent) take this view while 19 per cent agree with the alternative. These proportions contrast markedly with the opinions of Protestants who are sharply divided on this matter: 41 per cent concur with the first proposition, whereas 38 per cent believe the levels of unemployment benefit encourage idleness.

A divergence of opinion between the religious communities is also evident in relation to unemployed female single parents reliant on state benefits. Within the population as a whole, 23 per cent agree that they have either enough or more than enough to live on, while 70 per cent state that they are either 'hard up' or are 'really poor' (the comparable British figures are 26 per cent and 66 per cent, respectively). Catholics, however, are strongly disposed to perceive deprivation and poverty among benefit-dependant single mothers: 82 per cent believe them to be either hard up or poor, compared to 61 per cent of Protestants. The latter (at 29 per cent) are also twice as likely as Catholics (at 14 per cent) to agree that single mothers have at least enough to live on. This pattern of opinion is corroborated when respondents are asked to assess the sufficiency of a disposable income of £78 per week for jobless single mothers. While 34 per cent of the population at large believe this level of income to be at least adequate (a view shared by 38 per cent of the British population), this is true of 38 per cent of Protestants and 26 per cent of Catholics. Conversely, 57 per cent of Protestants perceive this income to consign single mothers to deprivation or poverty compared to 74 per cent of Catholics. (The respective figures for the wider populations in Northern Ireland and Britain are 65 per cent and 60 per cent.)

There are some interesting age effects among both women and men on this issue which indicate relative perceptions of deprivation and poverty. Older cohorts of both sexes, those at or beyond retirement age, are

significantly less likely than 17 to 34-year-olds to agree that jobless single mothers are either hard up or poor: 56 per cent of women and 53 per cent of men of pensionable age adopt this view, compared to 81 per cent of young women and 83 per cent of young men. Being born in the inter-war period clearly exerts attitudinal effects towards poverty that are different from those expressed by people born between the early 1960s and the late 1970s. The same generational effect is apparent in relation to unemployed single mothers on a fixed income of £78 per week. The perception of poverty and deprivation declines significantly with age: 79 per cent of women and 81 per cent of men aged between 17 and 34 years believe such mothers are either hard up or poor, compared to 52 per cent of women and 48 per cent of men of pensionable age.

What such age differentials suggest is that younger generations harbour higher aspirations concerning the unmet needs of jobless single mothers. *Inter alia* this implies that they are less disapproving of single parenthood than older cohorts brought up in a very different, more censorious, moral climate in which the incidence of poverty was much more common. Such generational effects are also evident in relation to other attitudes towards single mothers, as Table 10 shows.

Table 10

'Thinking about a single mother with a child under school age, which one of these statements comes closest to your own view?' (%)

	17-34		35-49		50-64		65+	
	M	F	M	F	M	F	M	F
She has a special duty to go out to work to support her child	6	8	8	4	17	12	7	14
She has a special duty to stay at home to look after her child	22	21	27	24	24	35	41	32
She should do as she chooses like everyone else	55	62	63	70	46	47	41	42

Note: Table excludes 'Don't knows'

Among the younger age groups, clear majorities of both sexes believe that single mothers should be able to make up their own minds, whereas older men and women are rather more disposed to take a home-centred view.   There is relatively little support across the age bands for the proposition that such women have a duty to go out to work, although it is rather more common among Protestants (13 per cent) than Catholics (three per cent). Yet there is a shared recognition among women and men of all ages and religious beliefs that a critical factor enabling single mothers of pre-school children to seek employment is the provision of child-care. Significant proportions of women (69 per cent) and men (78 per cent) agree that the government should cover the child-care costs of such a single mother who obtains employment.   Support for such a policy is also extended to a single mother with a child of school age: 62 per cent of all women and two-thirds of all men agree that government should subsidise employed single mothers by helping to pay for their child-care fees outside school hours.

There are, however, divisions of opinion concerning single mothers with school-age children.   Men under the age of 35, for instance, are significantly more likely both to agree that these women have a duty to go out to work (43 per cent) than their female cohort (17 per cent), and also to disagree that they should be free to choose (34 per cent) whether to work or stay at home, the viewed adopted by the overwhelming majority (75 per cent) of young women.   The home-centred alternative tends to be more popular among those of each sex aged at least 50 years, although the level of support it attracts is a modest 15 per cent as compared to 32 per cent of them who believe single mothers are duty-bound to find a job.   A plurality (46 per cent) of women and men aged 50 or more in fact agree that female lone parents with school-age children should be allowed to choose between home and work.

Religious affiliation also structures these attitudes.   More than one-in-three men (35 per cent) and 27 per cent of women of the Protestant faith believe single mothers with a child at school should be obliged to seek employment, compared to 18 per cent of male and 14 per cent of female Catholics.   There are also gender gaps among Protestants concerning whether or not such unmarried mothers should be free to choose between

employment and an exclusively domestic role. While 48 per cent of Protestant men agree with this alternative, a majority of their female co-religionists (61 per cent) do so. Catholics, especially women, are more likely to endorse this option: 51 per cent of male and 72 per cent of female Catholics endorse a free choice.

Within the wider population there are significant differences of view between the religious communities concerning the condition of single motherhood. Asked whether unmarried mothers 'who find it hard to cope have only themselves to blame', only a quarter of both men and women agree. However, Catholics are significantly less likely to adopt this view: 17 per cent of males and 14 per cent of females agree with the proposition, compared to 31 per cent and 39 per cent of, respectively, Protestant men and women. Catholics are also more likely to agree that unmarried mothers 'get too little sympathy from society': this view is adopted by 46 per cent of men and 49 per cent of women of the Catholic faith as compared with 26 per cent of male and 24 per cent of female Protestants. In general, Protestants appear quicker to affix individual blame and slower to accord social support to unmarried mothers.

Welfare Dependency
Attitudes towards the effects of the welfare system upon behaviour are also covered by the survey. As Table 11 indicates, respondents were asked to identify the extent to which they understood the welfare state both to encourage a dependency culture and weaken a sense of social solidarity.

Table 11
Attitudes towards the effects of the welfare system (%)

	Agree	Disagree	Neither
The welfare state: makes people less willing to look after themselves	40	33	25
Encourages people to stop helping each other	30	39	30

The proportions agreeing that the welfare state promotes dependency is more pronounced among Protestant women (47 per cent) and men (47 per

cent) than their Catholic equivalents (33 per cent and 26 per cent respectively). Though the attitudinal gaps are narrower, Protestants of both sexes are also more likely to agree that the welfare state undermines the readiness of people to help each other. This view is endorsed by 35 per cent of male, and 31 per cent of female, Protestants, compared to 31 per cent of Catholic men and 19 per cent of Catholic women. The latter are the most likely to disagree (48 per cent), followed by their male co-religionists (40 per cent), and women (36 per cent) and men (33 per cent) of the Protestant faith.

However, this apparent religious effect is complicated by the fact that Catholics are rather more likely than Protestants to be receiving state benefits (and much more likely to be unemployed), as well as the likelihood that the attitudes of welfare recipients will almost certainly be more positive towards those on benefit. Hence, is it being Catholic or being in receipt of benefit that leads to a more sympathetic attitude towards income dependency? In order to try and answer this, a logistic regression was carried out which modelled the tendency to be sympathetic on a 'welfarism scale' (see Heath et al., 1990, for information concerning the construction of the scale). The Appendix provides detailed results of the regression which, in summary, suggest that while being in receipt of benefits and being unemployed are most important in defining attitudes, being Catholic is of paramount importance. Also, supporters of the Alliance Party are notably more sympathetic and supporters of the Ulster Unionist Party are notably less sympathetic towards welfare dependants, even when all other factors are taken into account.

A related set of questions (see Table 12) probed attitudes towards various types of benefit dependants. The ambivalence in relation to the unemployed is marked. The population is narrowly split between those who regard them as work-shy and those who see their lack of employment to be no fault of their own. Whilst a plurality perceive the jobless to be 'doing the double', any belief that they may constitute one element of the undeserving poor does not extend to others in receipt of some form of social security: almost half of the population (47 per cent) believe that many beneficiaries of income maintenance are deserving of support.

Table 12

Attitudes towards benefit dependants (%)

	Agree	Disagree	Neither
Around here most unemployed people could find a job if they really wanted one.	38	40	20
Many people who get social security don't really deserve any help.	26	47	25
Most people on the dole are fiddling in one way or the other.	37	33	29

Moreover, an equivalent proportion (48 per cent) agree that those reliant on benefit 'are made to feel like second-class citizens', whereas 28 per cent

Table 13

Attitudes of Catholics and Protestants towards aspects of the Welfare system (%)

	Catholic		Protestant	
	Agree	Disagree	Agree	Disagree
The welfare state makes people less willing to look after themselves.	30	44	47	27
People receiving social security are made to feel like second class citizens.	58	22	42	33
The welfare state encourages people to stop helping each other.	25	44	33	35
Most unemployed people could find a job if they really wanted one.	27	52	45	34
Many people who get social security don't really deserve any help.	20	58	30	40
Most people on the dole are fiddling in one way or the other.	27	39	43	29
If welfare benefits were not so generous, people would learn to stand on their own two feet.	16	59	36	38

disagree that they are so stigmatised. Equally, a plurality of all respondents (46 per cent) disagreed that the 'generosity' of welfare benefits prevented people from learning 'to stand on their own two feet', compared to 30 per cent who agreed that it undermined a sense of self-reliance. As Table 13 underlines, it is Catholics who are more disposed to place a positive construction upon the effects of the welfare system on both individual and social behaviour.

Besides being much more likely to recognise the stigmatising effects of benefit dependency, majorities of Catholics are also more likely to adopt an expansive notion of the deserving poor; to reject the proposition that most of the jobless are workshy; and to disagree that the levels of benefit undermine self-reliance.

The Scope of Welfare
Reform of the welfare regime in Britain has taken a variety of forms, including the introduction of fiscal incentives designed to encourage the employed to invest in both private health cover and personal pensions. From the government's perspective, such tax breaks serve a number of purposes, including the promotion of Victorian notions of prudence and self-help, besides a hoped-for and longer-term reduction in claims on the Exchequer. The record of the largely deregulated personal pensions industry has however proven to be an extremely unhappy one, with millions left with less security for their post-employment years having opted out of occupational pension schemes. The growth of private medical cover has proven to be more popular, although the motives for taking out such policies may be rooted in fears for the future of the NHS rather than an ideological belief in the free market.

The 1995 survey indicates that nine per cent of the population is covered by a private health insurance scheme, mostly paid for by their employers. Those so covered are the most supportive of a two-tier health service, that is, those who agree that the NHS should be available only to those with low incomes on the assumption that they would have to pay consequentially lower national insurance contributions and taxation. Within the population as a whole, 22 per cent endorse this proposition and 76 per cent

oppose it: among those with private cover, the proportion in favour of a dual system rises to 34 per cent, yet a large majority (65 per cent) are opposed. Catholics are also marginally more likely to support a two-tier system than Protestants: 24 per cent of them take this view compared to 20 per cent of members of the Protestant faith. Among party identifiers, the level of support for a dual system is relatively uniform: SDLP voters emerge as marginally more disposed to support private medicine on the above terms (23 per cent), compared to 22 per cent of UUP, 21 per cent of Alliance, 20 per cent of DUP and 19 per cent of Sinn Fein voters.

Since 1993, however, there has been a decline of five per cent in support for a two-tier system and a corresponding increase in the proportion of the population opposed to its realisation. Indeed, since 1989 the idea that state health care should be available free only to those on low incomes has never appealed to more than 27 per cent of the wider population. For the majority, common welfare citizenship is heavily structured by a commitment to the NHS. Other aspects of the social security system do, however, seem more negotiable. For example, asked who should be mainly responsible for paying those who are off work because of sickness, the population seems more undecided, at least in regard to those who are ill for only a short period: 37 per cent opt for the government; 24 per cent for employers; and 37 per cent believe that the responsibility should be shared equally by the state and employers. However, for those who are off work for at least six months because of sickness, almost two-thirds (63 per cent) agree that the government should assume responsibility to maintain their income, compared to 13 per cent who opt for employers and 20 per cent who believe it should be a joint responsibility.

Despite its first priority as the beneficiary of increased social expenditure, a significant minority of the population believe that employers should be either mainly (11 per cent) or equally responsible (31 per cent) for ensuring that people have an adequate retirement pension, while 54 per cent agree that the government should be mainly responsible and only three per cent endorse individual responsibility via a Personal Equity Plan. In Britain, public opinion is more evenly divided: 47 per cent believe the government should be mainly responsible, nine per cent that employers should be, 37 per cent that the responsibility should be equally shared,

while six per cent endorse personal pensions. There are, however, as Table 14 shows, pronounced generational differences apparent among both women and men in Northern Ireland on this question.

Table 14

'Who do you think should be mainly responsible for ensuring that people have an adequate retirement pension?' (%)

	17-34		35-49		50-64		65+	
	M	F	M	F	M	F	M	F
Mainly government	28	48	53	50	67	60	76	66
Mainly employers	32	8	15	9	6	4	*	2
Shared equally	15	39	29	40	23	35	21	27
Other arrangement	25	2	3	*	3	0	3	*

Note: * *denotes less than one per cent. Table excludes 'Don't know'.*

While there are higher levels of support for reliance upon a state pension as age increases, this is more marked among men than women. Within each cohort women are also more likely than men to endorse the equal responsibility of employers and government. However, a plurality of young men favour occupational schemes and are almost as likely to endorse a personal as the state pension. In part, the age-related increase in support for the state pension reflects levels of expectations that were forged in the early post-war period. Among younger generations, the readiness to rely on a mix of occupational and state pensions, or in the case of the youngest men personal pensions, suggests a changing view of the role of the state in providing post-retirement income. Equally, the relatively buoyant support for a combined state and occupational pension arrangement suggests that a significant minority of the population anticipate the inadequacy of state provision in their later years.

The attachment to the state pension is also strongest among those at the foot of the occupational class scale where employment is less secure and levels of income are low. More than two thirds (69 per cent) of those in Social Class V believe government should be mainly responsible for

ensuring an adequate retirement income, compared to 55 per cent of those in Social Class I who enjoy greater resources to invest in a personal pension and are more likely to benefit from an occupational scheme. The most dependant (those in receipt of at least four types of benefits) are also those who place the heaviest reliance on a state retirement pension (64 per cent) while those who receive no benefits are the least likely (52 per cent) to place the onus on government.

One policy, common to both Labour and Conservative governments, designed to exert control over levels of social security expenditure has been to widen the scope of means-testing. Its progressive expansion has eroded the principle of universalism that underpinned the post-war welfare system and replaced it with an almost exclusively selective regime of income-maintenance. Yet, the attachment to this principle and the egalitarian motive it serves remains resilient. Overwhelming majorities of the population believe that, irrespective of income when in work, all individuals should receive the same level of unemployment benefit (73 per cent) and the same state retirement pension (75 per cent) – in Britain the corresponding proportions are 72 per cent and 69 per cent. However, this inclusive attitude towards welfare citizenship is significantly weaker in relation to the sole remaining universal benefit, viz. child benefit.

Respondents were asked whether high income earners should be entitled to either more, less, the same amount or no, child benefit. While 56 per cent agreed that they should receive the same amount as people on low incomes, 22 per cent believe they should receive less and 19 per cent that they should be wholly ineligible for child benefit. (In Britain a slim, combined majority – 51 per cent – choose the latter two options.) While 58 per cent of Catholics and 56 per cent of Protestants favour the retention of universalism, there is a wide variation of opinion among party identifiers. A narrow majority of DUP voters, for instance, believe high income earners should receive either less (32 per cent) or no (21 per cent) child benefit. The only partisans to express overwhelming attachment to equality are Sinn Fein supporters at 88 per cent, an attitude shared by smaller majorities of UUP (56 per cent), SDLP (56 per cent) and Alliance (54 per cent) voters. Both in Britain and Northern Ireland it does appear that any future attempt to limit access to child benefit to the less well off

will prove less controversial than any further rationing of other forms of benefit. Equally, one might surmise that having grown accustomed to a means-tested system the effects on the general population of its extension to child benefit may prove to be less than seismic.

Part of the explanation for more malleable attitudes towards child benefit may also be the introduction of new legislation designed to ensure that, in the event of a breakdown in a marriage, parents continue to provide for the financial needs of their children. While the introduction of the Child Support Agency has proved unpopular – especially among fathers – and its implementation has, to say the least, been problematic, the underlying principle that children should not suffer materially as a result of a failed marriage seems unexceptionable. The financial responsibility of fathers towards their children certainly strikes a chord in Northern Ireland, at least in the indirect sense that a near majority of the population (48 per cent) believe that when a marriage breaks up the woman either always or usually 'comes off worse' than her former partner. This is a significantly higher proportion than the British population (37 per cent): moreover, while 31 per cent in Britain believe the man either usually or always suffers more, this is true of just 22 per cent of Northern Ireland respondents. However, as Table 15 shows, there are large gender gaps on this issue.

Table 15

'As far as money is concerned, what do you think happens when a marriage breaks up?' (%)		
	Male	Female
The woman nearly always comes off worse.	19	31
The woman usually comes off worse.	20	25
Both usually come off about the same.	17	22
The man usually comes off worse.	24	12
The man nearly always comes off worse.	8	2
It varies.	7	5

Though many male respondents do believe that women tend to bear the heavier financial loss they are less certain than female respondents, the majority of whom agree that women invariably get the short end of the financial stick. Despite their ambivalence, an overwhelming majority of all men (85 per cent) concur with the general principle that if an unmarried couple split up fathers 'should always be made to make maintenance payments' for the upkeep of a child who remains with the mother – a view shared by 90 per cent of all women. Moreover, 89 per cent of all men and 91 per cent of all women agree that the father's maintenance payments should be means-tested. However, the sexes diverge on the matter of the mother's income. While 75 per cent of men agree that the mother's income should be taken in account in calculating the amount of maintenance, this view is shared by a smaller majority (59 per cent) of women.

The gender differences are sustained in the event of the mother marrying someone else. Asked whether the biological father should continue to pay maintenance, to stop, or whether any payments should depend on the step-father's income, 46 per cent of all women believe the payments should continue unaltered, compared to 32 per cent of all men. While a plurality of men (40 per cent) believe the payments should be contingent upon the step-father's income, a view shared by 38 per cent of women, they are twice as likely as women (27 per cent and 14 per cent, respectively) to believe that maintenance should cease in the event of the mother's marriage.

Irrespective of religious or political affiliation the principle of paternal maintenance is widely accepted, even where the couple are unmarried: music to the ears of the Treasury who see the implementation of the Child Support Act as a means of cost-saving. There is, however, a broad variation of view between the sexes concerning the basis on which maintenance is calculated and which is influenced largely by marital status. (Gender differences are especially apparent among the small number of respondents who are co-habiting, divorced or separated.) Separation and divorce are often rancorous episodes, during which pragmatism invariably sinks below a tide of mutual recrimination. The division of opinion among men and women, especially those who have been divorced or separated, suggests

that money continues to be a bone of contention whatever administrative arrangements are put in place to assure the upkeep of a child.

Conclusion

During a period of continuing uncertainty about the future direction of the welfare system, the population of Northern Ireland remains largely wedded to generous expectations about the levels of social protection the state should provide for its citizens. The primacy enjoyed by both the NHS and education spending, plus the attachment to a flat-rate, universally available state pension, implies that the public expects the government to maintain three of the most costly items of welfare provision. Yet, it is also the case that significant proportions of the population, especially younger cohorts, are prepared to countenance a role for the market in providing for pensions. The one remaining bastion of universalism – child benefit – also looks vulnerable to a means-tested assault, while the wider population, albeit structured by religious and political beliefs, clearly harbours conceptions of those considered to be the deserving and the undeserving poor.

There are, in effect, opportunities for a future reforming, or 'modernising', government to narrow the scope of welfare benefits. Thus, while 72 per cent of the population believe that 'ordinary working people do not get their fair share of the nation's wealth' and two-thirds agree 'there is one law for the rich and one for the poor', only a slim majority (52 per cent) endorse a policy of unfettered redistribution from the better to the less well off. Some of the latter, notably unmarried mothers, are simply not perceived to be particularly deserving cases. Even among women, it is only single mothers themselves who believe they should be the government's top priority for extra social benefit spending, leaving them generally isolated within the wider population.

The preference for the unemployed as the beneficiaries of social spending is also rather modest. That said, there is a commanding majority in favour of job creation: more than two-thirds of the public (69 per cent) believe that, faced with a choice, the government should accord a higher priority to keeping unemployment levels down rather than reducing inflation (30 per cent). This preference may, though, in part be explained by the fact that from 1993 to 1995 the annual rate of inflation hovered

between two and three per cent, encouraging the view that the battle against price rises may have been won, at least in the short-term.

While just over a half of respondents lend blanket support to the redistribution of wealth and income, there is an overwhelming belief that the income gap is too large: 87 per cent agree that the gap between those on high and low incomes is excessive, compared to nine per cent who believe the gap is about right and just two per cent that it is too small. The gap is, of course, influenced by fiscal policy. Between 1993 and 1995, the proportion of gross domestic product taken by taxation, including national insurance contributions, increased from 34 per cent to 36 per cent, much of it acquired through indirect taxation. The long-term shift from direct to indirect taxation (that is, VAT), coupled with the simplification of tax bands and the reduction, especially, of the tax levied on higher income-earners has compounded the regressiveness of the tax system in the UK. The population is clearly sensitive to the effects of these changes, especially the differential and negative implications they have had for the lower paid. Thus, more than three out of four of high, middle and low income earners agree that the level of taxation paid by those on low incomes is too high, while majorities (54 per cent each) of those on middle and low incomes believe that high income earners pay too little tax – not a view high earners themselves share, more than half of whom (52 per cent) believe they pay too much.

There is, however, a sense of fairness rather than an overwhelming mood of self interest apparent among higher tax payers. Asked whether to pay for extra public spending the government should increase the basic rate of income tax by 1p, by 5p for higher taxpayers, or raise VAT by one per cent on all goods and services, a narrow plurality of high income earners (32 per cent) choose the second alternative, even though more than half (57 per cent) agree that this would leave them and their families worse off. Middle and low income earners, by comparison, are much less inhibited about their perceived interests. Significant majorities of both (63 per cent of middle and 75 per cent of low earners) recognise that a VAT increase would leave them worse off and two-thirds of each favour a 5p increase for high income earners. In the event, the Government in its 1995 Budget reduced the basic

rate of income tax by 1p, an option that was supported by 28 per cent of middle, 27 per cent of low income earners and 30 per cent of high earners.

Ironically, perhaps, it is that part of the community most attached to the Union which expresses equivocation about the social effects of the welfare regime (see Table 13). This is confirmed by the attitudes of voters. A majority of UUP voters (54 per cent) and a plurality of DUP voters (39 per cent) agree that the welfare state 'makes people less willing to look after themselves', a view adopted by one-in-three of nationalist and republican voters. Equally, 45 per cent of UUP and 33 per cent of DUP identifiers agree that the generosity of welfare benefits discourage people from 'standing on their own two feet', compared to nine per cent of Sinn Fein and 18 per cent of SDLP voters.

There is an apparent paradox here: while the majority of unionist voters express pride in the social security system, they are more likely to concur with assertions concerning the deleterious effects of the benefits system both upon individuals and the wider society. The implication is that their negative attitudes are influenced by the perception of those they deem to be the benefit-dependant rather than the system itself. Conversely, Sinn Fein and SDLP voters are much more critical of the social security system and are less likely to agree with its assumed negative effects. Moreover, 74 per cent of Sinn Fein supporters and 71 per cent of SDLP voters agree that more should be spent on the poor even at the cost of increased taxes, compared to 46 per cent of both DUP and UUP voters. To that extent, the legacy bequeathed by the architects of the welfare state, Keynes and Beveridge, seems to have been inherited more by those electors who aspire to detach Northern Ireland from the UK than those determined to maintain the constitutional status quo.

References

HEATH, A., EVANS, G., LALLJEE, M., MARTIN, J. and WITHERSPOON, S. 1990. 'The measurement of core beliefs and values', CREST Working Paper No. 2, December 1990.

HMSO, 1995a. 'Employment Creation in Northern Ireland: The First Report of the Northern Ireland Affairs Select Committee', HC 37-I.

HMSO, 1995b. 'Government Observations on the First Report from the Northern Ireland Affairs Select Committee', Cmd 642.

JONES, C. 1993. 'The Pacific Challenge', in C. Jones (ed.), *New Perspectives on the Welfare State in Europe*, London, Routledge.

PLIATZKY, SIR LEO. 1984. *Getting and Spending: Public Expenditure, Employment and Inflation*, Blackwell, Oxford.

PLIATZKY, SIR LEO. 1985. *Paying and Choosing*, Oxford, Blackwell.

WILFORD, R. 1995. 'Welfare Attitudes', in R. Breen, P. Devine and G. Robinson (eds.), *Social Attitudes in Northern Ireland: The Fourth Report*, Belfast, Appletree Press.

Appendix

Table A1

Logistic regression modelling sympathy towards welfare dependency

	B	**S.E.**	**Wald statistic**	**Sig**	**R**
Receives state benefits	.6759	.1319	26.2704	.0000	.1219
Unemployed	1.2341	.2601	22.5154	.0000	.1121
Protestant	-.3258	.0717	20.6210	.0000	-.1068
Supports APNI	.5439	.2006	7.3490	.0067	.0572
Supports UUP	-.4305	.1807	5.6754	.0172	-.0474

Model chi-square 140.159 with 5 df, N=1230

3

Unleashing the Apathy of a Lost Generation? Community Relations among Young People in Northern Ireland

Lizanne Dowds and Paula Devine

Introduction

While policymakers and peacemakers struggle with the task of changing (or simply accommodating) entrenched attitudes, researchers have long been occupied with the equally frustrating task of searching for the political 'liberals' in Northern Irish society. This examination of the middle-ground has yielded up a fair number of 'unionist Catholics' (Breen, 1996) and a rather smaller number of politically independent individuals who reject religion altogether (Breen and Hayes, forthcoming; Breen, 1996; Trew, 1996). Yet in many countries this search would lead immediately to a close examination of social attitudes among young people – something that has not been carried out in Northern Ireland until now. Whether it be the rejection of nationalist symbols in Germany (Topf et al., 1989), the embracing of libertarian values in Britain (Ahrendt and Young, 1994) or the much vaunted cross-national 'postmaterialism' of younger generations (Inglehart, 1977; 1990), many young people indisputably tend towards the progressive. But evidence from Northern Ireland is mixed. Cairns (1992) demonstrated rather conclusively the lack of a 'generation gap' in Northern Ireland with regard to issues such as respect for life, sexual morality and attitudes towards authority. In this report we specifically set out to examine the evidence for and against the existence of a 'mindset' peculiar to younger people in Northern Ireland – with regard to

community relations, constitutional preferences, national identity and the resultant implications (if any) for community relations policies.

Unfortunately no analysis of community relations among the Northern Ireland population is possible without dividing respondents up into their respective Protestant and Catholic groupings.   Thus research itself continues to perpetuate and reinforce the image of a gaping divide between the two communities.   However there is a case for refining this practice. Those who say that they have 'no religion' are normally excluded from analyses according to 'religion' and treated as a somewhat quaint and separate group.   But, as said, research has also shown that it is here, if anywhere, that a clear middle-ground is to be found.   If rejection of religious upbringing were indeed to be linked to rejection of sectarian politics, then it is time to begin including this group on the continuum of differing social attitudes among those of Catholic or Protestant *background*.

Only 10 per cent of the Northern Ireland Social Attitudes survey (NISA) sample say that they have 'no religion' but when these people are grouped with others of the same religious background, they have an effect on the figures quite out of proportion to their numbers.   Seventy-four per cent of those who define themselves as 'Protestant' also think of themselves as 'unionist', but this figure falls to 70 per cent when those who have no religion now but were raised as Protestants are included in the sample. Ulster Unionist Party support drops by five percentage points when those who were raised as Protestants but who now have no religion are included in the 'Protestant' sample.

So the analyses carried out here define 'religious background' as current religion, except where respondents have no religion or simply prefer to call themselves 'Christians' in which case they are defined according to the religion in which they were raised.   This is done in the interests of including the attitudes of a wider and more diverse group of people who were brought up as Protestant or Catholic – and with apologies for imposing labels on people whose purpose in defining themselves as having 'no religion' may well have been to avoid this categorisation in the first place.   The rest of this chapter examines the attitudes of the 300 young people in our sample, the extent to which their attitudes are different from

those of older age groups, the specific question of whether young people are indeed more moderate, and the role that apathy may play in determining the views (or lack of them) of young respondents.

Identity

Most Catholics describe themselves as Irish, though a substantial minority refer to themselves as Northern Irish. Young Catholics are only marginally more likely to use the latter term – the biggest difference is that the elderly are *least* likely to say that they are Northern Irish (see Table 1). For Protestant young people the differences are more marked (see also Trew, 1996); they are noticeably more likely to use the 'Northern Irish' label and discernibly less likely to call themselves British. This tells us little about the relative saliency of each label (Gallagher, 1989) or the possibility that people use different labels in different contexts, but it may be one indication of a more 'moderate' position in terms of the British/Irish identity continuum.

Table 1

National identity among those of Protestant and Catholic backgrounds (%)

	Age of respondent							
	Protestant				Catholic			
	18-30	31-39	40-59	60+	18-30	31-39	40-59	60+
Ulster	10	10	12	14	2	0	1	4
British	56	72	61	69	11	8	17	13
Northern Irish	28	16	20	7	28	27	25	15
Irish	5	1	5	8	59	64	57	66

When respondents are further asked whether they consider themselves to be 'unionist, nationalist or neither unionist nor nationalist?' the tendency towards a moderate identity also becomes apparent among young Catholics (see Table 2). Catholics in general are rather more likely than Protestants to opt for being 'neither unionist nor nationalist' but it is young Catholics who most embrace the notion of being 'neither unionist nor nationalist'; 61

per cent do so compared with just under half of all other age groups. Although most Protestants of all ages will describe themselves as unionist, a much larger proportion of the young describe themselves as 'neither unionist nor nationalist'. This proportion decreases with increasing age so that the young are more than twice as likely as the elderly to use this term.

Table 2

Percentage of respondents describing themselves as 'unionist, nationalist, or neither unionist nor nationalist'

	Protestant				Catholic			
	18-30	31-39	40-59	60+	18-30	31-39	40-59	60+
Unionist	54	67	73	80	3	<1	1	0
Neither	45	33	26	19	61	48	47	49
Nationalist	0	0	<1	1	36	51	52	51

Constitutional Preferences

The possibility that young people may be more moderate in their political views is tentatively reinforced in relation to constitutional issues. NISA surveys have traditionally included a 'forced-choice' question on constitutional preferences:

> *Do you think the long-term policy for Northern Ireland should be for it ...*
>
> *...to remain part of the United Kingdom,*
> *or, to reunify with the rest of Ireland?*

Among researchers this question has typically been used as a measure of an individual's constitutional preference – though it has been criticised on the grounds that some respondents will answer in terms of what they think is best for Northern Ireland, even if this conflicts with their own personal preferences. Some critics have suggested that it may therefore underestimate the strength of a desire for a united Ireland, others that it allows for no scope for measuring the willingness for compromise within a basic unionist framework.

Just over one-third of all Catholics thought that Northern Ireland should remain part of the United Kingdom (see Breen, 1996 for a discussion of what he has termed these 'unionist Catholics') and this rises to 43 per cent among young Catholics. But there were few differences in the views of Protestants of different age groups (and 86 per cent overall would retain the union). However another set of questions were included for the first time in the 1995 survey which did not involve a straight forced choice between a United Ireland or retention of the Union, but offered the theoretical option of joint sovereignty or an independent state (the questions also offered each option with or without a separate parliament in Belfast – but results are presented here without showing this breakdown).

Table 3
Personal constitutional preferences (%)

| | Age of respondent | | | | | |
| | Protestant | | | Catholic | | |
	18-30	31-59	60+	18-30	31-59	60+
Remain part of the UK	72	83	88	15	22	26
Become part of the Irish Republic	0	3	1	34	30	22
Joint sovereignty	7	5	4	28	27	28
Independent state	8	4	1	8	6	4
Can't choose	11	4	3	13	13	19
N/A	2	1	3	4	3	1

As Table 3 shows, the apparent acceptance by young Catholics of the need to retain the Union seems to disappear. Across all age groups the notion of joint sovereignty appears to be the favoured 'compromise option'. But it is worth reiterating here that respondents are only asked to consider their *own* preferences and not 'the best long-term option for Northern Ireland'. With this in mind, young Catholics are *personally* less likely to favour the Union and slightly more likely to opt for a united Ireland or some other compromise.

For Protestants the picture is also interesting. Although the forced-choice question showed little variation across age groups – once other options are introduced everyone, but especially the young, appears much less certain about retention of the Union and more willing to go for other options (though not a united Ireland) or to be unable to choose between all the options. Again though, it must be remembered that the new question asks about personal preferences while the traditional question emphasises the best long-term future for Northern Ireland. It is also a moot point whether the 'independent state' is a compromise or a hard-line option (or both). Another new item sheds further light on the views of the Protestant sample.

And how much say do you think an Irish government of <u>any party</u> should have in the way Northern Ireland is run? Do you think it should have...

...a great deal of say,
some say,
a little say,
or - no say at all?

The results here are striking. For the first time it is clear that a substantial minority believe that an Irish government should not be entirely excluded from involvement in the way Northern Ireland is run (see Table 4).

Table 4
Percentage of Protestant respondents who believe that an Irish government should have:

	Age of respondent		
	18-30	31-59	50+
A great deal/some/a little say	33	30	23
No say at all	53	63	71
Can't choose	12	7	4

Although it would be overstating the case to suggest that young Protestants are more likely to believe that the Irish government should have

any say in the way Northern Ireland is run they are nonetheless the most uncertain about whether it should have 'no say at all' – further strengthening the thesis that this is a group with moderate views.

Perceptions of Prejudice and Discrimination

Majorities of both Catholic and Protestant respondents felt that there was 'a lot' or 'a little' prejudice against the 'other community' in Northern Ireland. For young Catholics this feeling was particularly pronounced with 80 per cent agreeing that there was a lot or a little prejudice against Protestants in Northern Ireland. The age pattern was much less pronounced among Protestants with younger respondents only slightly more likely than older Protestants to think that there was prejudice against Catholics.

When asked about discrimination from *specific* organisations or institutions, Catholic respondents hardly ever felt that the discrimination

Table 5

Percentage of Protestant respondents who thought that Protestants were treated better by:

	Age of respondent			
	18-30	31-39	40-59	60+
Army	45	22	10	5
RIR	41	32	17	8
RUC	30	20	13	5
District Council	18	12	8	5
Civil Service (in competition for Stormont jobs)	9	7	3	3
Housing Executive	8	1	0	1
Courts trying terrorist cases	5	3	1	2
FEC	2	0	0	1

A number of other organisations/institutions which were mentioned in the survey were excluded from this table because there appeared to be a general consensus among those of both community backgrounds that there was little or no discrimination involved. These included the way people were treated by the NHS, government employment schemes and courts trying non-terrorist cases.

went their way – it was rare indeed for any Catholic respondent to feel that Catholics were treated better than Protestants in any of the situations presented during the survey interview. In contrast (although the general view was that people were treated equally) many Protestant respondents believed that there were institutions which treated Protestants better than Catholics – and this was particularly pronounced among younger Protestant respondents (see Table 5).

This belief in the possibility of social injustice again gives some support for the thesis that younger Protestants have a more liberal mindset than their elder co-religionists when it comes to community relations issues. However, there is also some interesting support for the notion that attitudes of the young are bi-polar, or that there are some young people with quite the opposite views. The effect is much weaker but there are indications that some young Protestants may be notably more hard-line their older counterparts. Table 6 shows that although on the whole many fewer Protestants are prepared to say that Catholics are actually treated better than Protestants – the people who do say this are disproportionately likely to be young.

Table 6

Percentage of Protestant respondents who thought that Catholics were treated better by:

| | Age of respondent | | | |
	18-30	31-39	40-59	60+
Army	5	1	1	1
RIR	3	1	1	1
RUC	11	7	2	3
District Council	12	11	9	10
Civil Service (in competition for Stormont jobs)	19	17	21	15
Housing Executive	23	18	15	18
Courts trying terrorist cases	15	6	6	6
FEC	24	21	27	23

As said, there are too few Catholics who believe that Catholics are treated *better* in these situations to look at their attitudes according to age group. But looking at those who feel that there is discrimination against Catholics, again there is a tendency for this feeling to be stronger among younger Catholics than their older counterparts (see Table 7).

Table 7
Percentage of Catholic respondents who thought that Protestants were treated better by:

	Age of respondent			
	18-30	31-39	40-59	60+
Army	63	43	37	26
RIR	59	60	49	31
RUC	64	48	41	36
District Council	38	32	25	30
Civil Service (in competition for Stormont jobs)	34	32	28	22
Housing Executive	22	16	15	9
Courts trying terrorist cases	29	25	33	26
FEC	5	5	2	0

Political Support
The figures on party support (see Table 8) provide further evidence that there may be a particularly hard-line group as well as a more moderate element among young Protestants (assuming that the lack of *any* party identification can be interpreted as 'moderate', a point returned to). Protestants in the youngest age group are much less likely than their elders to vote for the Ulster Unionist party (UUP) and more likely to either say that they support no party at all or to opt for the Democratic Unionist party (DUP). Their votes are almost equally split between these three options. However, again consistent with the notion that there is a more politically non-traditional group among the young, they also seem to be more likely

than their older counterparts to favour the Green party as well as other unionist parties outside the two traditional mainstream groupings.

Table 8
Party political support among those with a Protestant background (%)

	Age of respondent		
	18-30	31-59	60 +
Ulster Unionist Party	26	45	54
Democratic Unionist Party	26	14	14
Alliance	5	12	15
Other Unionist	6	4	2
Green Party	5	1	0
None	27	18	9
Other party/answer	5	7	6

Interestingly, support for the Alliance party is lower among younger people – if those with a liberal mindset are indeed more numerous among younger people their liberal thoughts do not take them towards the most traditional middle of the road mainstream party.

Table 9
Party political support among those with a Catholic background (%)

	Age of respondent		
	18-30	31-59	60 +
SDLP	40	55	54
Alliance	8	8	9
Sinn Fein	8	5	6
Green Party	4	1	1
Workers' party	3	2	0
None	28	22	20
Other party/answer	10	6	11

The picture for young Catholics is quite similar in that young Catholics are also rather more likely to lack any political allegiance whatsoever (see Table 9). Sinn Fein support is fractionally higher among this group but support overall is clearly underestimated. Evans and Duffy (forthcoming) found age to be an important predictor of Sinn Fein support. Again Green party support is slightly higher among the young.

But perhaps what is most interesting about the findings on political support is the *lack* of support for the traditional main five parties (UUP, DUP, APNI, SDLP, SF). Only 56 per cent of young Catholics and 57 per cent of young Protestants actually say that they would vote for one of these five parties. This compares with 78 per cent of Protestants and 68 per cent of Catholics aged 60 or more.

Are Young People more Moderate?

The overall picture for young people is, therefore, mixed. Young Protestants are distinctly more likely to see themselves as Northern Irish and as 'neither unionist nor nationalist'. They are just as likely as their elders to feel that the best long-term future for Northern Ireland is to stay as part of the UK – at least when the only other option is a united Ireland. When other options are given they are much less certain about retaining the union and much less certain about excluding an Irish government from a say in the running of Northern Ireland. Younger Protestants are also much more likely than their elders to feel that Protestants are treated better than Catholics by a range of institutions – though there also appears to be a much smaller but distinctive group of young Protestants who feel the opposite. When it comes to party support there is further evidence of the heterogeneity of this group – young Protestants are both more likely not to support *any* party (or to support a 'non-traditional' party) *and* more likely to be DUP supporters.

Young Catholics are not markedly more likely to call themselves Northern Irish but they are more likely to say that they are 'neither unionist nor nationalist'. Given a straight choice between a united Ireland and retaining the union they are more likely to feel that the best *long-term future for Northern Ireland* is within the UK – but when given more

options and asked their *own* preferences, they are more likely than their elders to prefer some option other than the union. Young Catholics are particularly likely to acknowledge that there is a lot of generalised prejudice against Protestants in Northern Ireland, but in relation to the specific institutions mentioned they are more likely than their elders to feel that if there is discrimination, it goes against Catholics. When it comes to party support, young Catholics (like young Protestants) are the age group most likely not to support *any* party or to support a 'non-traditional' party. They are also fractionally more likely to support Sinn Fein.

There are indications then that young Protestants (or some of them) may be rather more liberal than their older co-religionists, though the picture is more equivocal for young Catholics. What is clear is that younger people of both religions do appear to have *different* attitudes from those in the older age groups, and that among young Protestants at least, these are often in a more moderate direction.

To look further at the idea that young Protestants and Catholics were 'different' from their elders we carried out a series of cluster analyses for each age group to see the extent to which there were 'natural' clusters of Protestants and Catholics based on the similarity of their attitudes. Cluster analysis is a statistical technique used to identify relatively similar groups of cases (people in this instance) whose attributes (in this case attitudes) are close enough that they tend to 'cluster' together. We included variables measuring:

- national identity
- party support
- sex
- level of education
- social class
- strength of unionism/nationalism
- whether respondent had no religion
- perceived prejudice against Catholics and Protestants
- perceived discrimination by particular institutions

We did not include information on their actual religion (or religious background). By imposing a two cluster solution on the data we were interested in the extent to which the two clusters that emerged formed an identifiable 'Protestant' and an identifiable 'Catholic' grouping.

The results were striking. For the younger age groups it was indeed the case that their attitudes were *least* likely to fall into natural 'Protestant' and 'Catholic' clusters – moreover this finding was mirrored in the two previous NISA surveys which included the same variables (see Table 10). However, what was equally interesting was that for every survey year and in every age group there was a very clear and identifiable 'Protestant' cluster (including almost no Catholics), while the other cluster included virtually all Catholics – but also a significant number of Protestants. Thus, while other research has shown that there is a large group of 'unionist Catholics' (Breen, 1996), they are still more similar to other Catholics in the rest of their attitudes than they are to most Protestants. In addition, clearly there is a group of Protestants – particularly among the young – who are closer to some Catholics in attitudes than they are to most other Protestants.

Table 10

Proportion of Catholics and Protestants in each of the two clusters by age and year of survey (%)

	1991		1993		1995	
	Catholic cluster 1	Protestant cluster 2	Catholic cluster 1	Protestant cluster 2	Catholic cluster 1	Protestant cluster 2
18-30	68	97	57	100	66	97
31-40	69	97	72	96	85	93
41-59	78	96	84	93	86	91
60+	87	96	91	95	85	95

But although there is clearly a younger group of Protestants who are closer to their Catholic counterparts than they are to their co-religionists, it would be unwise to assume that this is necessarily because they are more 'liberal' without first examining the role that apathy may play in shaping the political and social attitudes of young people.

The Importance of Apathy

When respondents say that they have no religion, or that they support no party, or that they are 'neither unionist nor nationalist', it is hard to know when this answer reflects a positive stance on political and religious issues and when it reflects a sense of apathy or a belief that politics is irrelevant to their lives. Similarly the apparent ambivalence over whether the Republic of Ireland should be involved in governing Northern Ireland may reflect thoughtful uncertainty – or disinterest. Attitude surveys may be better than other surveys at accepting 'don't know' answers from respondents but they are no better at dealing with the 'don't know and don't care' variety. The suspicion that some of these respondents are apathetic rather than determinedly middle-minded has some basis.

Interest in Politics

In Britain the lack of interest in politics evinced by young people has been well documented (see, for example, Park, 1995). Discussion has ranged around whether this is a life cycle effect (young people will become more interested in politics as they grow older) or a generational phenomenon (cohorts of the apathetic and disaffected will eventually replace current generations of the politically interested). In any event, Table 11 shows that young people in Northern Ireland are no exception in their lack of political interest. The only difference seems to be that Catholics aged 60 or more are equally as uninterested as their younger counterparts.

Table 11
Interest in politics among different age groups (%)

| | Age of respondent | | | | | |
| | Protestant | | | Catholic | | |
	18-30	31-59	60+	18-30	31-59	60+
A great deal/quite a lot	16	24	30	15	27	18
Some	32	36	29	33	32	30
Not very much	32	30	29	30	30	29
None at all	20	11	12	23	12	23

But even this question is hard to interpret definitively. 'No interest at all' may be a positive rejection of conventional politics rather than an indication of true apathy. Certainly other research does *not* indicate that age is an important predictor of levels of political trust and efficacy within a Northern Ireland population (Hayes and McAllister, 1996). Thus it is hard to say conclusively that lack of 'interest' combined with a 'neither unionist nor nationalist' stance implies apathy. The same is true for measures of electoral participation. The 1994 NISA survey included a question asking respondents if they had voted in the 1992 General Election (Table 12) and levels are characteristically low for young people. But is this because they don't care about the issues or because they reject a political system in which they see little scope for their views?

Table 12
Percentage voted in the 1992 General Election (of those eligible)

	Protestant	Catholic
Age of respondent		
18-30	66	68
31-59	81	76
60+	86	80

One way of trying to judge whether apathy plays a large part in forming the attitudes of young people is to look at those factors most strongly associated with a 'moderate' mindset and see if these are also consistent with an apathetic viewpoint.

Modelling a Moderate Mindset
A logistic regression model was devised looking at the factors associated with declaring oneself to be 'neither a unionist nor a nationalist'. We looked at this first for all respondents who were raised as Protestant and then again for young Protestants separately; we repeated this for those respondents raised as Catholics. The original models included demographic variables such as sex, social class, tenure and educational qualifications; measures of social contact such as having been to an integrated school or

having friends, relatives or neighbours of a different religion; measures of perceived prejudice or discrimination; and self-rated prejudice. Table 13 summarises the factors that are important in predicting whether a

Table 13
Factors important in explaining being 'neither unionist nor nationalist'

All Protestants	Young Protestants	All Catholics	Young Catholics
Describes self as 'not prejudiced'	Lives in a mixed area	Has friends of a different religion	Has friends of a different religion
Younger	Describes self as 'not prejudiced'	Has relatives of a different religion	Female
Feels that there is a lot of prejudice against Catholics in Northern Ireland	Describes religion as 'none'	Disinterested in politics	Attends church infrequently
Attended an integrated school	Feels that there is a lot of prejudice against Catholics in Northern Ireland	Younger	Believes that courts trying terrorist cases treat Protestants and Catholics equally
Believes that the FEC treats Protestants better than Catholics	Disinterested in politics	Female	
Feels that there is not a lot of prejudice against Protestants in Northern Ireland		Believes that courts trying terrorist cases treat Protestants and Catholics equally	
Has relatives of a different religion		Describes religion as 'none'	
Disinterested in politics		Believes that there is little prejudice against Catholics in Northern Ireland	

respondent is 'neither a unionist nor a nationalist' and lists these in approximate order of importance in each model. As expected, given the clarity of the results so far, being younger is significantly related to being 'neither unionist nor nationalist' among both Catholic and Protestant samples. Appendix A gives details of the models.

Looking first at the results for those raised as Protestants, what is most striking is the relative *lack* of impact of demographic factors and the predominance of factors that reflect social contact with, and perceptions of social injustice towards, Catholics. Thus Protestants who describe themselves as 'neither unionist nor nationalist' tend also to see themselves as unprejudiced, to feel that there is a lot of prejudice against Catholics, and to believe that there is specific discrimination against Catholics. They are also more likely to have relatives of a different religion and to have attended an integrated school.   This last is an interesting finding as evidence that social contact encourages a softening of attitudes has sometimes proved elusive. Nonetheless, the fact that having attended an 'integrated school' emerged so strongly in the Protestant sample is rather a curious result as relatively few people will have been to such schools; however respondents are known to define integrated schools rather broadly and thus many Protestants who attended a school in which there were any Catholics at all may have included themselves in this category. Interest in politics is of least importance over and above other measures indicating a generally liberal attitude. Whether this variable is measuring apathy or something else to do with a rejection of traditional politics (or both) is a moot point, but it is not of great relevance to being 'neither unionist nor nationalist' – much more important is the respondent's attitude towards the Catholic community group.   Therefore, for Protestants at least, this measure is probably quite a good indicator of a moderate mindset.

For Catholics a general disinterest in politics is rather more important in predicting being 'neither unionist nor nationalist', but this is still set against a general background of factors that are clearly more to do with social contact. Catholics who consider that they are not nationalists tend to have friends or relatives of a different religion; they also tend to believe that Protestants and Catholics are treated equally by the courts in terrorist cases, and they are quite likely to have rejected their religious affiliation.

Again, this is consistent with a moderate rather than an apathetic stance. What is distinctive about the Catholic sample, though, is that women are more likely to define themselves as 'neither unionist nor nationalist'.

But given that what we are looking at here is quite probably a measure of 'moderateness', are there any differences in the models for younger respondents that reveal why they are often so much more moderate than their elders? The answer for Catholics is no. Exactly the same kinds of factors emerge in both models. But for Protestants there are some differences. A rejection of religion is an important predictor of moderate attitudes in young people who were raised as Protestant, but this is not the case for the Protestant sample overall. The most likely explanation for the liberalism of younger Protestants is that they are simply more likely than their elders to hold the sorts of beliefs about inequality that *lead* to a more moderate stance.

The Implications for Electoral Behaviour
Although the 'neither unionist nor nationalist' is probably the nearest we can get to a liberal mindset it is impossible to disentangle completely apathetic disengagement from politics with a more positive decision to be non-aligned. But perhaps this does not matter, because the implications of this stance in terms of electoral participation are what is really significant. The 1994 survey included a new question asking if respondents had voted in the 1992 General Election (as part of a series of new questions looking at political trust and efficacy). What these data show quite clearly are that those who describe themselves as 'neither unionist nor nationalist' are much more likely *not* to vote. Moreover, given that young people are less inclined to vote in any case and that they (or at least young Protestants) are also most likely to be middle-minded, what this amounts to is that the liberalism that is most evident in young people is largely unreflected in actual voting patterns (see Table 14). Further analysis reinforces this grim picture. When modelling the choice of 'neither unionist nor nationalist' using 1994 data, *by far* the best predictor of this attitude among Protestant respondents is not having voted in the 1992 General Election. This leaves us with the sobering thought that (as this is written in the week that the

Table 14

Percentage of Protestants and Catholics who voted in the 1992 General Election

Age of respondent	Protestant		Catholic	
	'Unionist'	'neither'	'Nationalist'	'neither'
22-35	83	43	76	64
36-59	87	68	86	68
60+	89	75	86	71

Age given is that at the time of the 1994 survey in order to include only those respondents who would have been eligible to vote in 1992.

Numbers are small for some of these cells and results should be treated with caution

elections will be held to select the forum for discussions on the future of Northern Ireland) – within the present political context, the young, the liberal and the moderate will choose simply not to exercise their vote.

Conclusions and Implications for Community Relations Policies

On the face of it, some of these results must be encouraging for those responsible for community relations policy in Northern Ireland. Young Protestants (and young Catholics to some extent) do appear to be more moderate in their views, and perhaps initiatives such as Education for Mutual Understanding (EMU) have had some effect. Among all age groups there is some evidence that social contact with the 'other' community group does indeed encourage politically moderate views. Nonetheless there is a strong possibility that these signs of moderateness are simply generational effects; that is, as they grow older the attitudes of young people will simply harden into those of their elders (see also Evans and Duffy, forthcoming).

But by far the most worrying finding is that even if the moderate views of young people are transient, they appeared to find no clear expression within the political parties 'on offer' in 1992. Of course this would not necessarily be the case if other more 'acceptable' parties were to stand – and this might be good news for the plethora of newer political parties

advocating compromise that emerged in the May 1996 elections. In the event that these parties could manage to harness the votes of what is not (necessarily) an apathetic generation, it is not impossible that they could significantly shift the balance of politics in Northern Ireland over the next decade.

References

AHRENDT, D. and YOUNG, K. 1994. 'Authoritarianism updated', in R. Jowell, J. Curtice, L. Brook and D. Ahrendt (eds.), *British Social Attitudes: the 11th report*, Aldershot, Dartmouth.

BREEN, R. 1996. 'Who wants a United Ireland?', in R. Breen, P. Devine and L. Dowds (eds.), *Social Attitudes in Northern Ireland: the Fifth Report*, Belfast, Appletree Press.

BREEN, R. and HAYES, B. forthcoming. *Religious mobility and political identification in Northern Ireland.* (Queen's University Belfast, Department of Sociology).

CAIRNS, E. 1992. 'Political Violence, Social values and the generation gap', in P. Stringer and G. Robinson (eds.), *Social Attitudes in Northern Ireland: the Second Report*, Belfast, Blackstaff.

EVANS, G. and DUFFY, M. forthcoming. 'Beyond the sectarian divide: the social bases and political consequences of nationalist and unionist party competition in Northern Ireland', *British Journal of Political Science*.

GALLAGHER, A. M. 1989. 'Social identity and the Northern Ireland conflict', *Human Relations*, 42, 917-935.

HAYES, B. C. and MCALLISTER, I. 1996. 'Public support for democratic values in Northern Ireland', in R. Breen, P. Devine and L. Dowds (eds.), *Social Attitudes in Northern Ireland: the Fifth Report*, Belfast, Appletree Press.

INGLEHART, R. 1977. *The silent revolution.* Princeton, NJ: Princeton University Press.

INGLEHART, R. 1990. *Culture shift in advanced industrial society.* Princeton, NJ: Princeton University Press.

PARK, A. 1995. 'Teenagers and their politics', in R. Jowell, J. Curtice, A. Park, L. Brook and D. Ahrendt (eds.), *British Social Attitudes: the 12th report*, Aldershot, Dartmouth.

TOPF, R., MÖHLER, P. and HEATH, A. 1989. 'Pride in one's country: Britain and West Germany', in R. Jowell, S. Witherspoon and L. Brook (eds.), *British Social Attitudes: special international report*, Aldershot, Gower.

TREW, K. 1996. 'National identity', in R. Breen, P. Devine and L. Dowds (eds.), *Social Attitudes in Northern Ireland: the Fifth Report*, Belfast, Appletree Press.

Appendix

Table A1

Factors associated with being 'neither unionist nor nationalist' (respondents raised as Protestants)

	B	Sig	R
Describes self as not prejudiced	-2.1684	.0000	-.1653
Age		.0000	.1475
Age (young)	.6867	.0000	.1461
Age (middle)	-.0466	.6907	.0000
Feels that there is a lot of prejudice against Catholics in NI	-.9001	.0000	-.1353
Attended an integrated school	.7567	.0002	.1096
Believes that the FEC treats Protestants better than Catholics	.7694	.0013	.0913
Feels that there is not a lot of prejudice against Protestants in NI	.6425	.0015	.0899
Has relatives of a different religion	.2846	.0046	.0777
Disinterested in politics	.2248	.0094	.0689

Model chi-squared = 193.688 with 10 df

Table A2

Factors associated with being 'neither unionist nor nationalist' (respondents raised as Protestants and aged 18-30)

	B	Sig	R
Lives in a mixed area	.6987	.0014	.1977
Describes self as not prejudiced	-2.4462	.0022	-.1876
Describes religion as 'none'	-1.5429	.0046	-.1692
Feels that there is a lot of prejudice against Catholics in NI	-.7778	.0084	-.1534
Disinterested in politics	.4829	.0232	.1224

Model chi-squared = 55.914 with 5 df

Table A3

Factors associated with being 'neither unionist nor nationalist' (respondents raised as Catholics)

	B	Sig	R
Has friends of a different religion	.5540	.0000	.1574
Has relatives of a different religion	.4058	.0003	.1146
Disinterested in politics	.3013	.0005	.1109
Age	–	.0020	.1008
Age (young)	.4532	.0018	.0967
Age (middle)	-.3149	.0145	-.0694
Being a woman	.5939	.0017	.0979
Believes that courts trying terrorist cases treat Catholics and Protestants equally	-.6693	.0022	-.0945
Describes religion as 'none'	-1.3969	.0026	.0625
Believes that there is little prejudice against Catholics in NI	.3465	.0223	.0625

Model chi-squared = 133.707 with 9 df

Table A4

Factors associated with being 'neither unionist nor nationalist' (respondents raised as Catholics and aged 18-30)

	B	Sig	R
Has friends of a different religion	1.1641	.0000	.2649
Is a woman	1.0045	.0077	.1508
Attends church infrequently	.2614	.0126	.1372
Believes that courts trying terrorist cases treat Catholics and Protestants equally	-.7761	.0470	.4602

Model chi-squared = 45.430 with 4 df

4

Attitudes to Illicit Drug Use in Northern Ireland

Edgar F. Jardine

Introduction
The 1995 Northern Ireland Social Attitudes (NISA) Survey contained, for the first time, a series of questions to test public attitudes to illicit drugs. This chapter examines public views about the use of drugs, attitudes to legalising them and compares the responses of people in Northern Ireland with those of respondents in Great Britain (GB) who were asked the same questions in the British version of the survey. In the main face-to-face questionnaire we asked about two drugs, cannabis and heroin, in order to test if respondents differentiate between 'soft' and 'hard' drugs. The questions relating to both drugs were very similar although we also asked respondents whether they themselves had tried cannabis.

Historically, the use of illicit drugs is usually considered to have been lower in Northern Ireland (NI) than in other parts of the United Kingdom or in major urban areas in the Republic of Ireland. However the evidence from a range of sources confirms that in recent years there has been a substantial increase in the problem of drugs misuse in the province. Evidence provided by the Northern Ireland Office (NIO, 1996a) to the Northern Ireland Select Committee's Inquiry into Illicit Drug Use showed that the number of drug related offences recorded by the police increased almost five-fold between 1991 and 1995 and that arrests for drug related offences increased by 343 per cent over the same period. Seizures of all major classes of illicit drugs by the RUC are also much higher than five years ago. A similar pattern of seizures is evident from data provided by HM Customs and Excise. While the quantity and value of each major drug

class seized varies from year to year, as Table 1 shows, 1992 was a watershed year for drug seizures by Customs and Excise. Of particular note is the increase in Ecstasy seizures which, in 1995, accounted for almost all the total value of drugs seized by Customs and Excise. The Health Promotion Agency for Northern Ireland (HPA(NI)) has also noted a steady increase in the use of Ecstasy and other drugs such as Speed (amphetamine sulphate) and LSD which are associated with the 'clubbing' scene in Northern Ireland (HPA(NI) 1995a).

Table 1
HM Customs and Excise drugs seizures in Northern Ireland 1990-1995 by drug type

	1990	1991	1992	1993	1994	1995
LSD (Class A)						
Quantity (Tabs)	0	0	3504	271	2916	31
Value (£)	0	0	14016	1084	11664	124
Cocaine (Class A)						
Quantity (Gr)	0.5	2.7	2671.7	1	1108.4	12
Value (£)	40	219	213733	80	88672	960
Ecstasy (A)						
Quantity (Tabs)	0	0	993	229	6927.5	29798
Value (£)	0	0	19860	4600	138550	570945
Amphet. (B)						
Quantity (Tabs)	2.5	0	855.5	82.13	333	133
Value (£)	38	0	12832	1232	4995	1920
Cannabis (B)						
Quantity (Tabs)	121.3	1176	855.7	14553.2	29704.4	259.92
Value (£)	433	4198	3055	51955	106044	1233.13
Total						
Quantity (Gr)	124.3	1178.7	4382.9	14636.3	31145.8	404.92
Value (£)	511	4417	263496	58951	349926	575182

Surveys both of school children and adults are also beginning to provide evidence on the scale of drug misuse in Northern Ireland. The Northern Ireland Crime Survey, which was conducted in 1994, asked a random sample of people aged 16 and over if they had taken at least one of a range

of drugs.   While 80 per cent of respondents said they had never taken drugs, 23 per cent of men and 16 per cent of women admitted taking at least one of the listed drugs (NIO, 1996b).   Comparable data from a similar survey in Great Britain (GB) (Ramsey and Percy, 1996) produced rates of 33 per cent for men and 25 per cent for women, confirming the general perception of lower rates of use in Northern Ireland (see Table 2).   In both studies, the most frequently used drug was cannabis with much lower usage levels of amphetamines, LSD and magic mushrooms. Use of 'hard' drugs, such as heroin and cocaine, was negligible among respondents both in GB and NI.

Table 2

Percentage of males and females who have ever taken any illegal drug (%)

	GB	NI
Male	33	23
Female	25	16

In two comparable studies of drug use among school children (HPA(NI), 1994 and 1995b), it was found that fifth formers' exposure to illicit drugs had increased markedly between 1992 and 1994.   The proportion of respondents saying that they had been offered drugs rose from 26 per cent to 42 per cent while those who had ever used drugs increased from 16 per cent to 26 per cent.   Under six per cent admitted to 'currently using' drugs in 1992 compared to about 18 per cent in 1994. The majority of current drug users surveyed in 1994 (84 per cent) said that it would be 'quite easy' or 'very easy' to obtain drugs.   Cannabis was the most frequently used drug by these respondents although significant numbers had also used LSD, Ecstasy, poppers (amylnitrate) and Speed.

Research on drug use among young adults was extended through a survey of 16 and 17-year-olds drawn from sixth forms, further education colleges and Youth Training projects (Craig, 1996).   The study found that almost two-thirds of the sample had been offered drugs and just over 40 per cent had used drugs.   Taken together with the surveys of school-children, the progression in experience of drug use with age is clear.   While the HPA(NI)'s 1994 Health Behaviour of School Children (HBSC) study

found that 26 per cent of 15-year-old fifth form pupils had used drugs, Craig found that 36 per cent of 16-year-old and 43 per cent of 17-year-old sixth form pupils had done so. The major drugs of use among the 16 and 17-year-olds were cannabis, LSD and Ecstasy.

The Sample
The drug questions in the 1995 NISA survey were included in one of the two versions of the questionnaire and were hence only asked of half of all respondents to the survey. Analyses are reported in terms of the gender, age and religion of respondents. The sample was 54 per cent female while the age break-down was 18-30 years, 20 per cent, 31-59 years, 56 per cent and 60 years and over, 24 per cent. Of those respondents stating a religious affiliation, 57 per cent were Protestant and 41 per cent were Catholic.

Attitudes to Cannabis Use
We asked respondents whether they thought that more people in Northern Ireland were taking cannabis now than five years ago and whether they thought these numbers were likely to be more, less or about the same in five years time. The results were unequivocal with 82 per cent of respondents saying that cannabis use was more prevalent now than five years ago. Almost as many (79 per cent) anticipate that more people will be taking cannabis in five years time compared with now. GB respondents are notably less likely to agree either that cannabis use is more prevalent now or that future use is likely to increase (66 per cent in both instances) which may reflect the longer history of exposure to illicit drug use in GB than in NI.

Just less than one in ten respondents admitted to ever having tried cannabis, with men (13 per cent) being much more likely than women (seven per cent) to admit use. As Table 3 shows, this contrasts with the position in GB where one in five admit to having ever tried the drug. There is little difference in the percentage of men and women in the GB survey having tried cannabis (22 per cent compared to 20 per cent). In both GB and NI younger respondents (18-30) are much more likely to have used cannabis than those aged 31-59. The proportion of respondents aged 60 or over saying that they had tried cannabis was negligible. A significant

proportion of respondents report they had used infrequently (GB 60 per cent, NI 75 per cent) although 13 per cent of GB respondents and three per cent of NI respondents admit to having used cannabis frequently.

Table 3

Percentage of males and females who admit to using cannabis (%)

	GB	NI
Male	22	13
Female	20	7

We were interested to find out if respondents thought that the use of cannabis was a cause of crime and violence and whether use was considered to be damaging to health. The results are presented in Table 4. Almost 70 per cent of Northern Irish respondents (compared to just over half in GB) either agree or agree strongly that cannabis is a cause of crime and violence. There is little difference between the attitudes of men and women but older people are much more likely than younger people to strongly agree with the proposition.

Table 4

Percentage agreeing that cannabis is a cause of crime (%)

Age	GB	NI
18-30	38	48
31-59	46	70
60+	73	82

There is a widely held perception, shared by both men and women, that cannabis is dangerous to the health of users. Sixty per cent of Northern Ireland respondents either disagree or disagree strongly with the statement 'cannabis isn't nearly as damaging as some people think'. GB respondents are somewhat less likely to think that cannabis use is damaging (43 per cent). Again, people under 30 in both countries are less likely than those over 30 to think that cannabis use is damaging to health.

A series of questions was asked about legislative issues in relation to cannabis. While just 23 per cent of NISA respondents agree or agree strongly that people should not be prosecuted for possessing small amounts of cannabis for their own use, 70 per cent either disagree or disagree strongly with the proposition. GB respondents, by contrast, are more likely to say that people should not be prosecuted (41 per cent) with less than 50 per cent disagreeing. Older respondents take a less tolerant view of possession for personal use than younger people.

Attitudes to the prosecution of those who sell cannabis are particularly pronounced with 89 per cent of NI respondents and 78 per cent in GB agreeing to prosecution. NI respondents are much more likely to agree strongly with the statement than their GB counterparts. Strength of agreement increases with age for both groups.

Not surprisingly, just two per cent of NI respondents think that taking cannabis should be legal, without restrictions, while 23 per cent of men and 13 per cent of women (17 per cent overall), say that taking cannabis should be legal, but that it should only be available from licensed shops (see Table 5). However it is the view of a significant majority both of men (73 per cent) and women (83 per cent) that cannabis should remain illegal. Fewer GB respondents (64 per cent) agree that it should remain illegal while just under six per cent think it should be legal without restrictions although 27 per cent are prepared to accept it becoming legal if availability was controlled. Overall one in three GB respondents are prepared to contemplate the legalisation of cannabis. The differences between the attitudes of older and younger people to legalising cannabis are much more marked in GB than in NI with younger respondents holding more tolerant attitudes.

Table 5

Percentage of GB and NI respondents agreeing that taking cannabis should be... (%)

	GB	NI
...legal without restrictions	6	2
...legal, but from licensed shops	27	17
...remain illegal	64	79

We were interested to discover if respondents would discriminate in their attitudes to 'soft' and 'hard' drugs. The questionnaire contained a parallel set of questions to those asked about cannabis, only this time, the questions referred to heroin. From other evidence on drug misuse in Northern Ireland we expected to have few, if any, respondents who would admit to using heroin and no question on the use of heroin was therefore included. Our expectation was that respondents would indeed distinguish between cannabis and heroin and that this would be reflected in levels of disapproval of heroin use even higher than those recorded in relation to cannabis.

More than four in five respondents (83 per cent) think that the use of heroin is more prevalent now than five years ago, a view held by 86 per cent of women and 79 per cent of men. There is little variation by age, although younger respondents are more likely than older respondents to think there had been no change in the use of heroin over the period. As for the equivalent question on cannabis use, GB respondents are rather less likely (71 per cent) to report that heroin use had increased over the past five years.

The use of heroin is perceived to have a number of adverse consequences by a large majority of those surveyed. As Table 6 shows, no fewer

Table 6

Percentage of respondents citing adverse effects of heroin use (%)		
	GB	**NI**
Agreeing that 'heroin is a cause of crime and violence'	90	87
Disagreeing that 'heroin isn't nearly as damaging to users as some people think'	77	79
Agreeing that 'if you legalise heroin, many more people will become addicts'	72	70

than 87 per cent agree that heroin is a cause of crime and violence, a view shared equally by both men and women and by people of all ages (although older respondents are more likely to 'strongly agree'). Similarly, asked

'how much they agreed or disagreed' that 'heroin isn't nearly as damaging to users as some people think', 79 per cent record disagreement. Patterns of response to both questions are very similar in GB although there is a tendency for proportionately more GB respondents to 'strongly disagree' with the proposition. This pattern is repeated when respondents in both GB and NI were asked whether they thought many more people would become addicts if heroin was legalised. Some 72 per cent in GB and 70 per cent in NI think this would be so, with 37 per cent of the former and 30 per cent of the latter expressing strong agreement. The view is held consistently regardless of age although fewer NI respondents are likely to 'agree strongly'.

There is strong support (82 per cent) among NI respondents for the prosecution of people for possessing small quantities of heroin for their personal use, a position taken by rather fewer (70 per cent) GB respondents. There is little evidence that younger people are less disapproving overall although fewer strongly support prosecution. There is however almost total agreement (93 per cent and 95 per cent respectively) in NI and GB that people who sell heroin should always be prosecuted. Men and women agree equally strongly with the proposition. Age trends are similar in GB and NI, with older respondents more likely to strongly agree on prosecution. Consistent with the high levels of disapproval of heroin use confirmed repeatedly in the survey, it is not surprising that 90 per cent of NI respondents and 86 per cent of GB respondents take the view that heroin should remain illegal. Indeed only 10 per cent in GB and seven per cent in NI are prepared to offer qualified agreement to legalising heroin by agreeing that 'taking heroin should be legal, but it should only be available from licensed shops'. The consistency in the views of different age-groups in GB and NI on this question is remarkable.

Further light is shed on the high levels of disapproval associated with drug use from questions asked of respondents in the self-completion questionnaire. Almost three in four of those surveyed in Northern Ireland agree with the statement that 'The use of "soft" drugs leads to the use of "hard" drugs'. Older people (see Table 7) are more likely than younger people to agree with the statement and twice as likely to express strong agreement. GB respondents were rather less likely (69 per cent) to think

that the use of 'soft' drugs would lead to the use of 'hard' drugs although similar age response patterns are evident.

Table 7

Age differences in attitudes to illegal drugs in Northern Ireland

	18-30	31-59	60+	All ages
Percentage agreeing that...				
...the use of 'soft' drugs leads to the use of 'hard' drugs	59	78	77	74
...all use of illegal drugs is misuse	58	72	81	71
...the use of illegal drugs always leads to addiction	36	57	66	55
...the legalisation of drugs would lead to a considerable increase in misuse	68	70	69	69

Over 70 per cent of NI respondents and 57 per cent in GB either 'agree' or 'agree strongly' that 'all use of illegal drugs is misuse'. This varies from 58 per cent of 18-30 year olds to 81 per cent of the over 60s in Northern Ireland. The comparable figures for GB are 39 per cent and 78 per cent.

A related issue is whether the use of illegal drugs always leads to addiction. Just over half of NI respondents think it does. While there is little empirical evidence on which to make such a judgement, it is unlikely that the risk of addiction resulting from illegal drug use is as high as is publicly perceived. Although gender had little influence on response, there is a clear relationship with age, with 66 per cent of those aged 60 and over compared with 36 per cent aged 18-30 strongly agreeing with this statement both in NI and GB.

It is not surprising therefore that most respondents agree that the legalisation of drugs would lead to a considerable increase in misuse. Among NI respondents 69 per cent hold this view as do 64 per cent of respondents in GB. While there is no gender difference among the latter,

women in Northern Ireland are more likely than men to agree with the statement. Furthermore, in contrast to the tendency for the level of agreement to increase with age in GB, no discernible age differences are identified in the NISA survey. Just seven per cent of NI respondents and 10 per cent of those in GB agree that all illegal drugs should be made legal. We included a number of questions in the self-completion questionnaire about attitudes to treatment. Responses to these questions revealed much greater ambivalence than those which asked about other dimensions of the drugs issue. Two questions were designed to assess attitudes to compulsory treatment for drug addicts while further questions examined attitudes to other aspects of treatment.

A minority of respondents (28 per cent in NI and 35 per cent in GB) think that people who are addicted to drugs should decide for themselves whether to have treatment. Rather more (45 per cent and 43 per cent respectively) disagree with the statement. Conversely, half of GB respondents and 56 per cent in NI agree that the only way to help addicts is to make them have treatment.

There is little enthusiasm for the proposition that doctors must be allowed to prescribe drugs for those who are addicted to them. Fewer NI (22 per cent) than GB respondents (32 per cent) agree and, of those, a relatively small number express strong agreement. The preferred alternative for 56 per cent of NI respondents is to stop those addicted to drugs from using them altogether, a view also taken by half of those in the GB survey. Men in GB are a little more inclined than women to support total desistance, a difference not found in NI. The option finds less favour among younger respondents in both surveys.

Drug Use and Religious Affiliation
Differences in the attitudes of Protestant and Catholic respondents to issues included in the NISA survey have frequently been explored in previous NISA volumes and a number of chapters in the present volume. It is also almost invariably the case that differences are detected in the attitudes of the two main communities, irrespective of the topic being considered, and inter-community differences tend to be at least as important as intra-community differences.

Therefore, in addition to the analyses of the NISA data by age and gender we also looked for differences in inter-community attitudes to illegal drugs. The general trend to emerge from the data suggests that there are in fact very few substantive differences in the attitudes of Protestants and Catholics to the use of illegal drugs. Where differences are found they tend to be in the direction of more tolerant attitudes among Catholics. Given the links between age and attitudes identified earlier in this chapter and the different age profiles of the two communities (28 per cent of Catholic respondents in the sample were under 30 years compared with 19 per cent of Protestants), we undertook further analyses controlling for age. The religion effect however remained, suggesting that it is not solely an artefact of different age distributions.

In relation to heroin misuse, the most significant differences between the two communities relates to the slightly greater tolerance of Catholics to the prosecution of people for the possession of small amounts of heroin for their own use. Among Catholics, 13 per cent of respondents oppose prosecution of people in these circumstances compared to 10 per cent of Protestants. Both religious groups (93 per cent of Protestants and 95 per cent of Catholics) however hold similarly strong views about the prosecution of those who sell heroin. On other dimensions of heroin use, including the link between heroin use and crime and attitudes to legalising the drug, the attitudes of Protestants and Catholics are very similar. The results also show that both Catholics and Protestants hold similar views about most aspects of cannabis use. Catholic respondents are however slightly less likely to think that legalising cannabis will lead to more people becoming addicts (62 per cent compared to 68 per cent of Protestants), more likely to think that people should not be prosecuted for possessing small amounts of heroin (26 per cent of Catholics and 17 per cent of Protestants) and more likely to approve of the controlled availability of cannabis from licensed shops (20 per cent compared to 13 per cent of Protestants).

A similar pattern emerges in relation to questions asked on the self-completion questionnaire. In general, the responses from the two communities did not differ significantly with, for example, around half of both groups believing that the use of illegal drugs always leads to

addiction. Protestant respondents (79 per cent) are however a little more likely than Catholics (71 per cent) to agree that the use of 'soft' drugs leads to the use of 'hard' drugs. Rather fewer Catholics are prepared to accept that all use of illegal drugs is misuse (64 per cent compared with 78 per cent of Protestants).

In relation to attitudes to treatment, however, some significant differences between the attitudes of the two religious groups were identified. About one in two Catholics, compared with two thirds of Protestants, agree that the only way to help addicts is to make them have treatment. Similarly, 62 per cent of Protestants but only 46 per cent of Catholics disagree with the proposition that doctors must be allowed to prescribe drugs for those who are addicted to them.

Attitudes in Northern Ireland compared with Britain

One of the most interesting findings to emerge from the analysis so far is the contrast between attitudes towards drug use in Northern Ireland compared with Britain. Northern Ireland respondents are much more pessimistic about what they see as an increasing problem and are much more concerned, for example, that cannabis generates crime and violence. Furthermore, many more people in Northern Ireland than in Britain believe that people should be prosecuted even for possessing small amounts of cannabis for their own use. The reason for these highly disapproving and punitive attitudes is not immediately obvious, especially when set against a background of lower drug use (albeit increasing) than in Britain. In order to investigate the factors driving disapproval, a regression analysis was carried out for Northern Ireland and for Britain separately (see Appendix for detailed results). Various items measuring disapproval or tolerance towards drug-taking were scaled to form a 'disapproval' scale. The results showed that exactly the same kinds of variables were associated with disapproval in Britain as in Northern Ireland: older people, those who had never tried cannabis themselves, and those with generally authoritarian attitudes were most disapproving. The only variation in this pattern was that in Northern Ireland, having fewer educational qualifications was also independently associated with higher levels of disapproval. Thus there did not appear to be anything special about Northern Ireland respondents that

would lead to their higher levels of disapproval – unless it was simply that NI respondents were generally *more likely* to be authoritarian/older and less likely to have tried cannabis. In order to test this a further regression was constructed, combining data from Northern Ireland and Britain, and including place of residence as an additional variable. The results showed that people living in Northern Ireland were still significantly more likely to be disapproving, over and above the effects of their being authoritarian or older. This finding bears further investigation but it is worth noting that the message that 'drugs are bad' has been fairly well absorbed within Northern Ireland culture, and that further efforts in the area of national advertising campaigns may have little added value without much more specific targeting of the actual populations at risk.

Conclusion

In this chapter we have described the attitudes of the Northern Ireland public to the use of illegal drugs and drawn comparisons with Great Britain. The findings provide new insights into community attitudes to drug use and a baseline against which to measure future trends.

The analysis has demonstrated that illegal drugs evoke a strong response from the Northern Ireland public. While respondents' attitudes to cannabis and heroin differ, disapproval of all illegal drug use is widespread, particularly among older people. Younger people tend to be more tolerant of drug use and more likely to have taken cannabis than older respondents. Craig (1996) also found considerable tolerance of drug use among her sample of 16 and 17-year-olds. Relatively high levels of tolerance of drug use are evident, even among respondents who had never used drugs.

There is widespread agreement that drug use is more prevalent now than five years ago and that cannabis use will continue to increase in the future. The majority of respondents think that the use of cannabis and heroin causes crime and violence and that people who sell these drugs should be prosecuted. There is, however, a significant minority who oppose the prosecution of people who are found to have small quantities of drugs for personal use and almost one in five respondents think that cannabis should be available either without restriction or from licensed shops.

Compared with Northern Ireland, GB respondents report more tolerant attitudes to drug use and are rather less inclined to support prosecution for personal use or to disapprove of the use of cannabis or heroin being legalised. The differences do however have to be read in the context of significant levels of disapproval of drug use among both British and Northern Irish respondents.

The results of this survey provide a particular challenge for agencies which are attempting to discourage use of illicit drugs in the community. There is compelling evidence from the survey of high overall levels of disapproval to the use of drugs among the general public, suggesting that the messages arising from media coverage and from drug prevention campaigns have been well absorbed. However, some of the least disapproving are young people and it is among this group that the drugs problem is principally located. This suggests the need for very specific targeting of educational programmes and advertising campaigns designed to inform young people of the general risks of illicit drug use and the dangers of drugs associated with the 'clubbing' scene. Furthermore, even holding negative attitudes about drug use may not guarantee desistance. Prevention programmes therefore, in addition to ensuring that young people have the right information, must include the development of the necessary inter-personal skills to enable them to deal effectively with an offer of drugs made in a social situation and in the presence of their peers.

References

CRAIG, J. forthcoming. 'Almost Adult. Some correlates of alcohol, tobacco and illicit drug use among a sample of 16 and 17 year-olds in Northern Ireland', *Northern Ireland Statistics and Research Agency Occasional Paper No. 3*, Belfast, Northern Ireland Statistics and Research Agency.

THE HEALTH PROMOTION AGENCY FOR NORTHERN IRELAND. 1994. *The Health Behaviour of School Children in Northern Ireland (1992)*, Belfast, The Health Promotion Agency for Northern Ireland.

THE HEALTH PROMOTION AGENCY FOR NORTHERN IRELAND. 1995a. *Health No. 18*, Belfast, The Health Promotion Agency for Northern Ireland.

THE HEALTH PROMOTION AGENCY FOR NORTHERN IRELAND. 1995b. *The Health Behaviour of School Children in Northern Ireland. A report on*

the 1994 survey, Belfast, The Health Promotion Agency for Northern Ireland.

HEATH, A., EVANS, G., LALLJEE, M., MARTIN, J. AND WITHERSPOON, S. 1990. 'The measurement of core beliefs and values' CREST *Working Paper No. 2*, December 1990.

NORTHERN IRELAND OFFICE. 1996a. *Memorandum to the Northern Ireland Select Committee Inquiry into Illicit Drug Use*, Belfast, Northern Ireland Office.

NORTHERN IRELAND OFFICE. 1996b. 'Experience of Drugs in Northern Ireland. Preliminary findings from the 1994/95 Northern Ireland Crime Survey', *Research Findings 1/96*, Belfast, Northern Ireland Office.

RAMSEY, M. and PERCY, A. 1996. 'Drug Misuse declared: results of the 1994 British Crime Survey', London, Home Office.

Appendix

A factor analysis was carried out to determine which items should be included in a general drug-use 'disapproval' scale. Items used in the scale included:

- Doctors must be allowed to prescribe drugs for those who are addicted to them
- The UK should aim to become a drug-free society
- Adults should be free to take any drug they wish
- All adults have a duty to prevent young people from using illegal drugs
- The use of 'soft' drugs leads to the use of 'hard' drugs
- All illegal drugs should be made legal
- The best way to treat people who are addicted to drugs is to stop them from using drugs altogether
- Taking illegal drugs can sometimes be beneficial
- The use of illegal drugs always leads to addiction
- You can never trust someone who is addicted to drugs
- People who are addicted to drugs should decide for *themselves* whether they have treatment
- Taking drugs is always morally wrong
- All use of illegal drugs is misuse
- We need to accept that using illegal drugs is a normal part of some people's lives
- The legalisation of drugs would lead to a considerable increase in misuse
- The only way to help addicts is to *make* them have treatment

Table A1
Multiple regression – Estimation of drug-use disapproval in Great Britain and Northern Ireland

	Great Britain			Northern Ireland		
	Beta	B	SE	Beta	B	SE
Age	-.12	-.05	(.01)	-.11	-.05	(.02)
Whether ever taken cannabis	-.29	-.47	(.04)	-.24	-.47	(.07)
Level of education	ns	-.01	(.01)	-.17	-.05	(.01)
Libertarianism	-.45	-.45	(.03)	-.38	-.39	(.04)
Adjusted R squared	.42			.33		

Standardised and unstandardised coefficients are presented with standard errors in parentheses.
ns = Not significant at 1% level.
The 'authoritarian/libertarian scale' is a standard scale based on respondents attitudes to a range of items measuring conformity, punitiveness and moral traditionalism (see Heath et al., 1990 for details of its construction).

Table A2
Multiple regression – Estimation of drug-use disapproval – Great Britain and Northern Ireland combined

	Great Britain and Northern Ireland		
	Beta	B	SE
Age	-.12	-.06	(.01)
Whether ever taken cannabis	-.27	-.47	(.04)
Level of education	-.08	-.03	(.001)
Libertarianism	-.41	-.42	(.02)
Lives in Northern Ireland	-.11	-.15	(.03)
Adjusted R squared	.40		

Standardised and unstandardised coefficients are presented with standard errors in parentheses.
ns = Not significant at 1% level.
The 'authoritarian/libertarian scale' is a standard scale based on respondents attitudes to a range of items measuring conformity, punitiveness and moral traditionalism (see Heath et al., 1990 for details of its construction).

5

Family, Friends and Neighbours

Marina Monteith and John Pinkerton

Introduction

Relationships of mutual obligation have been the subject of study by a number of academic disciplines, each bringing its own perspective and focus of interest. Social psychologists have examined friendships and love (Argyle and Henderson, 1985); sociologists have looked at family, kinship and primary groups (Giddens, 1993); and in social policy, the capacity of these networks for social care has been explored (Langan, 1992; St. Leger and Gillespie, 1991). But this interest has tended to raise questions rather than provide clear messages about the extent and utility of these relationships. This questioning has a resonance both within popular consciousness and amongst social care professionals. There is at the very least a nagging doubt, and for some open disbelief, about the continued existence of binding social ties within families, neighbourhoods and friendship circles.

Such questioning reflects real changes within the family affecting membership, size, age structure and roles (Gittins, 1993). It also reflects a greater openness about the dark side of family life, such as child abuse and domestic violence (Dallos and McLaughlin, 1993). Change has also had its impact on neighbourhoods with new patterns of employment, housing and leisure loosening previously tight relationships based on shared locality. As for friendship circles, they seem too loose and contingent to substitute for family and neighbourhood.

Research in Britain and the USA on social relationships have shown strong links with health and happiness. People who have a supportive social network including spouse, family and several friends tend to be

happier, in better health and to live longer. Over a decade ago Campbell (1981) found that health and happiness were affected more by people's social relationships than by income levels, social status or education attainments. Research on women's well being (Aneshensel, et al., 1981) found that having a husband who was a confidante reduced the rate of depression. Research on marital relationships has found that a close confiding relationship is important for mental health, and couples, whether married or cohabiting, with this type of relationship are less likely to have mental health problems.

Other family ties also have a bearing on an individual's health and provide a source of support in times of need. Parents' health has been found to be better if adult children living away from the parental home see them often. Research in the USA has also found that contact with brothers and sisters and other close kin is important as a major source of help in times of need. Studies of patients with mental health problems have found that they are lacking in close family relationships, rather than being short of friends (Leavy, 1983). Similarly, there is research evidence that spouse support is particularly important for emotional and mental well-being. Baldwin and Carlisle (1994), in their literature review of social support for disabled children and their families, also found that spouse support was one of the most important social coping resources for parents, providing both practical help and emotional support. In addition, they found support of a practical nature was often offered by the extended family.

Jenson and Whittaker (1987) reported that social and community resources can play a key role in the success of social care interventions and in the maintenance of this success. Maluccio and Whittaker (1988), in their work on family preservation services, found that social support was important in helping families avoid children being placed in care, shortened the duration of such placements and enabled children to return to their families. Combining family support with family psycho-education is advocated as an important component for the successful management of mental ill-health (Dallos and Boswell, 1993).

There is evidence that people are willing to provide major help for kin, but are less willing to provide similar help for friends or neighbours – or to ask for it from them. Argyle and Henderson (1985) suggested that kin

were a source of 'serious help' while friends were, on the whole, not seen as a source of such help. An exception to this was the help provided amongst young people as part of intense friendships during the period between adolescence and marriage. However, in general, a sense of obligation to help was closely associated with a blood tie, especially where the relative was a child or an aged parent. Often this obligation entails domestic work and is carried out by women, in situations such as a person being ill or having a baby, or where elderly parents need help with household chores (Lang and Brody, 1983). It seems clear from existing research that the parent-child bond is a strong connection within supportive networks.

Moving beyond close family to more distant kin and friends, there is evidence of supportive networks but of a different sort. Friends were likely to provide emotional support in the form of being a confidante, giving emotional support and building self esteem. Friends talked over problems, compared notes and shared experiences. By contrast the support from more distant kin was likely to be practical assistance. Friends were also important in participating in leisure activities and shared common interests.

Neighbours are another source of support within the social network. MORI (1982) carried out a major survey in relation to neighbours, interviewing 1801 adults in Britain. They found in the main that neighbours talk, entertain, provide mutual help and take joint action. Neighbours provided practical help with minor matters, but were unlikely to be approached for more demanding types of help; for example, while 46 per cent had asked neighbours to look after plants or pets and 47 per cent had asked neighbours to keep house keys for tradespeople to enter in an emergency, only three per cent sought financial help from neighbours, three per cent sought help from neighbours about unemployment and four per cent asked advice about marriage break-up.

The Northern Ireland Social Attitudes (NISA) survey, through its questions on attitudes, expectations and experiences of giving and receiving support and help, provides some important clues as to the actual state of family, friendship and neighbourhood networks in Northern Ireland. The survey data in this area provides useful information on attitudes and expectations which people hold about types and sources of contact and

support. It also suggests patterns within the actual experiences of giving and receiving different types of help.

Based on NISA information, this chapter considers the existence and importance of emotional support and practical help as an aspect of social relationships in Northern Ireland. It draws attention to what is generally known about such relationships; considers the Northern Ireland picture as suggested by the NISA data; looks at some comparative international figures; and then in conclusion suggests that to make the most of the apparently strong presence of support networks requires increasing attention to the detail of these networks.

Attitudes and Expectations
Respondents in the NISA survey were asked if they agreed or disagreed with a number of statements concerning contact with close family, other relatives and friends, as well as statements about sources of help. Table 1 sets out these statements and the proportions who agreed or disagreed with these. Overall, the survey found that family networks were felt to be important and should be maintained through contact. This family network was seen as involving not only close family but also other relatives such as aunts, uncles and cousins. The majority of respondents agreed that people should keep in touch with both close and extended family members and that they themselves tried to do so. Family was also felt to be a potential source of help, and that parental support for their children did not end when the children left home. Friends seemed to be viewed as less important than family, as most respondents disagreed with the statements that they would rather spend time with friends than family, and that friends were more important to them than family members (69 per cent and 83 per cent respectively disagreed). The proportion of respondents who agreed that this network of close family and extended family should be maintained by keeping 'in touch' increased with age. There were no significant differences by sex when respondents were asked whether they agreed that people should keep in touch with close relatives or other relatives in the family. However, when the statement said 'I try to stay in touch...' there were significant differences by sex. Women were more likely than men to

agree (59 per cent compared with 50 per cent) that they tried to stay in touch with all their relatives, 'not just close family'.

Table 1

	agree	neither	disagree	can't choose
People should keep in touch with relatives like aunts, uncles and cousins even if they don't have much in common	69	22	9	0
Once children have left home, they should no longer expect help from their parents	16	12	71	1
People should always turn to their family before asking the state for help	53	18	27	3
On the whole, my friends are more important to me than members of my family	5	11	83	1
People should keep in touch with close family members even if they don't have much in common	80	13	6	1
People are too quick to blame the family for social problems	51	26	21	2
I try to stay in touch with all my relatives, not just my close family	54	21	23	2
I'd rather spend time with my friends than with my family	11	18	69	2

Attitudes to contact and support (%)

The survey also posed a number of hypothetical situations and asked respondents who they would turn to for help in each situation. These situations covered types of practical and emotional support which could be sought either within the close social network or outside of it. Choices of support included spouse or partner, close family members, other relatives, friends, neighbours, work colleagues, church representatives, organisations and professionals. The resulting data provide a snapshot of the expectations around social support held by people in Northern Ireland.

Starting with low level practical needs, respondents were asked who they would turn to for help if there was some household or garden jobs they couldn't really do alone (for example, someone to hold a ladder or help move some furniture). Over half of the respondents (54 per cent) said they would turn first to their spouse or partner for help. Expectations of close family rose to over four fifths (84 per cent) when taken to include fathers (eight per cent) and mothers (five per cent), sons (nine per cent) and daughters (three per cent), and brothers (five per cent) and sisters (three per cent). By contrast, under a tenth of the respondents would turn first to a neighbour (four per cent) or a friend (three per cent) for mundane, practical help. Second choices for help were distributed across the social network with children (27 per cent) the most often cited, followed by parents (14 per cent), and siblings (14 per cent), then friends (12 per cent) and neighbours (11 per cent) and other relatives (9 per cent).

Turning to deeper, though still essentially practical, needs, respondents were asked who they would first turn to if they were ill and had to stay in bed for several weeks necessitating help around the home, with shopping and with other tasks. Again, the majority reported that they would first turn to their spouse or partner for help (54 per cent). Next came close female relatives (mother 16 per cent, daughter nine per cent, sister five per cent). It was also these close female relatives (39 per cent) who were the most popular second choice of help. Although close male relatives tended not to be the first choice for this type of help (five per cent), they accounted for almost a quarter (23 per cent) of the second choices. Included in the other sources of help cited as a second choice were other relatives (11 per cent), moving ahead of friends (eight per cent) and neighbours (five per cent).

A different pattern of responses emerged when a hypothetical question was put regarding financial assistance. Respondents were asked who they would first turn to for help if they needed to borrow a large sum of money. Almost one third of adults (31 per cent) said they would first approach a bank, building society or other financial institution, in other words, they would go outside the informal network completely. A fifth, however, did say they would turn firstly to their spouse (20 per cent) and a similar proportion said they would firstly ask their parents (father 10 per cent,

mother nine per cent). Under a tenth would seek help from their children (seven per cent) and just under that would approach siblings (six per cent). Although only a very small proportion (three per cent) named other relatives as a first source of financial help, this rose to just over a tenth (11 per cent) as a second choice.

Turning now to deeper emotional needs, respondents were asked who would be the first source of support they would turn to if they felt down or depressed and wanted to discuss how they felt. Once again partners or spouses tended to be the first source of support followed by female relatives. Almost half (48 per cent) the respondents cited partners and a fifth would have first approached a close female relative (mother six per cent, daughter six per cent, sister six per cent). However the pattern of responses is notably different from the areas of practical support in that almost a fifth of respondents (17 per cent) would expect to discuss emotional problems with a close friend. Friends (24 per cent) were also an important second choice of support – though a larger proportion of respondents identified a close female relative (30 per cent) as their main second choice of support.

The relationship with a spouse is clearly the major source of practical and emotional support – but what about when there is a difficulty in that relationship? Respondents were asked about seeking help regarding an unresolved problem with a spouse or partner. This provoked a very different pattern of responses than for the other hypothetical questions. One fifth of respondents would have sought help from a friend in these circumstances, while 15 per cent would have first approached their mother, 11 per cent would go to a sister and 10 per cent to a daughter. The main expected source of support for personal problems with a partner would therefore seem to be a close female relative (mother, daughter or sister), covering over a third of the respondents, followed by friends (20 per cent). A tenth of respondents (10 per cent) would expect to go to the spouse him- or herself. A similar, though slightly lower proportion (nine per cent), would first turn to close male relatives (brother four per cent, son four per cent, father two per cent). A small but significant number of respondents (seven per cent) would go outside their informal network to clergy or priests.

In summary it would seem from this data that partners or spouses are expected to be the main source of emotional and practical support for people in Northern Ireland and are usually the first choice of help when a problem arises. People feel they would only go elsewhere within the family when advice is needed about a problem with a spouse or partner. Close family (parents, siblings, children) are also viewed as a major source of practical and emotional support, whereas other relatives tend to be viewed as a source of practical help only. Although neighbours are not often perceived as a first choice of support, a substantial number of people reported that neighbours would be their second choice for practical help. Friends are also seen as an important second choice for help but as a source of emotional rather than practical support. Finance is the only area in which the close social network is not the mainstay of support. When people needed to borrow money, they preferred to go outside the social network to the formal financial systems such as banks or building societies.

Experiences of Providing and Receiving Help and Assistance

As well as covering attitudes and expectations in hypothetical cases the NISA survey provided information on actual experiences of giving and receiving practical help and support. In particular, the survey focused on regular help or care if someone is ill, disabled or pregnant and providing financial help.

Respondents were asked about their experiences during the last five years of providing help or care for an adult relative, friend, neighbour or colleague because of pregnancy, an illness, disability or other problem. About half the respondents (48 per cent) had provided such help or care and in the main this was provided for either a partner, spouse or another close family member, particularly female family members. Of those providing care or help, three-quarters (76 per cent) named close family as the recipients (spouse/partner 20 per cent, parents/parents-in-law 36 per cent, children seven per cent, siblings 13 per cent). Close female relatives (excluding spouse or partner) were more likely to have been provided with help or care than close male relatives (41 per cent and 15 per cent respectively). This may be partly explained by the inclusion of pregnancy in the question as a circumstance when care might be given. Under a tenth

(eight per cent) of the respondents had been involved in providing care for other relatives. The same proportion (eight per cent) had provided support to friends and only half that proportion were involved in helping neighbours. Thus, people's *expectations* of the importance of close family networks is consistent with their commitment in practice to providing help and support.

When this experience of providing regular help or care is analysed by class, religion and age, no significant differences are found. There is however a significant difference according to gender – though this is perhaps not as great as might have been expected. Women were more likely than men to have provided care or help (53 per cent of women compared to 43 per cent of men). Again this is consistent with the expectations described earlier.

The survey also asked respondents if they themselves had *received* such help or care from another adult in the past five years because of pregnancy, illness, disability or other problems (see Table 2). The pattern of responses

Table 2
Help provided/received within social network (%)

	provide help/care to	receive help/care from	lend money to	borrow money from
Spouse	20	43	5	8
Other close family	56	49	73	72
Other relative	8	2	6	10
Friend	8	2	11	5
Neighbour	4	2	2	*
Other person	3	2	3	4

on receiving help was again consistent with the expectations expressed by respondents. One quarter had received care or help, and of these, 43 per cent said that this care or help had come from their spouse. An additional two-fifths (42 per cent) also identified a close female relative (mother 19 per cent, daughter 13 per cent, sister nine per cent) as their source of help.

Again, while there were no significant differences by religious affiliation, age group or social class between those who had received care or help and those who had not, there were significant differences by gender. A higher proportion of women (30 per cent) had received care or help in the past five years than men (18 per cent).

Respondents were also asked about actual financial help they had either received from, or given to, other adults in the past five years. The questions were 'have you loaned or given anyone £100 or more to help with a problem' and 'have you personally received a loan or gift of £100 or more'. It is important to note that the questions were worded in such a way that the focus is on financial help given or received from another adult, and so unlike the hypothetical situation question, formal financial institutions were not considered. Over a quarter of respondents (29 per cent) had *lent or given* money to someone in the past five years, and over a fifth (22 per cent) had *borrowed or been given* money of £100 or more. Close family relationships are crucial in giving and receiving of help, but the most likely source of financial help is from parent to child (46 per cent) rather from spouse to partner. Of those who lent money, a third did so to their son or daughter and just under a quarter lent to a sibling or sibling-in-law. Slightly more than a tenth of respondents had lent to friends. Others borrowed from siblings and parents-in-law (both nine per cent), children (seven per cent), and grandmothers and friends (both five per cent).

Table 3
Percentage of age group who lent or borrowed money in last 5 years

Age	lent or gave money	borrowed/was given money
18-24 years	14	31
25-34 years	32	37
35-44 years	39	27
45-54 years	25	14
55-64 years	30	12
65+ years	33	5

Respondents in younger age groups were more likely to have been *given* as well as less likely to have *lent* money (Table 3). Gender differences are also obvious as money was more likely to be lent by men than by women. Unsurprisingly, class was also important and money was more likely to be lent by those in professional, managerial or technical classes than in other social classes.

International Comparisons

The International Social Survey Programme (ISSP) allows for some comparisons of the NISA survey findings to be made with data collected from seven other countries in 1986, although the time lag between the two sets of data makes comparability difficult.

From the NISA survey, spouses or partners emerged as the major source of help. Table 4 sets out the percentages of respondents naming spouse or

Table 4

	with domestic help	help when ill	help when depressed
NI	54	54	48
Britain	63	65	53
USA	50	52	40
Australia	63	64	51
West Germany	54	59	54
Austria	51	53	48
Hungary	43	53	44
Italy	42	41	33

Percentage naming spouse or partner as first source of help (%)

Source: Figures for NI are taken from 1995 NISA.
Figures for other countries are taken from 1986 ISSP

partner as the first source of help in three different situations. Britain and Australia tended to top the 'league table', although Northern Ireland was not far behind. In contrast, countries like Italy were consistently low.

Table 5

First source of help over a problem with spouse or partner

	Friend	Parents	Clergy/Priest	No-one
NI	20	17	7	7
Britain	21	18	2	8
USA	30	14	13	5
Australia	28	12	6	10
West Germany	28	14	2	20
Austria	21	20	3	19
Hungary	13	20	*	19
Italy	28	14	2	14

note: * less than 0.5 percent
Source: Figures for NI are taken from 1995 NISA
        Figures for other countries are taken from 1986 ISSP

Where the *problem* is with a spouse or partner, Northern Ireland was similar to most countries with a friend being the most popular source of help though with a notably lower percentage than for four of the other countries (Table 5). The proportion of people in Northern Ireland choosing a friend, parents or 'no-one' was very similar to Britain. However, Northern Irish people were more likely than British people to cite the clergy or priest as a first source of help (though much less likely than Americans).

Turning to finance, most other countries showed a similar pattern to Northern Ireland, with the most frequently cited first source of help for borrowing money being a bank or similar financial institution (Table 6). Italy was the only country where more people would approach parents before the banks. Although Northern Ireland respondents were more likely to seek help from a bank than from any other source, they were nonetheless the country least likely (apart from Italy) to approach a bank at all. From these comparisons it is reasonable to suggest that while there is variation between countries, there is also a considerable degree of similarity. Northern Ireland does not stand out as exceptional in how support is perceived within social networks, or in what are felt to be appropriate sources of help for particular problems.

Table 6
First source of help for borrowing money

	Bank	Parents	Children
NI	31	20	7
Britain	38	17	6
USA	39	20	6
Australia	42	16	5
West Germany	45	18	5
Austria	37	18	6
Hungary	42	19	11
Italy	24	29	8

Source: Figures for NI are taken from 1995 NISA
Figures for other countries are taken from 1986 ISSP

Summary and Conclusions
Overall then, what does the NISA survey suggest about the actual state of family, friendship and neighbourhood networks as a source of social support? The data certainly provide evidence that close social networks do still exist in Northern Ireland and that they are important sources of help and assistance with both emotional and practical problems. It is important, however, to recognise that these networks exist with differing degrees of strength, are strongly gendered, and that there are differences in sources of help depending on the problem arising.

At the core of these close social networks lies the relationship with spouse or partner. Beyond that lie strong bonds of reciprocity within the immediate family – especially between mothers and daughters. These close family relationships are expected to, and do seem to, provide regular help or care in situations of pregnancy, illness and disability. In particular, there seems to be evidence of a strong female support network, with women providing much of the help or care, as well as being more likely to receive this kind of support.

In addition, there are wider ties of expectation and experience of support involving more distant relatives, friends and neighbours. From the survey's hypothetical situations and questions about people's perceptions of sources of support, it appears that friends supplement close female family members as an important source of emotional support. Other relatives and neighbours provide support but to a lesser extent and of a practical nature. Only in the area of financial support are these various informal networks set aside in preference for formal institutions.

It would seem therefore from the NISA survey data that there is evidence of important supportive networks in existence in Northern Ireland. In addition to this overall picture reinforcing the popular self image of Northern Ireland people as close and supportive, these findings give an important message to social care professionals. It is not enough that they recognise the existence of these informal networks as complementary to their own services. Formal services need to be tailored to go with the grain of the informal networks. To do this successfully requires a detailed appreciation of the different types and strengths of networks and the way that different networks meet different needs. Professionals aiming to build on existing support systems need to be aware of situations when spouse support is the most appropriate, when extended family members can play a role and when neighbours might provide help. Detailed knowledge of social support networks is crucial to inform intervention practices and the NISA survey has made a useful contribution to further developing that knowledge.

References

ANESHENSEL, C. S., FRERICHS, R. R. and CLARK, V. A. 1981. 'Family roles and sex differences in depression', *Journal of Health and Social Behaviour*, 22: 379-93.

ARGYLE, M. and HENDERSON, M. 1985. *The Anatomy of Relationships*, Harmondsworth, Penguin.

BALDWIN, S. and CARLISLE, J. 1994. *Social support for disabled children and their families: a review of the literature,* Edinburgh, HMSO.

CAMPBELL, A.1981. *The Sense of Wellbeing in America: Patterns and Trends*, New York, McGraw-Hill.

DALLOS, R. and BOSWELL, D. 1993. 'Mental Health' in R. Dallos and E. McLaughlin (eds.), *Social Problems and the Family London,* London, Sage.

DALLOS, R. and McLAUGHLIN, E. 1993. *Social Problems and the Family*, London, Sage.

GIDDENS, A. 1993. *Sociology,* Cambridge, Polity Press.

GITTINS, D. 1993. *The Family in Question*, London, Macmillan.

JENSON, J. M., and WHITTAKER, J. K. 1987. 'Parental involvement in children's residential treatment', *Children and Youth Services Review*, 9: 81-100.

LANG, A. and BRODY, E. 1983. 'Characteristics of middle-aged daughters and help to their elderly mothers', *Journal of Marriage and the Family,* 45: 193-202.

LANGAN, M. 1992. 'Who cares? Women in the mixed economy of care', in M. Langan and L. Day (eds.), *Women, oppression and social work,* London, Routledge.

LEAVY, R. L. 1983. 'Social support and psychological disorder: a review', *Journal of Community Psychology*, 11: 3-21.

MALUCCIO, A. N. and WHITTAKER, J. K. 1988. 'Helping the biological families of children in out-of-home placement', in W. W. Nunnally, C. S. Chilman and F. M. Cox (eds.), *Troubled relationships*, Newbury Park, California, Sage Publications.

MORI, 1982. *Neighbours and Loneliness*, London, Market Opinion Research International.

ST. LEGER, F. and GILLESPIE, N. 1991. *Informal Welfare in Three Belfast Communities,* Belfast, SSI/DHSS.

TRACY, E. M. 1990. 'Identifying Social Support Resources of At-Risk Families', *Social Work,* May 1990.

TRACEY, E. M., WHITTAKER, J. K, PUGH, A., KAPP, S. N. and OVERSTREET, E. J. 1994. 'Support Networks of Primary Caregivers Receiving Family Preservation Services: An Exploratory Study', *Families in Society: The Journal of Contemporary Human Services*, October 1994.

6

Class, Community Polarisation and Politics

Mary Duffy and Geoffrey Evans

Introduction
In his chapter from the first volume of this Social Attitudes series, O'Dowd
(1991) points to how, against the intensity of the ethno-national division
that lies at the heart of the conflict in Northern Ireland, social class has
been considered a relatively minor factor in shaping politically salient
attitudes and identities (see also Curtice and Gallagher, 1990). This, he
suggests, has been in stark contrast to its perceived role in Britain where,
despite debate as to whether its significance has recently begun to decline,
class position remains the key source of social cleavage and a central
predictor of political attitudes and allegiances (for example, Marshall et al.,
1988; Evans, 1993).

Since then, much and little has changed. Much, in so far as class has
been given a more central role in research into the changing intra-group
dynamics in Northern Ireland. So, on the Catholic side, O Connor (1993)
devotes a whole chapter to the class issue, which, indeed, emerges as one
of the central themes throughout. The focus is on the much-heralded
expansion of the Catholic middle class and the increasing occupational
diversity of Catholics (Cormack and Osborne, 1994; Knox et al., 1995),
and on the effect such changes are having on attitudes and traditional
political aspirations. O Connor's interviewees paint this newly emerging
group as middle-of-the-road, fence-sitting moderates whose success has
'taken the edge off the grievance', and who have been depoliticised and
lured away from their traditional group loyalties by the material benefits of
direct rule. This growth is, it is argued, redefining mainstream Catholic
nationalism, creating fissures and new tensions within a previously

coherent group. Catholics are no longer seen as a tight community with a unified sense of political identity: 'There was a sense of togetherness among Catholics – that's been lost ... there's a painful and angry division now between those educated, mobile, skilled and in work, and those who are not ... this causes all the resentment of unequal fortunes – but in this case, heightened by a sense of political betrayal' (O Connor, 1993: 19, 17).

Conversely, looking at Protestants, the focus has been squarely on the working class: on the nature of loyalism, on the strains along class lines that continue to define party competition among unionists, and on the 'explosion of resentment' that increasingly marks working-class Protestant reactions, not only towards Catholics, but also towards their own middle class (Bruce, 1994; McAuley, 1994). McAuley emphasises the salience of class as a factor in unionist politics, echoing many of the ideas in Nelson's (1984) earlier work. So, just as Nelson pointed to the 'social grievances of people left out of the new affluence, squeezed on one side by the middle class, on the other by Catholics' (Nelson, 1984: 53), so Bruce (1994: 61) sees the same divisions, if anything exacerbated by the apparent relative success of the Catholic community: '... a zero-sum game; if we are losing, it must be because Catholics are gaining'. Most recently, the fringe loyalist parties newly entering the political process (the Progressive Unionist Party, the Ulster Democratic Party) are regarded by many as having grown to give a voice to a frustrated working class who were being inadequately served by the two main unionist parties, and that such growth is indicative of a greater class consciousness among the Protestant working class (Price, 1995).

But in other respects, little has changed, in that much of the discussion about the role of class still relies heavily on anecdotal evidence which, while important and suggestive, may not paint a generally representative picture, and does not easily allow for the consideration of how class position relates to other factors which might influence attitudes. There are exceptions, but the area remains under-explored. Even Rose (1971), in his seminal work based on his 1968 survey, did not fully explore the class within religion angle, despite the fact that his own results showed 39 per cent of Catholic respondents and 39 per cent of Protestant respondents felt

they had more in common with someone of the same class than of the same religion.

In this chapter, we use data from the 1995 Northern Ireland Social Attitudes (NISA) survey to examine systematically the significance of class for perceptions and attitudes in Northern Ireland. For a number of reasons, we are not able to look at change over time: problems of comparability are created by differences of measurement, some of which are related to the huge changes which have taken place in Northern Ireland over the last three decades (not least, the party options and political system), and others which pertain to changes in survey methods (different measures of social class are used in the two main long-term comparison points (Rose, 1971; Moxon-Browne, 1983)). However, we do not necessarily need to look beyond the contemporary data to address at least some of the questions raised above – if the latter reflect real processes taking place in the Catholic and Protestant communities, then we would expect this to be evident in clear class differences, across a range of measures, within each religious group. Perhaps the Catholic middle class have, in diverging from other Catholics, become more like Protestants – this can be examined here. And for Protestants, we can adopt a similar perspective: looking at the contemporary data, to what extent do the working class differ in their economic and political views from their middle-class co-religionists? We should thus be able to assess the extent to which social class challenges religious affiliation in defining a range of attitudes – to repeat the question Rose (1971) posed in looking at economic factors in his 1968 survey: are the working class and the middle class more alike across religious groups than Protestants and Catholics across the classes?

This chapter also introduces an additional factor into the picture: men and women often do not have identical views on the issues facing Northern Ireland. But, if class differences have received relatively little attention from survey analysts, this is even more true of differences between men and women. There has been some coverage of women's issues in earlier volumes of this series, but the issues with which sex is seen to matter are rarely explicitly political: instead authors tend to examine areas such as women and work, and women's changing role in a modernising society.

And, even where sex does emerge as a significant differentiating factor in core political attitudes (for example, Breen, 1996), this is rarely picked up or further explored. This may be partly due to the same reason O'Dowd saw for the lack of research into class: compared to the overwhelming significance of ethnicity, other sources of group difference come a pale second. Yet, although it is true that women in Northern Ireland have not, until very recently, had much direct involvement in the political process, in terms of community and political action women have been distinctive in being often involved in cross-community initiatives and efforts aimed at religious conciliation (the Peace Movement, in the mid-seventies, for example). Thus, given that women are now becoming more involved in mainstream politics – many of the parties actively trawling for women to enter their ranks (Rooney, 1994) – if they also hold different attitudes to men, this may have important effects on the political dynamic. Recent examples of women's greater involvement in politics with an explicitly cross-community slant (not least, the performance of the Women's Coalition in the 1995 Northern Ireland election) also serve as a warning that, on questions of politics and community relations, it would be unwise to assume that working-class women are just like working-class men, or that the growing band of female professionals and semi-professional workers simply reflect the views of 'the middle class'. Of course, such assumptions do hold sometimes, but, on other occasions, consideration of differences between men and women might change the picture of class and religious divisions that would otherwise be portrayed.

The chapter is structured in several parts. We begin with a look at current class profiles, noting unemployment levels and sex differences within the religious groups. We then examine the extent to which, for both Protestants and Catholics, class position is reflected in differing economic experiences and in differing levels of class consciousness. Following this, we look at aspects of community relations, in particular at perceptions of discrimination and attitudes to religious integration in various contexts. The final section moves onto the most explicitly politicised issues: partisanship, national identity, constitutional preferences, trust in governments. In all of these areas, we examine class and religion as sources of differences in perceptions and attitudes; where pertinent we also

describe differences between men and women and how these might affect divisions between classes and religious groups.

Class Profiles

We start with a description of the demographic distribution of classes by religion and sex. Figure 1 shows class profiles by religion for 1995. Our measure of class is that developed by Goldthorpe and his colleagues (see Erikson and Goldthorpe, 1992). Unlike the standard Registrar General's classification this index of social class has received careful checks on its validity and also captures some of the important social divisions blurred by the traditional manual/non-manual distinction (Marshall et al., 1988; Evans, 1992). In assigning class, married respondents (of either sex) who cannot be classified according to their own positions are given the class of their spouses. For this general picture of the sizes of the demographic divisions in Northern Ireland we use an elaborated version of the classification which identifies, as a distinct group, those in sales and personal service jobs, who are usually included with routine office workers to form the routine non-manual class. Farmers are also given their own category, rather than including them with the petty bourgeoisie, as is typically done for Britain; and there remains a small residual group of those who cannot be classified – mainly because they have never had a job (mainly the young and women). The first thing to note is that, whatever the evidence of shifting class profiles and an expanding Catholic middle class, the 1995 data show relative profiles that are still marked by the familiar disparities. Thus, while Catholics and Protestants are both more concentrated in the working class than in any other group, Catholics have a larger working class and Protestants remain more likely to be in the salariat, within which they also tend more to the higher professional occupations than do Catholics. Distribution by religion is fairly even across the intermediate classes (although, for example, within the petty bourgeoisie, Catholics are less likely than Protestants to have employees).

The picture of relative Catholic disadvantage is continued in more subjective measures of economic standing. Analyses show that, on a range of indicators tapping evaluations of current and expected economic

Figure 1

Distributions of class by religion (%)

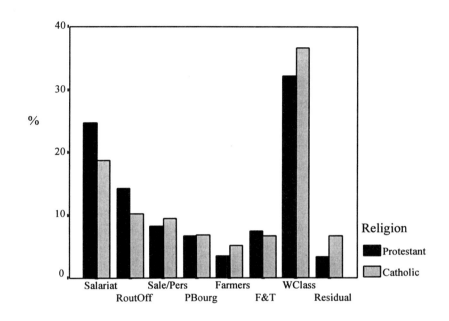

RoutOff = Routine office workers
Sale/Pers = Sales and personal service workers
Pbourg = Petty bourgeoisie
F&T = Foremen and technicians
Wclass = Working class

situations, Catholics of all classes consistently report greater economic difficulty than Protestants. This is true even when we take account of differences in household size (Catholic households being larger on average), and it fits with official statistics which indicate that, for a given social class, Protestants are likely to have higher incomes than Catholics (PPRU Monitor, 1993).

However, as Table 1 illustrates, the differences in class distribution between Catholics and Protestants are not the same for men and women. Catholic and Protestant women hardly differ at all in their class profiles, have a similar proportion of working class as have Protestant men, and both have around seven percent less of their groups in the salariat. The

smaller intermediate classes are strongly sex biased, sales and personal being almost entirely a female group, foremen and technicians typically mostly men. Catholic men, however, are quite another matter: 42 per cent are working class, compared with 29 per cent of Protestant men. Conversely, there are only 15 per cent of Catholic males in the professional and managerial classes, compared with almost twice that proportion from the Protestant male group. This pattern of relatively better off Catholic females compared with Catholic males is supported by official statistics which show a larger female professional and managerial class: in the 1991 Census, 27 per cent of Catholic females were in the professional and

Table 1
Class distributions, by religion and gender (%)

| | Protestants | | Catholics | |
	M (315)	F (466)	M (265)	F (302)
Salariat	28	22	15	21
Routine Office	8	19	4	16
Sales/Personal	1	13	3	15
Petty Bourgeoisie	12	3	10	4
Farmers	7	1	10	*
Foremen & Technicians	13	4	10	4
Working Class	29	34	42	32
Residual	2	4	5	8
[Current Unemployed]	6	3	18	4

* in all tables, less than 1%

Note: percentages for current unemployed are calculated separately. In the main table, the unemployed are assigned a class according to their last job.

managerial classes, compared with 24 per cent and 28 per cent of Protestant men and women respectively, and only 22 per cent of Catholic men (Gallagher et al., 1994).

The general impression of Catholic disadvantage being concentrated among the men is also indicated by the information on current levels of

unemployment. While levels vary from three per cent to six per cent for the other three groups, for Catholic men it is no less than 18 per cent. These figures, it should be noted, ought to be interpreted with care, as the ratio of Catholic male to Protestant male unemployment is somewhat exaggerated compared with recent results from more reliable data (see Gudgin and Breen, 1996: 1) and since the NISA data show considerable fluctuation in the percentage profiles over the years 1989-1995, especially for Catholic men and women. Nevertheless, the relative patterns of unemployment displayed here are in keeping with the findings from a series of studies (for example, Aunger, 1975; Osborne and Cormack, 1986; Gudgin and Breen, 1996) on employment and unemployment differentials which show that, despite a changing economic environment, Catholic men (the young and the working class especially) are consistently more likely to be unemployed than their Protestant equivalents, even when differences in their distributions by occupation are held constant. Moreover, differences in educational achievement are likely to become an increasingly important factor in the future of shifting class profiles, perhaps even more within than across religious groups. Research has established a pattern of increasing educational attainment among Catholic women in particular, especially at the university level (Osborne et al., 1988, p. 291-3). This sex differential among Catholics is clear in the 1995 data: Catholic men are doing much less well than the other three groups and the differentials remain when we look only at those under thirty-five years old (see Appendix, Tables A1 and A2).

These findings give some indication that any interpretation of the potential effects of a changing class profile might require sex differences to be taken into account. The growth of a female Catholic middle class, and the continued concentration of Catholic men in the working class and amongst the unemployed, points to the possibility of a starker contrast between Protestant and Catholic men than would be revealed by a 'non-gendered' analysis. Clearly, even though the main thrust of this chapter is about class, it is important to consider sex differences also where they condition the extent of division between classes. Unfortunately, however, there is a cost to incorporating this extra complexity into the analysis, in that the size of the 1995 NISA survey is not such as to allow us to fully

explore the full range of class divisions and their relations to both religion and sex. Even without distinguishing men and women the size of the intermediate classes is undesirably small. Our intention, therefore, is to concentrate on the largest and traditionally most significant classes – the 'salariat' of professional and managerial occupations, and the 'working class' composed of unskilled, semi-skilled and skilled manual employees. Also, as preliminary analyses showed that those in sales and personal work take a similar position to those in the working class on many issues – they are also, objectively, in jobs that are badly paid and low status – we follow the lead of other researchers and combine this group with the working class. The intermediate classes we shall consider in subsequent analyses using larger data sets.

The method of analysis and presentation we adopt is to test statistically for the effects of class, religion and sex (and the interactions between these characteristics) on each of the perceptions and attitudes we examine. Where significant differences between men and women are found they are presented, otherwise we focus on the differences between Protestants and Catholics, the middle class and the working class.

Class Consciousness

Although it is the ethnic divide that dominates social and political relations at the general level, class consciousness and an awareness of class conflict may also be important factors, especially at the intra-group level. Nelson (1984: 128), for example, is not alone in talking of how the stirring of 'a new class consciousness' created tensions and divisions within the Protestant community in the aftermath of direct rule and remains evident today, while both Bruce's (1994) work on loyalist identity and O Connor's (1993) study of Catholics paint a working class very aware of their position, not only compared to that of the other religious group, but also relative to their own middle class.

Table 2 shows how the two classes split in terms of middle/working-class identity for each religious group. (Since class identity was not measured in 1995, we use combined data from the 1989, 1990 and 1994 NISA surveys instead. Combining the years increases the sample size and makes for more robust estimates: there were no significant over time variations).

Respondents were asked: *Most people see themselves as belonging to a particular social class. Please tell me which social class you would say you belong to.*

Table 2

Class identity, by religion, class and sex (%)

| | Protestants | | | | Catholics | | | |
| | Salariat | | Working Class | | Salariat | | Working Class | |
	M	F	M	F	M	F	M	F
Middle	56	53	19	21	53	37	5	14
Upper Working	23	28	10	14	30	25	4	6
Working	21	17	64	61	16	37	81	70
Poor	0	3	6	5	2	2	10	10

In general, Catholics of both classes are more likely to define themselves as working class than are Protestants. The Catholic salariat are somewhat more likely to see themselves as working class, while a quarter of the Protestant working class feel middle class. This is contrary to Rose's (1971: 286) conclusion that that 'Catholics are not particularly likely to think of themselves as lower class, nor are Protestants likely to upgrade themselves'; and it is not surprising, if we take into account the evidence that Catholics of any class feel worse off than do Protestants. In addition, we have already indicated that Catholics are more likely to be in the lower ranks of the professional and managerial classes, which might in part account for the slightly greater tendency for the Catholic middle class to assign themselves to the working class. The more pronounced difference among the working classes may be partly due to Protestants 'upgrading' themselves, but is more likely explained by the proportion of currently unemployed in the Catholic group: 11 per cent of the Catholic working class are not currently employed, compared with one per cent of the Catholic middle class and five per cent of the Protestant working class. This reasoning is also supported by the sex differences within class. In fact, it is only Catholic women in the salariat who differ from Protestants

in class identity: 37 per cent feel middle class, compared with more than half of those in each of the other three groups. And, in the working class, it is the Catholic men who are most likely to assign themselves to the working class (81 per cent, against 70 per cent of the Catholic female working class). Catholic men are clearly more class polarised on identity than are Catholic women.

But measuring class consciousness requires more than looking at patterns of self-assigned class. In Britain, class consciousness is also associated with the adoption of certain class-typical positions on a range of economic issues concerned with welfare provision, income redistribution, public ownership and the like (Marshall et al., 1988; Evans, 1993). These have long been considered the 'bread and butter' of British politics and can be seen as tapping the 'left-right' dimension around which politics have traditionally been organised (Evans, Heath and Lalljee, 1996). Together with, and linked to, social class, left-right ideology has been seen as a central factor in defining who votes for what party in Britain (Heath et al., 1991). However, in Northern Ireland, politics have been conducted primarily around a religious, rather than an economic, divide; and, although class politics are alive and well within the ethnic blocs (Evans and Duffy, 1997), the potential for cross-religious class politics has been seen as limited, evidenced by the demise of the Northern Ireland Labour Party and the modest electoral fortunes of the Alliance Party of Northern Ireland (see also Duffy and Evans, 1996). It is therefore interesting to examine, first, the extent to which Northern Irish respondents are like the British in their views on economic issues, and, second, whether it is religion or class that best defines differing positions.

Figure 2 shows mean left-right ideology scores for Protestants and Catholics in Northern Ireland and for the British working class and salariat generally. The ideology scale is comprised of five items and has been widely applied and validated in Britain (Evans, Heath and Lalljee, 1996). Lower scores indicate support for government intervention and redistribution of income, while higher scores indicate a more pro-market, less egalitarian orientation.

Figure 2

Left-right ideology, by class, in Northern Ireland and Britain (higher scores indicate a more right-wing position)

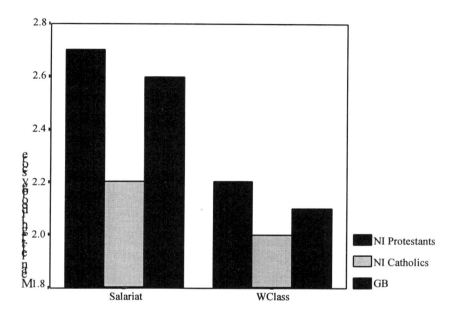

Catholics, in general, are more left wing than are Protestants, the Catholic middle class having the same mean score as the Protestant working class. Mean scores and degree of polarisation are almost identical for Northern Irish Protestants and British respondents. It is the Catholic position that is unusual, because, although there is a significant difference between the mean scores of the salariat and the working class, these scores are much closer together than for Protestants, and, in fact, the mean score of the Catholic salariat is the same as that of the Protestant working class. Again, the more left-wing general position of Catholics may in part reflect higher welfare dependency and unemployment, though this has limited explanatory power in the salariat. What it clearly provides, however, is evidence *against* the thesis advanced by several of O Connor's

interviewees that the Catholic middle class are abandoning the values of their group on their 'upwards spiral that leads to selfishness' (O Connor, 1993: 29).

As Figure 3 shows, within the two classes, for both Protestant and Catholic, there are also sex differences. Among Protestants, although

Figure 3

Left-right ideology, by religion, class and sex (higher scores indicate a more right-wing position)

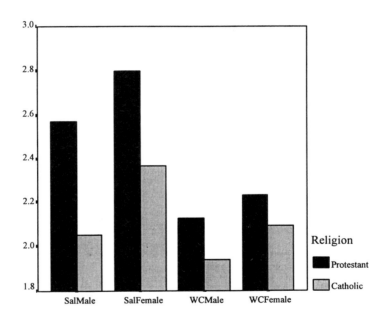

salariat females score slightly higher than salariat males, this is not statistically significant, and the main difference is by class rather than sex. However, among Catholics it is clear that the class difference seen in Figure 2 was due to a sex difference within the salariat group: while Catholic salariat men are just as left wing as working-class men, Catholic women share a similar position to Protestant salariat men (with a significantly lower mean score than Protestant salariat women).   This

means that, unlike the pattern for Britain, where in the 1995 British Social Attitudes survey (BSA) no differences are found between women and men on these issues, women in Northern Ireland generally, and among Catholics especially, are more right wing than men.

Community Relations

Prejudice and discrimination
Objectively, the situation in Northern Ireland has changed considerably since the issue of discrimination brought Catholics onto the streets in the late 1960s: the institution of direct rule from Westminster, various political changes, a series of economic reform packages, the formation of a Fair Employment Commission and general changes in the nature of the employment market. While economic disparities between Catholics and Protestants remain, it is also true that some Catholics have done very well. Research in the later years of the Troubles, and contemporary research especially, makes much of these changes and of how, whatever the actual or objective nature and extent of change, perceptions of change – of one group succeeding at the expense of another – have been increasingly important in shaping attitudes. Bruce, for example, comments that 'for unionists the crucial point of the last twenty years has been loss' (Bruce, 1994: 53) And, indeed, if it is the case that working-class Protestants have been most sorely hit by the decline of traditional industries and have watched their group decline as Catholics have apparently done better, we might expect to find this group more sensitive to issues of discrimination and prejudice.

Alternatively, any growth in the Catholic middle class, especially in areas traditionally reserved for Protestants – the changing religious composition of the student body in the Law department at The Queen's University of Belfast, and the implications of this for the religious make-up of the legal profession, is a good example – might be creating greater competition at the top end of the market. This, in addition to Fair Employment legalisation, which is often seen as hitting the middle class most, might create stronger feelings of anti-Protestant discrimination among the salariat. In general, it may also be the case that, on job

allocation, perceptions of discrimination among the salariat are greater than among the working class because members of the latter are more likely to work in jobs and areas where the religious composition of the workforce is more homogeneous and, therefore, less open to direct competition with members of the other religion.

To test some of these ideas, we look at perceptions of prejudice and discrimination across a range of situations. The question format was: *Thinking of [Protestants/Catholics] – do you think there is a lot of prejudice against them in Northern Ireland nowadays?* We begin, in Table 3, with perceptions of anti-Protestant prejudice.

Table 3

Perceptions of prejudice against Protestants, by religion and class (%)

	Protestants		Catholics	
	Salariat	Working Class	Salariat	Working Class
Lot	20	21	11	14
Little	52	48	52	57
Hardly any	28	28	35	27
Don't know	*	4	2	3

Responses by class are very similar within each religious group. Although Protestants are a little more likely to say there is 'a lot' of prejudice against their group, Catholics too perceive significant levels of anti-Protestant prejudice. Among Protestants, there is no evidence to suggest that the working class are more likely to perceive their religious group as victims of discrimination than are the salariat. When we compare these figures with the equivalent for anti-Catholic prejudice (see Table 4), the pattern by religion changes, while class differences are similarly trivial. Protestants feel that there is much less general prejudice against Catholics – less, in fact, than they see against Protestants. The Catholic salariat and working class are as likely to perceive prejudice against Catholics, as are the Protestant salariat and working class. There are no significant sex differences in these patterns among either Protestants or Catholics.

Table 4
Perceptions of prejudice against Catholics, by religion and class (%)

	Protestants		Catholics	
	Salariat	Working Class	Salariat	Working Class
Lot	17	15	22	29
Little	49	44	61	54
Hardly any	33	37	18	15
Don't know	1	3	0	2

Next, in Table 5, we consider a set of items which refer to more specific aspects of treatment by the authorities. Respondents were asked to say whether they thought that Catholics were treated better, Protestants better, or both groups equally, in relation to a number of different areas, including

Table 5
Protestant opinions about which group is treated better, by class (%)

	Salariat			Working Class		
	District Councils	Fair Emp Legislation	The RUC	District Councils	Fair Emp Legislation	The RUC
Catholic Better	13	35	3	7	17	5
Protestant Better	10	0	21	11	1	12
Both Equal	56	55	69	60	64	73
Don't know/Depends	21	10	7	22	18	10

in the allocation of District Council jobs, by the Fair Employment Commission (FEC), and by the Royal Ulster Constabulary (RUC). Class differences are found, but mainly for Protestants.

Among Protestants, the most pronounced effect of class is on the Fair Employment question, where more than a third of the Protestant salariat think that Catholics are better treated, compared with only 17 per cent in

the working class. It is possible that the higher proportion of 'don't know' responses in the latter group is in part because some respondents did not know what the FEC does, but it is also likely that the working class are less directly affected by fair employment legislation. Clearly, fair employment is *the* sensitive issue, one where Protestants feel they get a bad deal; and it is the Protestant middle class who seem to feel this most strongly. It is possible that Bruce is correct in his claim that: 'The main cause of Protestant hostility to fair employment legislation is that they do not believe that a fair liberal democracy is possible in the Irish context ... they see (it) as a device to further nationalist interests under the guise of equitable social policy: another stick to beat the Prods' (Bruce, 1994: 55, 59).

Regarding the RUC, few Protestants say that Catholics get better treatment, and there is no significant tendency for the salariat (from among whom many RUC officers come) to feel this more than members of the working class. There is no evidence here of any of the supposed Protestant resentment of the RUC (especially among the working class), which Bruce (1994) has suggested has been evident in responses to a series of politically volatile situations, beginning with the policing of demonstrations against the Anglo-Irish Agreement. It is possible that such resentment has been occurring, but is more a temporary 'blip' during certain periods of trouble and does not filter through to long term attitudes.

Table 6

Catholic opinions about which group is treated better, by class (%)

	Salariat			Working Class		
	District Councils	Fair Emp Legislation	The RUC	District Councils	Fair Emp Legislation	The RUC
Protestants Better	5	3	0	2	3	*
Catholics Better	29	3	43	30	5	51
Both Equal	51	89	42	54	84	42
Don't know/Depends	15	5	15	14	8	7

Catholic responses to the same set of issues (Table 6) show much less variation. There is a slightly greater tendency for the Catholic working class to see the RUC as treating Protestants better, but elsewhere the salariat and working class have similar views. Overall, Catholics in general feel that they are less fairly treated than Protestants feel their group is. Note, however, that fair employment is the area in which Catholics feel there is most fair treatment – 86 per cent of all Catholics feel treatment of the religious groups is fairly equal (the figure is 59 per cent among Protestants). It is no surprise that, where Catholics feel they are being dealt a reasonably fair hand, Protestants feel that they are getting a raw deal.

Religious Integration
Given the importance attributed to integration as a source of harmony, it is valuable to ask whether people are willing to engage in mixing and whether they support official measures to facilitate communal integration. If there is to be any reduction in the barriers between the two communities, we should hope to see some signs of a softening of attitudes with regard to these issues. Unsurprisingly, therefore, attempts to devise ways of improving community relations in Northern Ireland through increased contact (for example, through the Education for Mutual Understanding (EMU) programme), and assessments of whether relations have been improving or deteriorating over the past few decades have been the focus of much recent discussion (see, for example, Gallagher, 1996).

Any differences between the two religious groups in their openness to increased integration is, of course, important. However, given that a distinction has often been made between a more liberal, more moderate middle class and more narrow-minded working class (Lipset, 1981; Heath and Evans, 1988), it is also interesting to go beyond religion and see if the middle class are indeed more positive about, and supportive of, integration.

It is well-known that religious segregation – residential, but also across a range of other areas – is an important feature of Northern Irish society. It is also known that segregation is highest in working-class areas. We begin, therefore, by showing levels of reported integration across three areas: among friends, in the neighbourhood, and among relatives.

Figure 4

Levels of reported integration, by religion and class (higher scores indicate greater integration)

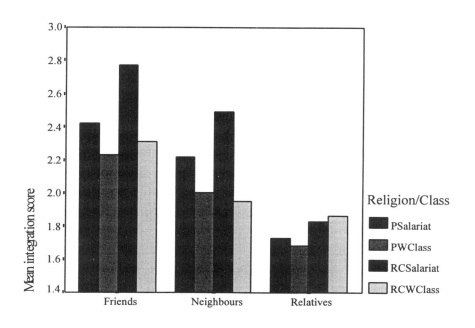

From Figure 4, we can see that classes within the religious groups differ in the expected ways (greater working-class segregation), with respect to integration by residential area and friendship, but not for relatives. The more consistent pattern for relatives is not surprising, since endogamy is still the norm across all classes. It can also be seen that the Catholic salariat report living in more integrated areas than do the Protestant salariat – this disparity may well result from the differential size of the religious groups.

Next, we look at some indicators of individual support for integration and at support for government intervention to encourage integration in various situations. These should be seen in the context of very strong agreement across the board that better inter-group relations would be facilitated by more mixing: well over 90 per cent of both Protestants and

Catholics agree that this is the case (Catholics showing slightly greater endorsement).

On more specific attitudes, first, consider the degree to which people themselves are supportive of mixing with members of the other community. Respondents were asked if they were in favour of more mixing or more separation in several important areas of their lives. To each issue, responses were coded along a five point scale from 'much more separation' to 'much more mixing'. In Figure 5, we present the mean score on a combination of four items for which individual scores were highly

Figure 5

Support for integration, by religion, class and sex (higher scores indicate stronger support)

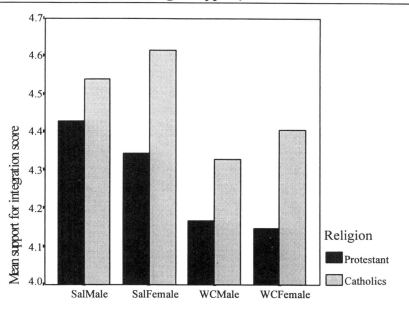

correlated: secondary/grammar schools, neighbourhoods, workplaces, leisure activities. Higher scores indicate a more pro-integration stance. Overall, Catholics are more pro-integration than are Protestants and, within religious groups, the salariat are more supportive of mixing. There are no

significant sex differences, though there is a tendency for Catholic women in both classes to be more integrationist than their male counterparts. On a range of other measures, including attitudes to mixed marriages and mixed primary schools, this general pattern holds, though the levels of support vary: for example, all groups give somewhat lower levels of endorsement to mixed marriages than to most of the other, less controversial, issues.

Politics

Party Support
Although religious affiliation remains the best single predictor of party support and of attitudes to a range of politicised issues such as national identity and preferences about the constitutional status of Northern Ireland, it cannot account for all of the variation in these.   Nor can it explain divisions within the religious groups. Social class has been used to explain intra-religious differences in partisanship specifically and, by implication, to account for party competition strategies within the nationalist and unionist communities (Evans and Duffy, 1997).   In this section, we examine responses to a number of questions that tap into some of the most central elements of political orientations in Northern Ireland.

Previous research on the link between class and party support has looked mainly at the parties people say they would vote for. Here, before looking at actual patterns of support, we examine whether people are *partisans* of a particular party or not. Respondents were asked: *Generally speaking, do you think of yourself as a supporter of any one political party?*

Table 7

Percentage saying they are supporters of a particular party, by religion, class and sex

	Protestants		Catholics	
	Salariat	Working Class	Salariat	Working Class
Males	49	32	21	25
Females	42	33	30	19

Table 7 shows how Protestants are far more likely to consider themselves supporters of a specific party. The lower levels of partisanship among Catholics have been noted before (Evans and Duffy, 1997) and may not necessarily be indicative of political apathy. Indeed, some evidence that apathy is not the explanation is provided by responses to the question: *How much interest do you generally have in what is going on in politics?*

The problem of what 'politics' might be taken to mean notwithstanding, interest scores were very similar for the two religious groups. Thus, the lack of defined party affiliation among Catholics may be more a consequence of the limited party options available to them (for example, where do the considerable group of Catholic non-nationalists (see Breen, 1996) 'go' politically?) than symptomatic of more general lack of political awareness or involvement.

There is a marked class difference among Protestants, with the salariat, regardless of sex, being far more likely to have a party identification. Looking at Catholics overall, we find no significant class difference (26 per cent of the salariat state a party, versus 22 per cent of the working class). Among women, however, the pattern is the same as for Protestants generally: higher levels of partisanship in the salariat.

If we next look at expressions of support for particular parties, we see the familiar (see Evans and Duffy, 1997; Duffy and Evans, 1996) patterns of class allegiance within religious groups. Party identification was measured as a composite of responses to three questions. Respondents were first asked the question above on whether they were supporters of a particular party. If they said no, they were asked: *Do you think of yourself as a little closer to one political party than to others?* And if they still answered no, they were asked: *If there was a general election tomorrow, which political party do you think you would be most likely to support?*

Table 8 shows that there are strong class effects for both Protestants and Catholics, but that these are more marked in the former group. The single most salient feature of party support is the almost total lack of cross-religious appeal of the four main (confessional) parties, indicating that religious affiliation remains, unsurprisingly, *the* main predictor of party support. Neither do any of the findings on class show anything new: the working-class nature of Democratic Unionist Party (DUP) support, and the

Table 8
Party identification, by religion and class (%)

| | Protestants | | Catholics | |
	Salariat	Working Class	Salariat	Working Class
UUP	48	42	0	*
DUP	8	23	0	*
SDLP	1	1	60	48
Sinn Fein	0	0	1	8
APNI	22	5	16	6
Other	9	4	7	4
None	8	19	14	26
Other/Don't Know/NA	3	6	3	6

cross-class appeal of the Ulster Unionists are well-known. So, too, is the almost total lack of middle-class support for Sinn Fein and the slight middle-class bias in the following of the Social Democratic and Labour Party (SDLP). The Alliance Party (APNI) remains clearly a middle-class party, though the split in levels of salariat/working-class support is sharper among Protestants. Beyond this, note that the SDLP gains a larger relative slice of salariat support among Catholics than does the UUP among Protestants, and that Catholics in general, and the working class in particular, are far more likely than Protestants to express no party affiliation, even when pressed. This relates back to the above discussion of Table 7, and the same possible explanations apply. Rather more surprising is the absence of sex differences in either religious group. What might be termed the more 'extreme' parties on either side are not more likely to be supported by men, and there is no evidence that women are choosing more moderate or neutral parties.

National Identity

Moving away from participation and party politics, we look next at the key political questions of national identity and constitutional preference. Together, these can be regarded as forming the core around which the Northern Ireland conflict is built, around which religious labels become merely 'proxy words' (Moxon-Browne, 1983: 3) to represent a conflict which is fundamentally a clash of national allegiances and the political/constitutional aspirations associated with these.

Looking at patterns of national identity (see Table 9), we find that the salariat of both religious groups, but especially Catholics, are more likely to adopt a Northern Irish identity than are the working class. This suggests that there is some mileage in claims that Northern Irish has emerged as the preferred identity for the middle classes. The assumption is that this is the compromise choice for moderates who do not want to be drawn into, or identified with, one or other side in the conflict.

Table 9

National identity, by religion class and sex (%)

	Protestants		Catholics	
	Salariat	**Wk Class**	**Salariat**	**Wk Class**
Men				
British	56	67	15	5
Irish	8	3	49	75
Ulster	8	15	6	-
Northern Irish	23	13	30	20
Other	5	2	-	-
Women				
British	61	64	19	15
Irish	9	6	51	59
Ulster	6	15	-	4
Northern Irish	22	12	28	21
Other	2	2	2	1

However, there are several problems with the suggestion that Northern Irish is a middle-class label of moderation. First, there is a large portion of the Catholic working class who also adopt a Northern Irish identity (as large as among the Protestant salariat, in fact): feeling Northern Irish is not, therefore, the reserve of the well off. But, second, over half of the Catholic salariat (indeed, of both class groups), and around two thirds of salariat Protestants, prefer their traditional label of identity. Without over time data, it is impossible to say if this figure is declining as more of the younger people grow up with the Northern Irish label. However, although neither Rose (1971) nor Moxon-Browne (1983) had Northern Irish as an option on their identity questions (this, in itself, is significant), they did have the traditional labels: looking at Rose, there is a very significant shift towards Britishness for Protestants, only 39 per cent of whom felt British in 1968, while, among Catholics in general, Irish identification is down slightly (76 per cent in 1968). Among Catholics as a whole, however, it is true that, in 1995, feeling Northern Irish, as opposed to Irish, is associated with a significantly less nationalist position (on a seven point scale of unionism (1) to nationalism (7), those who feel Northern Irish score 4.5, compared with 5.1 for Irish identifiers), and this, again, gives support to the 'Northern Irish for neutrality' argument. Among Protestants, feeling Northern Irish, rather than British or 'Ulster', is also associated with a less strongly unionist position (3.1 versus 2.7 and 2.4 respectively).

Overall, class differences among Catholics are trivial, though the working class is somewhat less likely to choose a British identity than the middle class, and the middle class feel a little less Irish than the working class in general. However, when we look at the pattern by sex, we find that this is due to a marked difference among the men only (otherwise, for both religious groups, sex is not an important source of differentiation). It is not the working class in general who look less towards Britain than the salariat; it is the Catholic male working class who are significantly more Irish and less British than any other group. Higher unemployment rates among Catholic men mean they are likely to be quite welfare dependent, but this does not as a group make them more likely to identify with Britain. Since it is well-known that working-class men are more directly involved in the conflict (and therefore may have had more negative experiences of the

security forces), it is not surprising that they are the least likely to assign themselves a British identity.

In the Protestant group, unsurprisingly, the profile is very different. A trivial number of Protestants feel Irish in each class. It is interesting how much this has shifted since Rose's survey, where 20 per cent of Protestants considered themselves Irish. The shift probably reflects the changing meaning attached to the Irish label, which, since the Troubles, has become more associated with a political, 'nationalist' position.

The final thing to note about Protestant profiles is the use of the Ulster identity. Much research points to how this is more a label for the working class than for the middle class, again perhaps because of the extremist (paramilitary) undertones the label may carry, and this is supported by these findings. Few in the salariat adopt the Ulster label as their badge of identity, a significant move away from pre-Troubles patterns found by Rose (1971). And, in fact, the decline in numbers calling themselves Ulster people has been general across the classes: 32 per cent of all Protestants chose the 'Ulster' label in 1968. Of course, this is also, in part, explained by the choice of a Northern Irish option in the 1995 survey, which makes absolute comparisons with past results very difficult.

Constitutional Preferences

If O Connor's interviewees are correct in their sense of the Catholic middle class abandoning traditional nationalist aspirations in their move up the socio-economic ladder, we should find significant differences in constitutional preferences between the classes. The question asked was: *Do you think that the long term policy for Northern Ireland should be for it to ... remain part of the UK/reunify with the rest of Ireland/other.* To increase the numbers, data from the 1994 and 1995 surveys are combined in Table 10, since there were no significant differences between responses in the two years.

The profiles for Catholics do not differ significantly by class, in general, though the working class are more likely to express no preference. The majority of both the working class and the salariat would like a united Ireland in the long-term, compared with roughly half that proportion who want to stay part of the UK. Thus, on these data, and looking back to the

previous section on identity, only the first part of what one of O Connor's interviewees has to say survives this superficial analysis: 'They (the Catholic middle class) have a desire for their Irishness (but they) haven't got the same desire for a united Ireland' (O Connor, 1993: 32-3).

Table 10

Long-term constitutional preference, by religion, class and sex (%)

	Protestants				Catholics			
	Salariat		Working Class		Salariat		Working Class	
	M	F	M	F	M	F	M	F
Part of UK	83	85	94	86	31	28	22	37
United Ireland	10	8	-	8	64	59	63	49
Other	7	3	4	2	6	4	4	2
Don't know	-	4	2	4	-	9	10	11

However, this does not mean that class has no effect on constitutional preferences: it could be that there are effects in two directions here, some of the working class wanting to stay with the better welfare provisions of the United Kingdom, others wanting to try their fortunes in a united Ireland. Clearly, however, middle-class Catholics have not abandoned the traditional position any more than their working-class counterparts. Here is another major issue, then, on which we can find no evidence that the middle class hold attitudes which are very different from those held by the working class.

For Protestants, there is no preference split of the kind seen among Catholics. Protestants remain steadfastly opposed to changing the constitutional status of Northern Ireland, and their support for the Union with Britain is the same irrespective of class. This result stands even when they are presented with a much wider range of alternatives in another question on constitutional preferences (see Evans, 1996). There is also a small sex difference within the Protestant working class, with men almost unanimously endorsing the Union and slightly more of a spread across other response options among the other three Protestant groups. This fits

with the idea that unionism and loyalism are strongest among working-class Protestant men.

In the Catholic group, there is a more complicated, and perhaps more significant, pattern by class and sex. Among the salariat, male and female preferences are similar, but differ considerably among the working class, where men show the lowest and women the highest levels of support for the UK link. Such a pattern may be linked to the greater levels of direct involvement in the conflict among working-class men, while women may be more politically conservative and somewhat more likely to prefer the status quo to some radical overhaul, especially one that might involve violence. This fits uncomfortably, however, with evidence that working-class men are not more likely than women to support Sinn Fein, though it is possible that support for Sinn Fein has a different meaning for men than for women. It also does not explain why it is only working-class women who show the more pro-UK preference. And, indeed, if it is true that growth in a Catholic middle class may be more a female than a male phenomenon in the future, and if the constitutional preferences seen here are a reasonable reflection of group attitudes, then simple shifts in proportions should mean that the Catholic middle class will become *more,* rather than less, in favour of a united Ireland. This, of course, is directly against the popular view of such growth signalling a move away from the traditional Catholic nationalist position.

Trust in Government
Bruce makes much of the increasing numbers of unionists who are sceptical of British government policy towards Northern Ireland. He argues that, in the wake of the 1985 Anglo-Irish Agreement especially, unionists have become more distrusting of British political motives, more resentful of Irish government 'interference', and more threatened by the prospect of a 'slippery slope' to a united Ireland. The corollary of this is an intense suspicion of, and increasing antagonism towards, the Irish government. Given that much is also made of the concentration of feelings of threat and inadequacy among the working-class, it is interesting to see whether there are class differences in perceptions of the British and Irish governments. Moreover we might expect this to tie into findings on

national identity and constitutional preference, those more pro-UK and more British being less sceptical about British government. Among Catholics, if we follow the logic of the argument that the middle class have had a better deal from the current constitutional arrangement and from many of the policies introduced under direct rule, we might expect a more favourable view of the British government among the salariat.

In Table 11, we examine attitudes relating to trust in the British government, and in Table 12 to trust in the Irish government. Respondents were asked: *Under direct rule from Britain, as now, how much do you generally trust British governments of any party to act in the best interests of Northern Ireland? And if there was a united Ireland, how much do you think you would generally trust an Irish government to act in the best interests of Northern Ireland?*

Table 11

Percentage saying they would mostly/always or never trust a British government, by religion and class

| | Protestants | | Catholics | |
	Salariat	Working Class	Salariat	Working Class
Mostly/Always	22	29	26	20
Never	6	12	7	11

The first thing to note is the striking similarity across religious groups in the proportions who trust the British government 'mostly' or 'almost always'. There is a slight tendency for the Protestant salariat to trust less than working-class Protestants, and for the Catholic salariat to be more trusting than the Catholic working class, but these differences are small. At the other extreme, levels of most distrust are also similar, and relatively low, across religion. But it is the comparisons with the distributions in Table 12 that are most striking. These show that trust in the Irish government is similarly high across classes in the Catholic group, almost half of whom say they would trust a Dublin government most of the time.

Table 12

Percentage saying they would mostly/always or never trust an Irish government, by religion and class

| | Protestants | | Catholics | |
	Salariat	Working Class	Salariat	Working Class
Mostly/Always	21	12	48	42
Never	24	34	4	3

However, Protestants are much more sceptical. Although more than one-fifth of the Protestant salariat would have a lot of trust in an Irish government (a similar figure to Catholic levels of trust in Britain), this is matched by almost a quarter of the same class group who would never trust Dublin. This is evidence of striking polarisation on this issue within the middle-class Protestant group. There is polarisation, too, among the Protestant working class, but it shows a much stronger lean towards absolute mistrust of an Irish government: where the split between most and least trust is almost even among members of the salariat, in the working class the proportion is three times greater than that expressing high levels of trust. More than one third of working-class Protestants would have no trust at all, fitting with the view that the most intense threat is felt among the economically disadvantaged. Not surprisingly, Catholic levels of total mistrust in an Irish government are low in both classes. There is no evidence of significant sex differences in attitudes on these issues.

Conclusions

The complex patterns of evidence presented in the previous pages clearly bear quite significantly upon the issues raised in the introduction. The general picture we have observed has mainly concerned the importance of religion and class – in that order – as influences on perceptions and attitudes in Northern Ireland. Sex differences are to be found, and in places they do challenge certain stereotypes about men, women and class in the province, but they have a less pronounced presence in their consequences for social and political attitudes. Most of the relevant findings concern the

presence – or otherwise – of divisions within religious groups along lines of social class.

Consider, first, that the widely held view of the working class on both sides of the sectarian divide being more polarised than their respective middle classes is given only partial support. Class differences of an expected sort surface in the context of attitudes towards integration (a finding that also survives multivariate tests – see Evans, 1996): Catholic and Protestant middle-class respondents report being both more integrated in reality and more pro-integration in their attitudes. Nevertheless, when we examine prejudice and politics this picture becomes more complex. In terms of views on prejudice and discrimination, both in general, and by specific authorities, the notion of a Protestant 'siege mentality' being particularly pronounced among the working class, does not receive much support. Indeed, levels of 'resentment' at the FEC and at the possibility of positive discrimination in favour of Catholics appear to be higher in the Protestant middle class. Where the Protestant working class are less compromising, however, is in their political views: they are slightly more unionist in their long-term aspirations, somewhat less trusting of an Irish government, more likely to identify with 'Ulster', and, of course, more likely to support the DUP (although this in itself does not appear to derive very strongly from the DUP position on the Union, but from the DUP's role in articulating the economic interests of the Protestant working class (Evans and Duffy, 1997).

As for the Catholic middle class, we find little evidence that they have defected from nationalist political goals, thus creating class divisions on the national question. On the constitution, trust in the Irish government, and national identity, they display similar levels of pro-nationalist views as do the working class. It is unsurprising, then, that in the wake of the disturbances at Drumcree during the 1996 Protestant marching season, we are now hearing talk (Douds, 1996: 18) of a reawakening of the 'hitherto silent Catholic middle class' about whom O Connor comments. The fact that the Catholic middle class are more compromising on questions concerning communal integration and tend to support parties that are less hard-line on the nationalist question does not indicate a rejection of the goals of nationalism.

It is important to note, moreover, that these views tend to apply to both men and women, so the continued growth of a feminised Catholic middle class would not, in and of itself, suggest that levels of Catholic nationalism will decline. Thus, the indications that Catholic girls are doing better than boys at school, that girls are less likely to be unemployed, and that they make up a disproportionate number of the newly emerging Catholic middle class, does not appear to open up the way for a long-term reduction in support within the Catholic community for changes to the constitution. The general point seems to be that, even if middle-class Catholics – especially women – are more right-wing on economic issues, this does not translate into lack of commitment to nationalism. The political and economic questions are separate.

Interestingly, both middle-class and working-class Protestants share ambivalence towards the British government with Catholics of both classes. This is also the only issue that we have examined on which religion has little or no effect, and it is noticeable in that it focuses on the role of the British government – a body that is clearly distinct from the political groupings in the province itself, and whose long-term reliability and motives regarding the national question remain unclear (or perhaps too clear...) to people on both sides of the debate.

The evidence suggests, then, that class differences are different for Protestants and Catholics. Despite the high levels of Protestant commitment to the Union with Britain, the Protestant middle and working classes appear to be more divided on political attitudes and voting preferences than do these classes among Catholics. Moreover, the relatively low-key nature of differences between men and women, and their diverse nature, do little to support the notion that it is working-class *men* who are the most polarised section of the two religious communities. This is despite the evidence that Catholic men tend to be particularly disadvantaged. Thus, even though in Northern Ireland some women have been involved in certain cross-communal initiatives, we can find little evidence that women are more moderate or compromising in their views. They are just as likely to be nationalist if Catholic, or unionist if Protestant, while on economic issues, women are distinctive for being more right-wing than men of the same class or religion. This suggests that, even if sex roles

are changing, and if, as a consequence, women take a more direct and directive role in community relations and politics, the implication is that they are unlikely to introduce a distinctive viewpoint into the long-established agenda of constitutional disputes.

For our final point, we return to the issue on which we opened the chapter: that of class differences. The key observation on which we shall end is a simple one: despite the cynicism expressed by the Catholics interviewed by O Connor on issues concerning the national question, in general middle-class Catholics share many of the political views of working-class Catholics; while, among Protestants, there is at least some evidence that, to a greater degree than their middle-class co-religionists, the working-class display some of the insecurities and hard-line views that writers such as Bruce have suggested are redolent of a 'siege mentality'. This asymmetry is an important feature of the relationship between social structure and politics in Northern Ireland and provides a basis for further understanding of the intra-sectarian political dynamics on which any long-term resolutions of the current conflicts may well depend.

References

AUNGER, E. 1975. 'Religion and occupational class in Northern Ireland', *Economic and Social Review,* 7, 1-18.

BREEN, R. 1996. 'Who wants a United Ireland? Constitutional preferences among Catholics and Protestants', in R. Breen, P. Devine and L. Dowds (eds.), *Social Attitudes in Northern Ireland*, Belfast, Appletree Press.

BRUCE, S. 1994. *The Edge of the Union: The Ulster Loyalist Political Vision*, Oxford, Oxford University Press.

CORMACK, R. J. and OSBORNE, R. D. 1994. 'The evolution of a Catholic middle class', in A. Guelke (ed.), *'New Perspectives on the Northern Ireland Conflict'*, Aldershot, Gower.

CURTICE, J. and GALLAGHER, T. 1990. 'The Northern Ireland dimension', in R. Jowell, S. Witherspoon and L. Brook, (eds.), *British Social Attitudes: the 7th report,* Aldershot, Gower.

DOUDS, S. 1996. 'All croppies together', *Fortnight,* 353, 18-9.

DUFFY, M. and EVANS, G. 1996. 'Building Bridges? The Political Implications of Electoral Integration for Northern Ireland', *British Journal of Political Science,* 26, 123-40

ERIKSON, R. and GOLDTHORPE, J. H. 1992. *The Constant Flux: A Study of Class Mobility in Industrial Societies,* Oxford, Clarendon Press.

EVANS, G. 1992. 'Testing the validity of the Goldthorpe class schema', *European Sociological Review,* 8 (3), 211-231.

EVANS, G. 1993. 'The decline of class divisions in Britain? Class and ideological preferences in the 1960s and the 1980s', *British Journal of Sociology,* 44, 449-71.

EVANS, G. 1996. 'Northern Ireland during the cease-fire', in R. Jowell, L. Brook, A. Park, and K. Thomson (eds.), *British Social Attitudes: the 13th report.* Aldershot, Dartmouth.

EVANS, G. and DUFFY, M. 1997. 'Beyond the sectarian divide: the social bases and political consequences of unionist and nationalist party competition in Northern Ireland', *British Journal of Political Science,* 27, 47-81.

EVANS, G., HEATH, A. and LALLJEE, M. 1995. 'Measuring Left-Right and Libertarian-Authoritarian Values in the British Electorate', *British Journal of Sociology,* 47, 93-112.

GALLAGHER, T. 1996. 'Community relations, equality and the future', in R. Breen, P. Devine and L. Dowds, (eds.), *Social Attitudes in Northern Ireland,* Belfast, Appletree.

GALLAGHER, A. M., OSBORNE, R. D. and CORMACK, R. J. 1994. *Fair Shares? Employment, Unemployment and Economic Status,* Belfast, Fair Employment Commission.

GUDGIN, G. and BREEN, R. 1996. *Evaluation of the ratio of unemployment rates as indicators of fair employment,* Belfast, Central Community Relations Unit.

HEATH, A. and EVANS, G., 1988. 'Working class conservatives and middle class socialists', in R. Jowell, S. Witherspoon, and L. Brook, (eds.), *British Social Attitudes: The 1988 Report,* Aldershot, Gower.

HEATH, A. JOWELL, R., CURTICE, J., EVANS, G., FIELD, J. and WITHERSPOON, S. 1991. *Understanding Political Change: The British Voter 1964-1987,* Oxford, Pergamon.

KNOX, C., MCILHENEY, C. and OSBORNE B, 1995. 'Social and Economic Influences on Voting in Northern Ireland', *Irish Political Studies*, 10, 69-96.

LIPSET, S. M. 1981. *Political Man: The Social Bases of Politics,* Garden City, Doubleday.

MARSHALL, G., NEWBY, H., ROSE, D., and VOGLER, C. 1988. *Social Class in Modern Britain,* London, Hutchinson.

MCAULEY, J. W. 1994. *The Politics of Identity,* Newcastle upon Tyne, Avebury.

MOXON-BROWNE, E.A. 1983. *Nation, Class and Creed in Northern Ireland*, Aldershot, Gower.

NELSON, S. 1984. *Ulster's Uncertain Defenders,* Belfast, Appletree Press.

O CONNOR, F. 1993. *In Search of A State: Catholics in Northern Ireland*, Belfast, Blackstaff Press.

O'DOWD, L. 1991. 'Social Class', in P. Stringer and G. Robinson (eds.), *Social Attitudes in Northern Ireland: 1990-91 edition,* Belfast, Blackstaff Press.

OSBORNE, R. D. and CORMACK, R.J., 1986. 'Unemployment and Religion in Northern Ireland', *The Economic and Social Review*, 17 (3), 215-225.

OSBORNE, R. D., MILLER, R. L., CORMACK, R. J. and WILLIAMSON, A. 1988. 'Trends in Higher Education Participation in Northern Ireland', *The Economic and Social Review*, 19 (4), 282-301.

PPRU MONITOR, 1993. *Religion 1988-90/91,* Belfast, Government Statistical Publication.

PRICE, J. 1995. 'Political Change and the Protestant Working Class', *Race and Class, 37* (1), 57-69.

ROONEY, E. 1995. 'Women in political conflict', *Race and Class, 37* (1), 51-6.

ROSE, R. 1971. *Governing Without Consensus,* London, Faber and Faber.

Appendix

Table A1
Educational achievement, by religion and sex (%)

	Protestants		Catholics	
	M	F	M	F
Degree	12	8	3	9
Higher Education	15	12	6	12
'A' level	14	9	17	6
'O' level	15	20	18	22
CSE	10	11	11	8
None	35	41	45	42

Table A2
Educational achievement among the under-35s, by religion and sex (%)

	Protestants		Catholics	
	M	F	M	F
Degree	14	13	4	11
Higher Education	21	13	8	13
'A' level	25	17	27	10
'O' level	19	32	30	38
CSE	8	12	12	12
None	15	13	21	15

7

Transport in Northern Ireland: Finding the Way Forward?

Iain Bryson, Paula Devine and Lizanne Dowds

Introduction

For the first time in the Northern Ireland Social Attitudes (NISA) survey series, attitudes to transport issues have been included as a substantial module of questions. Not before time. Transportation is increasingly a global problem with policies on transportation (or the lack of them) impinging directly on the environment, economic efficiency and the 'liveability' of towns and cities over the world. The growth in population (particularly urban populations) and increasing household incomes have led to a rise in private car ownership and thus a tendency to travel more as well as increased demand for both roads and car parking facilities. It has been estimated that the number of motor vehicles world-wide could grow from 580 million in 1990 to over 800 million by the year 2010 (Walsh, 1994). Faitz et al. (1994) suggest that the forces driving this level of growth range from demographic factors (urbanisation, increasing population and smaller households) to economic factors (higher incomes and declining car prices), to social factors (increased leisure time and the status associated with private car ownership), to political factors (powerful lobbies and governments that view the automobile industry as an important generator of economic growth).

Up until quite recently the main aim of transport policy has been to build new roads to meet the growing demands, not only from business and industry, but also from individual car owners. As recently as 1989 the 'Roads to Prosperity' White Paper continued this trend by announcing a £12 billion road-building policy. However, in recent years, government

policy on transport has undergone something of a sea-change with the acknowledgement that unrestrained traffic growth is environmentally and economically unacceptable. The resultant focus on seeking to change travel habits sits somewhat uneasily with conservative ideals of providing freedom of choice and market-led approaches to public transport; nonetheless the policy of restraining car use (in line with EU policy) is now explicit. In January 1995, Malcolm Moss (the Northern Ireland minister for the environment) outlined seven key principles concerning future transport policy in Northern Ireland. This was followed by the Department of the Environment's publication 'The Way Forward', setting out the policy direction in more detail. In the rest of this chapter we look at public opinion in Northern Ireland as it relates to the government's stated framework for action. Where appropriate, we compare attitudes in Northern Ireland with those in mainland Britain, and we end by examining the resistance to changing car use and the notorious gap between environmentally friendly attitudes and behaviour.

Protecting the Environment
Protecting the environment is a key principle listed in the Department of the Environment's 'framework for action' and within it the issues of road safety, vehicle emissions, pedestrian/vehicle conflict and impact on the natural and built environment are given priority. The survey has something to say about public attitudes to most of these, albeit at a very general level. When asked what is the 'greatest threat to the countryside' respondents in Northern Ireland are much more likely than those in Britain to name pollution (of land, air or water) as the greatest problem. Forty-one per cent of Northern Ireland respondents named this as the biggest threat compared with 28 per cent of respondents in Britain. Concerns in Britain are spread much more widely across different issues (see Table 1). Northern Irish people tend to be a little less concerned than their British counterparts about industrial development, new road building, changes to the natural appearance of the countryside, and traditional methods of farming. However these are relative figures, and just because the greatest number of people choose pollution as the biggest threat does not mean that they are

Table 1
Perceived 'greatest' threat to the countryside

	Northern Ireland	Great Britain
Land and air pollution, or discharges into rivers and lakes	41	28
Litter and fly-tipping of rubbish	28	24
Industrial development like factories, quarries and power stations	9	14
New housing and urban sprawl	10	9
Building new roads and motorways	3	7
Changes to the ordinary natural appearance of the countryside, including plants and wildlife	2	7
Changes to traditional ways of farming and using farmland	3	6
Superstores and out-of-town shopping centres	2	3
The number of tourists and visitors in the countryside	<1	1

correspondingly overly concerned about this. Respondents were also asked how 'serious' they thought various traffic and transport problems were. On each of the three items shown in Table 2, respondents in *Britain* are actually rather more concerned than respondents in Northern Ireland about vehicle emissions, noise pollution and traffic congestion. Nonetheless a massive 86 per cent of respondents in Northern Ireland pointed to vehicle emissions as a serious problem, 85 per cent thought the same about traffic congestion and a rather smaller 68 per cent felt that noise pollution was a serious problem. These figures are strikingly high and therefore encouraging, but of course there is nothing here to suggest that respondents acknowledged that *they themselves* might be a part of the problem (and hence a part of the solution). The question of whether traffic congestion is seen as a problem because it prevents the respondent from arriving swiftly at his/her destination, or that fumes and noise from *other* cars are inconveniences to their journey is a moot point.

Table 2

Now thinking about traffic and transport problems, how serious a problem is...

	Northern Ireland	Great Britain
% saying 'serious' or 'very serious' problem		
Exhaust fumes from traffic in towns and cities	86	96
Traffic congestion in towns and cities	85	93
Noise from traffic in towns and cities	68	78

Interestingly, the first set of questions that actually force respondents to consider the possible costs of protecting the environment result in rather more muted levels of support. As Table 3 shows, respondents were asked

Table 3

The costs of protecting the environment

	Northern Ireland	Great Britain
% 'agree' or 'strongly agree'		
Ordinary people should do more to protect the environment, even if it means paying higher prices	63	67
Industry should do more to protect the environment, even if it leads to lower profits and fewer jobs	57	61
The government should do more to protect the environment, even if it leads to higher taxes	55	61
% 'disagree' or 'strongly disagree'		
People should be allowed to use their cars as much as they like, even if it causes damage to the environment	45	51

to weigh the costs of the protecting the environment against higher taxes, fewer jobs and profits within industry, higher prices and restricted car usage. So while nearly nine out of ten people think that vehicle emissions

are a serious problem, *less than half* would accept restraint on car use for the sake of the environment. Somewhat more would swallow the need for higher prices (or say they would), but enthusiasm begins to wane when faced with the possibility of fewer jobs and higher taxes. All in all, support for the environment is still evident, but the patterns in the data suggest that facing citizens with hard reality of the costs of environmentalism could erode support fairly swiftly.

Improving Public Transport
Over half of Northern Ireland respondents never travelled by local bus (54 per cent) and only 12 per cent did so more than twice a week. Regular rail travel is even rarer with a mere one per cent using trains more than twice a week while 80 per cent never travel by train at all. This is not to say that there is no support for increased spending on public transport: when asked whether respondents would like to see more or less government spending on public transport, 43 per cent said they wanted more or much more spending on local bus services and 40 per cent said the same about local train services. However, again this must be set in context, and while a solid four in ten respondents might say that they support spending on public transport, three in ten would still like to see more or much more spending on new *roads*. Public transport might be a slightly higher priority than new road building, but there is not a great deal in it.

As Table 4 shows, support for public transport *versus* 'roads' is slightly lower in Northern Ireland than in Britain. About half of respondents were prepared to give buses a higher priority than cars in towns and cities, to improve public transport even if the road system suffers and to subsidise uneconomic bus services. Rather fewer were prepared to subsidise uneconomic rail services – accessible train routes may be so few and far between that they are seen as irrelevant to people's everyday travel needs. What this amounts to is quite a lot of support for extra spending on public transport among a population who use it relatively rarely, coupled with luke-warm support for giving preference to public transport over cars. This is consistent with the view that Northern Ireland simply does not have the public transport system capable of seriously competing with the

Table 4
Support for public transport

	Northern Ireland	Great Britain
% 'agree' or 'agree strongly'		
Buses should be given more priority in towns and cities, even if this makes things more difficult for car drivers	53	61
UK should do more to improve its public transport system even if its road system suffers	48	58
% 'disagree' or 'disagree strongly'		
Local bus services that do not pay for themselves should be closed down	55	66
Local rail services that do not pay for themselves should be closed down	41	62

convenience of car usage for most people. The survey did not include in-depth questions on improving public transport, but it did ask car users why they *really* needed a car (see Table 5).

Table 5
Reasons why respondents said they 'really' needed a car (%)

	Northern Ireland	Great Britain
No convenient bus or train route to where you need to go	54	48
Bus or train does not run often enough	46	41
Live too far from a station or a bus-stop	36	24
Cost of bus or train travel is too high	33	45

Both in Northern Ireland and in Britain, the most common reason given is that there is simply no convenient bus or train route to where people need to go, and this answer is rather more commonly given in Northern

Ireland than in Britain (which of course would be expected given that a greater proportion of the population lives in rural areas). Interestingly, the cost of bus or train travel is a relatively unimportant reason in Northern Ireland in comparison with other reasons to do with convenience, accessibility and frequency (though this is certainly not the case in Britain where cost is quite an important factor). Most tellingly, respondents who said that they would find it inconvenient not to have access to their car were asked if they would use public transport more if it were 'better or less expensive'; a full 64 per cent said that they would use their car just the same as now.

Providing for Pedestrians and Cyclists

It has been suggested by many people (for example, Godlee (1992)) that transportation is a public health as well as an environmental issue, because of the effects of pollution and traffic accidents. But another public health issue that the survey figures cannot fail to highlight is the lack of exercise resulting from over-dependence on cars. Twenty-nine per cent of survey respondents in Northern Ireland would rarely 'go somewhere on foot at least fifteen minutes walk away'; in fact they would do this less than once a month. A full fifth of respondents said that they would *never* walk for more than fifteen minutes. At the other end of the scale, only a quarter said that they would go somewhere on foot (at least fifteen minutes walk away) *every day*. The figures are rather better in Britain with a third saying that they would walk this length every day. A similar picture is evident for cycling; 80 per cent of Northern Ireland respondents never cycled (the equivalent figure is 77 per cent in Britain).

However, any measures that are designed to improve facilities for pedestrians are likely to receive solid public support; three-quarters of Northern Ireland respondents were 'in favour' or 'strongly in favour' of many more streets in cities and towns reserved for pedestrians only. When asked whether they would like to see more or less government spending on improving facilities for cyclists and pedestrians, even if 'everyone's taxes may have to go up to pay for it', 63 per cent still wanted more or much more money spent and only three per cent wanted to spend less.

Influencing the Future Use of the Car

Nobody, least of all the Department of the Environment (as indicated in their recent publication) imagines that it is going to be easy to wean motorists away from their cars and off our congested roads. And certainly, the public attitudes reported so far give little reason to be optimistic. This is not to say that respondents are unaware of the problems associated with increasing car usage: Table 1 demonstrated that respondents are well aware of the existing problems of congestion, noise and fumes. Further questions indicate pessimism about the future: 87 per cent think that traffic congestion and 70 per cent think that traffic noise will be 'one of the most serious problems facing the UK in the next twenty years'. Nonetheless, it is clear that any measures that set out explicitly to deter drivers from using their cars may well be deeply unpopular. Table 6 shows that only about a fifth of the population (and this includes people who don't drive cars as

Table 6

Popularity of measures to deal with traffic problems

	Northern Ireland	Great Britain
Many more streets in cities and towns reserved for pedestrians only	74	68
Only vehicles with permits for essential business allowed in city centres in working hours	51	49
Banning company cars except where they are essential for employees in their work	46	49
Motorists charged for driving in city centres in working hours	23	25
Drivers charged tolls on all motorways	22	22
Shops and offices encouraged to move out of town and city centres	22	21
Much higher parking charges in towns and cities	14	17

well as drivers) would favour motorway tolls or charges for driving in city centres during office hours. Even fewer (14 per cent) would accept much

higher car-parking charges in towns and cities. However it is important to remember that car drivers are pedestrians as well, and measures to keep traffic out of city centres altogether are much less unpopular. As noted above, 74 per cent approve of pedestrianised streets and about half of respondents would support city centres being closed to traffic except for vehicles with permits for essential business. Interestingly, half of respondents were not averse to banning company cars – though this may be yet another reflection of a willingness to keep somebody else's car off the road. Views in Britain are extremely similar to those of respondents in Northern Ireland, despite the fact that traffic problems in mainland Britain are clearly rather different.

But of course the group most of interest here is car drivers themselves and their attitudes towards deliberate restrictions *versus* the freedom to use their cars as they wish. Who are the 'hard-line' drivers who feel that they should be allowed to use their cars as much as they want, regardless of the effects on the environment? Who are the drivers who believe that cars have too easy a time and that tolls or higher parking charges would be a good thing? What would it take to turn the former car drivers into the latter *and* reduce the extent to which they use their cars? It is hard to make predictions about this from a national survey, when local conditions in cities and towns across Northern Ireland (as well as people's individual circumstances) vary so much. But in fact the survey can shed some light on these issues and give some preliminary indications about which groups of drivers are likely to be the most and the least intransigent.

We selected only car drivers who used their cars at least once a week (though in fact 98 per cent of these actually used their cars every day or two to five times a week) and looked at four groups of drivers; the first group represented the most 'hard-line' car users, and the other three groups represented drivers whose attitudes implied that they would be most open to measures restricting car use:

Group 1
Drivers who believed that 'people should be allowed to use their cars as much as they like, even if it causes damage to the environment'.

Group 2
Drivers who believed that 'car drivers are still given too easy a time in the UK's towns and cities'.

Group 3
Drivers who believed in 'much higher parking charges in towns and cities' as a measure to deal with traffic problems.

Group 4
Drivers who believed that tolls should be charged on all motorways

Each group of drivers was examined in relation to:

- Age
- Gender
- If they had children aged five or less
- If they appeared to be commuters (they were employed and used their car every day or nearly every day)
- If their household had one or more company cars
- If they had a long-standing health problem or disability
- Their score on a general 'environmentalism' scale (see Appendix)
- Their score on a 'perception of traffic problems' scale (see Appendix)
- The type of area they lived in (city, suburbs, small city or town, village, farm)
- Driving frequency

Perhaps surprisingly, the extent to which respondents proved to be really 'hard-line' road users had nothing to do with whether they were anti-environmentalist, nor the extent to which they acknowledged that there were indeed traffic problems. What seemed to be of sole importance was the perceived necessity of their car. Those who lived in country areas, who had a disability or who commuted were most adamant about the right to use cars as much as they like, even if it damaged the environment. Campaigns to raise awareness of traffic problems and encourage more responsible car use are unlikely to have much effect on this particular group of people. Though, of course people who have disabilities and who

live in rural areas may well be accepted as essential users in any case. However commuters are an interesting group and they would almost certainly be seen as a target for changed travel behaviour. Furthermore their apparent unwillingness to reduce their car usage may be rather less intransigent than it first appears. Despite their hard-line attitudes, commuters are also significantly more likely than other groups of drivers to accept that 'cars drivers are still given too easy a time in the UK's towns and cities'. They are joined in this belief by drivers who are generally pro-environmentalist, by male drivers and by those who actually live in small cities and towns. The last is hardly a surprising result and these respondents are almost certainly responding as irritated residents rather than 'drivers'.

For all three items that measure the apparent willingness of drivers to accept changes/restrictions in car use, the group consistently most receptive is the pro-environmentalists. This is a predictable finding but it is worth giving this some consideration in the context of future advertising campaigns to alter travel behaviour. What is important about these drivers is that they are *generally* environmentalist – not that they are concerned about traffic noise, congestion and fumes. People who are 'environmentalist' on our scale are those who think that government, industry and ordinary people should all 'do more to protect the environment', even if it costs us all more money (see the Appendix for details of the construction of this scale). Something more than a national survey is needed to unravel this finding but designers of future advertising campaigns should be cautious about restricting the focus to traffic issues in an effort to reduce car use. What may be more useful is setting such campaigns within a generally 'environmentalist' promotion. Other groups who would advocate much higher car parking charges in an effort to deal with traffic problems include, people who do *not* have a disability, and those who do *not* have children aged five or less. Groups in favour of toll charges on motorways also include men, and those who do *not* live in the country.

Clearly then, the drivers apparently least receptive to change include those living in country areas, the disabled, women, and those with small children. Any envisaged improvements to public transport would need to

address the concerns of these groups (more and better rural bus routes, accessibility for disabled and child-friendly child-secure public transport). It may be that providing a real alternative to car travel for such groups is impossible but services such as kneeling buses, Busy Bus, Easibus and Dial-a-Ride schemes reflect innovative approaches to the differing needs of public transport users. Nonetheless these schemes are largely confined to urban areas and therefore have little impact on the needs of rural communities.

The gap between environmental attitudes and behaviour
Finally, it is worth ending on a note of caution concerning the potential for conflict between a respondent's attitudes and their actual behaviour, as this has clear implications for any future policy initiatives. The survey asked respondents whether they agreed or disagreed with a fairly unequivocal statement:

I do what is right for the environment, even when it costs more money or takes more time.

The results show that regular car drivers are more likely than other groups to declare themselves environmentalists according to this item. In fact over half (57 per cent) of those people who say that they do what is right for the environment (even when it costs more money or takes more time) are car drivers who use their cars every day or nearly every day. A further note of irony is provided by figures on walking and public transport. Of those drivers who say that they do what is right for the environment, 20 per cent *never* go somewhere on foot at least fifteen minutes walk away, and 58 per cent say that they would still use their cars as much as they do now ever if public transport were better or less expensive. Even weaning 'environmentalists' away from their cars may prove to be something of an uphill struggle.

References

DEPARTMENT OF TRANSPORT. 1989. *Roads to Prosperity*. London, HMSO.

DEPARTMENT OF THE ENVIRONMENT FOR NORTHERN IRELAND. 1995. *Transportation in Northern Ireland: The Way Forward*, Belfast, HMSO.

FAIZ, A., SINHA, K. and GAUTAM, S. 1994. *Air pollution characteristics and trends*, Washington, The World Bank.

GODLEE, F. 1992. 'Transport: A public health issue', *British Medical Journal, 304*: 48-50.

WALSH, M. P. 1994. *Motor Vehicle Pollution Control: An Increasingly Critical Issue for Developing Countries,* Washington, The World Bank.

Appendix

Construction of environmentalism scale

The following items were used in the construction of the environmentalism scale:

- *The government should do more to protect the environment, even if it leads to higher taxes*
- *Industry should do more to protect the environment, even if it leads to lower profits and fewer jobs*
- *Ordinary people should do more to protect the environment, even if it means paying higher prices*

Answer responses ranged on a five point scale from 'strongly agree' to 'strongly disagree'. 'Don't know' answers were recorded into the mid-point response 'neither agree nor disagree'. These items scaled reliably (with a Cronbach's alpha of .82) and the resultant scale was thus a reasonable choice, though it should be noted that many other items could also be said to measure 'environmentalism' or various facets of it.

Construction of 'traffic problems scale'

This scale was felt to be rather different from the former in that awareness of traffic problems did not necessarily imply environmentalism. Noise, congestion and fumes may be seen as inconveniences to drivers and as problems for residents/pedestrians without necessarily being seen as environmental issues. Six items were used in the construction of this scale. A Cronbach's alpha of .76 suggested that the resulting scale was adequate for our purposes. The items were as follows:

- *And thinking about traffic and transport problems, how serious a problem is congestion on motorways?*
- *And how serious a problem is increased traffic on country roads and lanes?*
- *And how serious a problem is traffic congestion at popular places in the countryside?*
- *And how serious a problem is traffic congestion in towns and cities?*
- *And how serious a problem are exhaust fumes from traffic in towns and cities?*
- *And how serious a problem is noise from traffic in towns and cities?*

Answer responses ranged from 1 to 4 from 'A very serious problem' to 'Not a problem at all'. There was no neutral mid-point and 'Don't know' answers were treated as missing information.

Table A1

Logistic regression modelling drivers who believed that 'people should be allowed to use their cars as much as they like, even if it causes damage to the environment'

	B	Wald statistic	Sig	R
Lives in a country village	1.0830	10.5301	.0012	.1469
Lives in a farm or home in the country	.8967	7.7856	.0053	.1209
People who have a disability	-.7464	4.6585	.0309	-.0820
Commuter	.5800	307281	.0535	.0661

Final model chi-square = 19.706, p=.0006.

Table A2

Logistic regression modelling drivers who believed that 'car drivers are still given too easy a time in the UK's towns and cities'

	B	Wald statistic	Sig	R
Pro-environmentalists	-.3673	28.4593	.0000	-.2429
Men	-.8491	10.1603	.0014	-.1349
Commuters	.7027	7.0739	.0078	.1064
Lives in a small city or town	.4796	3.4450	.0634	.0568

Final model chi-square =55.814, p=.0000.

Table A3

Logistic regression modelling drivers who believed in 'much higher parking charges in towns and cities' as a measure to deal with traffic problems

	B	Wald statistic	Sig	R
Pro-environmentalists	-.2831	13.3212	.0003	-.1811
People who do *not* have a disability	.9967	4.9397	.0262	.0923
Those who do *not* have children aged five or less	-.7841	3.1952	.0739	-.0588

Final model chi-square =22.791, p=.0000.

Table A4

Logistic regression modelling drivers who believed that tolls should be charged on all motorways

	B	Wald statistic	Sig	R
Pro-environmentalists	-.3099	23.7873	.0000	-.2170
Does *not* live in a farm or a home in the country	-.8092	6.2656	.0123	-.0960
Men	-.5153	4.3540	.0369	-.0713

Final model chi-square =40.717, p=.0000.

8

Economic Beliefs and Politics in Northern Ireland

Bernadette C. Hayes and Ian McAllister

Introduction

Economic issues such as unemployment, public ownership, the rights of workers, and the redistribution of income and wealth have traditionally represented one of the most fundamental cleavages within British politics, the so-called left-wing/right-wing division (Heath et al., 1985; 1990; 1991). From its inception, it was differences in support for these 'bread-and-butter' issues which not only set the Labour party apart from its Conservative counterpart, but also gave British politics its class-based character. In contrast to the working class, which has been more likely to favour full employment, redistribution and public ownership, and to vote Labour, members of the middle class have tended to reject such collectivist orientations and cast their vote for the Conservative party. Although there is some evidence to suggest that the traditional class-basis of these economic beliefs has now declined, current voting studies indicate that differences in economic orientation are still important, and not infrequently remain the most important single consideration in determining electoral choice (Evans et al., 1996; Sarlvik and Crewe, 1992; Heath et al., 1990; Rose and McAllister, 1990).

Despite the political importance of these differences within Britain, the role of economic issues in determining party support and electoral outcomes has rarely been empirically investigated in Northern Ireland. Popular opinion as well as a number of academics have emphasised the religious nature of the conflict and not its material bases (Benson and Sites,

1992; Moxon-Brown, 1991; MacIver, 1987; Bruce, 1986; O'Brien, 1972). The popular image of Northern Ireland politics is of a sectarian conflict between two monolithic religious communities, Protestant and Catholic. As Bruce, in epitomising this view, blatantly asserts: 'The Northern Ireland conflict is a religious conflict. Economic and social differences are also crucial, but it was the fact that competing populations in Ireland adhered and still adhere to competing religious traditions which has given the conflict its enduring and intractable quality' (1986: 249).

Despite this popular interpretation, however, there has also been much discussion about the economic roots of the problem (McAuley, 1994; Bew et al., 1979, 1995; Aughey, 1989; Rowthorn and Wayne, 1988; Gaffikin and Morrisey, 1987; O'Dowd et al., 1980; Birrell, 1972). Liberals as well as Marxists have suggested that the conflict is ultimately reducible to material differences – real or imagined – between social groups, and if these can be rectified, then the ethno-nationalist basis of the problem would disappear (Whyte, 1990). Policy makers, too, have been quick to identify economic strands in the Northern Ireland problem, since an economic solution is easier to devise and implement than a non-economic one (Cormack and Osborne, 1991; Smith, 1988; SACHR, 1987; McCrudden, 1983). As Cormack and Osborne, in exemplifying this policy position, briefly explain: 'Whether being Protestant or Catholic is merely an ethnic label or confessional identity matters little in this context. What is important is the issue of the advantage or disadvantage associated with being *identified* as a member of one or other of the two communities' (1991: 9).

There is little doubt that the Northern Ireland problem has an economic dimension. The claims of the Northern Ireland Civil Rights Movement in the 1960s were largely based on grievances associated with inequalities in access to socio-economic resources, notably housing (O'Dowd et al., 1980). Indeed, one of the defining events that gave rise to the civil rights movement was the occupation of a council house in Caledon, County Tyrone, which had been allocated to an unmarried Protestant woman over the claims of a large Catholic family. These claims were confirmed by the Cameron Commission in 1969, which was established to inquire into the origins of the disturbances. Since then, there has been much research to

show that there are economic disparities between Catholics and Protestants, although few have been able to demonstrate that they are the consequence of systematic discrimination (Smith and Chambers, 1991; Kelley and McAllister, 1984; Hewitt, 1981; Birrell, 1972).

The British government has also emphasised the economic problems associated with the conflict. This was illustrated by the establishment of affirmative action policies in the 1970s and by the many attempts at economic interventionism, designed to try and stimulate job creation (Jay and Wilford, 1991). For example, even during the strict monetarist policies of the Thatcher years, Northern Ireland's expenditure programme suffered only a marginal decline as compared to that in Britain. More specifically, whereas public expenditure per head in Northern Ireland was about 33 per cent greater than in Britain in 1980, by 1986 it had further increased to 42 per cent (Gaffikin and Morrissey, 1990). The United States government has also supported this view as reflected in their commitment to the International Fund for Ireland since 1985, and more recently in the economic aid pledged by President Clinton after the 1994 IRA ceasefire (Guelke, 1994).

In conclusion, contrary to popular interpretations, economic conditions and the political conflict in Northern Ireland remain closely associated. Despite this relationship, however, the extent to which economic beliefs differ between Catholics and Protestants, the causes of any variations, and how they differ from their British counterparts, has rarely been investigated empirically. In this chapter, we examine popular economic beliefs in Northern Ireland, how they differ by religion, and their contribution to both party support and to preferences for a constitutional solution. We also examine how they differ from economic beliefs in Britain. The data come from the 1995 Northern Ireland Social Attitudes Survey, which asked a range of questions about economic beliefs, largely based on parallel questions asked in the British Social Attitudes Survey.

Economic Beliefs in Northern Ireland and Britain

Popular economic beliefs are shaped by many influences. There are individual experiences within the labour market, the experiences of others communicated through family and friends, and the information and images

that are portrayed by the mass media. Most importantly, from a political perspective, political parties and interest groups help to define the economic beliefs that become salient by deciding which economic issues they will politicise and by informing voters about the advantages and disadvantages that are associated with the various alternative economic policies. In Britain and most other established democracies, economic issues form the substance of party political debate, and voters are generally well-informed about the performance of the economy and about the policies that the competing parties believe will improve it (Sanders, 1992; Heath et al., 1985, 1991). In Northern Ireland, the dominance of the constitutional issue in party politics means that while citizens will probably hold some opinions on economic issues, these will have relatively few political consequences, since the major parties do not articulate them.

Attempts to establish political parties in Northern Ireland based on economic rather than on constitutional appeals have met with little success (Bell, 1990; McAllister, 1983; Bew et al., 1979). The longest-running attempt to establish the primacy of economics in politics was the Northern Ireland Labour Party (NILP). Although the NILP had some electoral success in the 1960s, when communal tensions were low, it failed to develop beyond a loose coalition of moderate nationalists and unionists, united only by a common interest in trade unionism. Wisely, the Alliance Party, which occupied substantially the same biconfessional space within the party system after 1970, made no claims to class solidarity (McAllister and Wilson, 1978). Equally, the Social Democratic and Labour Party, despite its title, remains essentially a Catholic nationalist party.

To analyse the economic beliefs in Northern Ireland, the Northern Ireland Social Attitudes surveys conducted since 1989 have consistently asked respondents' views on five questions, ranging from the redistribution of income and wealth, to views about business management. The percentages of respondents who agreed with each of the five questions are shown in Table 1. The surveys show comparatively strong support for economic reformist views. On each of the five questions in each survey there is a majority in favour of the left-wing viewpoint, ranging from the redistribution of income and wealth (favoured by 50 per cent in 1994) to the belief that ordinary working people do not receive their fair share of the

nation's wealth (73 per cent in both 1990 and 1995). Based on these data, the Northern Ireland electorate would have to be characterised as more left than right-wing, at least as far as economic beliefs are concerned.

Table 1

Economic beliefs in Northern Ireland, 1989-95					
			(% agree)		
	1989	**1990**	**1991**	**1994**	**1995**
1. Government should redistribute income from the better-off to those who are less well off.	57	58	56	50	53
2. Big business benefits owners at the expense of workers.	57	60	59	59	63
3. Ordinary working people do not get their fair share of the nation's wealth.	69	73	72	55	73
4. There is one law for the rich and one for the poor.	66	67	58	62	68
5. Management will always try to get the better of employees if it gets the chance.	57	68	65	64	67
N	866	869	906	1,519	1,510

The trend across the surveys is for these reformist opinions to have strengthened over the six year period covered by the surveys. In the case of the final item, the role of management in dealing with employees, there has been a 10 percentage point increase in views agreeing with the statement, although that change appears to have taken place between 1989 and 1990, rather than more gradually over the period. The only exception to this general trend concerns opinions about the redistribution of wealth, where there has been a decline in support for the proposition, by four percentage points over the survey period. In general, however, these results tend to support the view that there is relatively little change in public opinion about fundamental economic issues; the change that has taken place is more likely to occur at the elite level, where policy is made,

rather than at the mass level (Studlar and McAllister, 1992).

Based on the lower socio-economic attainments of Catholics compared to Protestants, together with a longer history of attempts to articulate working-class economic grievances in constitutional nationalist politics, we might expect left-wing economic beliefs to be more prevalent among Catholics than Protestants. This expectation is confirmed by the first part of Table 2, which shows significant differences in economic opinions based on religion. On average, 13 per cent more Catholics than Protestants

Table 2

Economic beliefs by religion and nation

	(% agree)					
	Northern Ireland			Great Britain		
	Prot	Cath	All	Eng	Wales	Scot
1. Government should redistribute income from the better off to less well off.	46	63	53	47	46	60
2. Big business benefits owners at the expense of workers.	59	71	64	63	60	69
3. Ordinary working people do not get their fair share of the nation's wealth.	68	81	74	68	68	73
4. There is one law for the rich and one for the poor.	62	76	68	72	79	80
5. Management will always try to get the better of employees if it gets the chance.	64	72	67	66	63	63
N	626	468	1,095	2,669	187	225

support the left-wing view on each of the five questions, ranging from a difference of a substantial 17 percentage points on the redistribution of

wealth, to 8 per cent on the role of management.   These are major differences which do suggest a much stronger economic reformist base of support among Catholics than among Protestants.

In comparing the economic beliefs of the two Northern Ireland communities with those found in the three nations in Britain, Protestants are much closer in their views to the English than are Catholics. In turn, the economic beliefs of Catholics are closest to the Scottish. The only significant variation in Protestant-English opinion occurs on the question of the application of the law to rich and poor, with Protestants taking a more objective view of the operation of the legal system compared to the English. Overall, however, the extent of these differences should not be over-estimated: averaged across the five questions, 63 per cent of Protestants agreed with the propositions, as did 63 per cent of the English and Welsh respondents; similarly, 73 per cent of Catholics agreed with them, compared to 69 per cent of the Scottish respondents.

The Socio-economic Roots of Economic Beliefs

In societies where economic beliefs form the basis for party political conflict, there are clear links between social structure and economic opinions. Although political parties often seek to blur the overlap between social divisions and party support for reasons of electoral expediency, there is an established historical relationship between lower socio-economic status and the vote for left-wing parties, and between higher socio-economic status and voting for right-wing parties. Although partisan dealignment – the process whereby voters have deserted the major political parties – has weakened this relationship during the past quarter of a century, socio-economic status remains one of the strongest influences on voting behaviour in advanced industrial society (Franklin et al., 1992).

The definition of socio-economic status requires clarification. Traditionally, social status has been measured by inherited and acquired human capital, such as education and occupation respectively, with occupation being by far the most important social variable influencing party support (Rose, 1974). More recently, as class distinctions have become blurred, different aspects of social status have become politically important (Dalton, 1996). The most important of these new economic

lifestyle measures are share ownership or 'popular capitalism', a British phenomenon stimulated in the main by the privatisations of the Thatcher years, and housing ownership, which was also central to Thatcher's microeconomic policies (Garrett, 1994). Economic lifestyle is reflected here in trade union membership, income, share ownership and owner-occupied housing.

The absence of any Northern Ireland parties emphasising socio-economic divisions suggests that we might expect a weak relationship between socio-economic factors and economic beliefs, at least when compared to the pattern that is found in the rest of Britain. Figure 1 tests this hypothesis, by regressing education and three different aspects of occupation on the five measures of economic beliefs combined into one scale. The scale runs from 0 to 10, with a low score denoting economic conservatism, and a high score economic radicalism. A factor analysis, the results of which are reported in the Appendix at Table A1, shows that for both Britain and Northern Ireland these five items form a single factor. The figures are partial regression coefficients, which show the unit change in the dependent variable induced by a unit change in the independent variable. The figures in parentheses are standardised regression coefficients, which show the relative weight of the variable in question in predicting economic beliefs. The significance of the paths themselves is denoted by the thickness of the line. The variables, their coding and their means and standard deviations are presented in the Appendix at Table A2.

Contrary to our expectations, the results in Figure 1 show that when the human capital model is applied to Northern Ireland it is a stronger predictor of economic beliefs than it is in Britain. Overall, the model predicts just over 15 per cent of the variance in economic beliefs in Northern Ireland, compared to just over seven per cent in Britain. Admittedly, some of this difference is explained by the effect of religion in Northern Ireland – which is the second most significant variable in the equation, after tertiary education – but even if we remove religion from the model, the socio-economic variables still account for 12 per cent of the variance, appreciably more than in Britain.

Education is a more important predictor of economic beliefs in Northern Ireland than it is in Britain, which may reflect the diversion of political

Figure 1
Socio-economic influences on economic beliefs

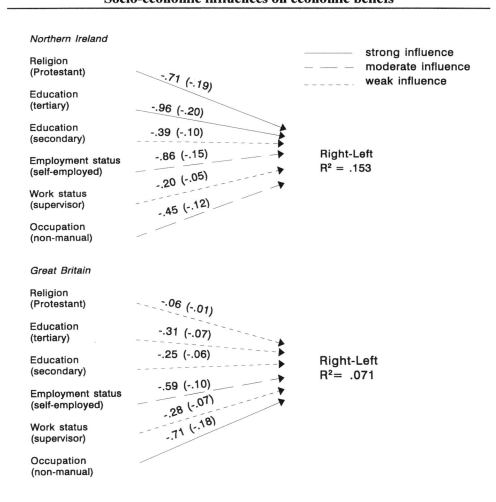

Figures are unstandardised (bs) and standardised (betas) partial regression coefficients that measure the independent impact of each predictor when controlling for the effects of all other variables in the model. Standardised regression coefficients are in parentheses. Control variables included in the model but not shown are gender, marital status and age.

debate in the province away from material concerns, so that it is only the better educated who adopt firm views on such matters. By contrast, two of the three occupation measures – manual versus non-manual occupation, and the supervision of employees in the workplace – are more important predictors in Britain than in Northern Ireland. The exception is self-employment, which is more closely allied with economic beliefs in Northern Ireland than in Britain. The British results clearly show the historical legacy of the class-party alignment, so that the non-manual/manual distinction is more important than the other two occupation measures combined.

The economic lifestyle measures, like those for human capital, also show more significant effects in predicting economic beliefs in Northern Ireland than in Britain – 16 per cent as against 10.5 per cent (Figure 2). Once again, although religion is important in Northern Ireland but not in Britain, this does not account for the disparity; when religious affiliation is dropped from the model, the economic lifestyle measures still account for just over 13 per cent of the variance. Income and owner-occupancy are more important predictors in Northern Ireland; shareownership and trade union membership are more important in Britain. The latter is easily explained by the incapacity of the trade union movement to organise effectively in Northern Ireland, at least in comparison to Britain, and by the greater wealth in Britain, which allowed many to take advantage of the privatisations of the 1980s. In fact, since 1980, not only has the number of individuals who bought shares in privatised companies more than tripled in Britain, but recent estimates suggest that they now constitute between 20 to 30 per cent of the electorate, or 10 to 13 million people (Garrett, 1994: 111). It is not immediately clear why income and housing should be more important in the province, though it may be a consequence of having a smaller proportion of wealthy people in Northern Ireland, and fewer shareowners. For example, in contrast to Britain, where a quarter of respondents were shareholders, the equivalent figure for the Northern Ireland sample was much lower at only 18 per cent.

In summary, the results contradict our hypothesis that the predominance of the constitutional issue in party political debate has weakened the link

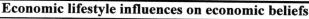

Figure 2
Economic lifestyle influences on economic beliefs

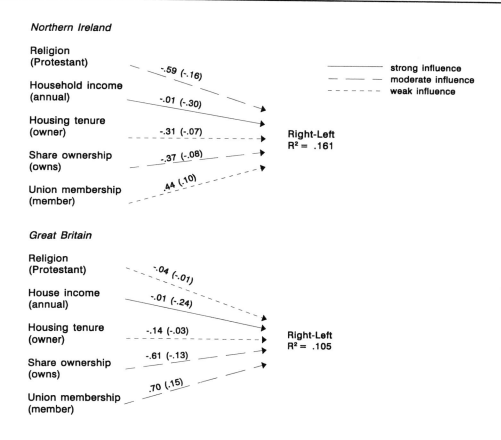

Figures are unstandardised (bs) and standardised (betas) partial regression coefficients that measure the independent impact of each predictor when controlling for the effects of all other variables in the model. Standardised regression coefficients are in parentheses. Control variables included in the model but not shown are gender, marital status and age.

between socio-economic status and economic beliefs. This may indicate that competitive political parties have a lesser role in defining and articulating economic issues than they do with non-economic issues. The imperatives of a post-industrial economy would appear to influence most individuals in much the same way, regardless of whether parties emphasise

economic issues. The results imply that if a constitutional solution ever attracted broad agreement in Northern Ireland and the major parties were forced to abandon their traditional appeals, the main pre-requisite for a modern, competitive party system – an electorate divided on questions of economic management – is already well-established.

The Political Dimension

Although economic beliefs are largely absent from party competition in Northern Ireland, economic considerations do frequently surface in politics, albeit in a more muted way than would be found in other competitive democracies. At the party political level, the support of the Protestant and Catholic communities for their respective unionist and nationalist parties has not entirely stifled socio-economic factors. Within the Catholic community, there has been a tradition of socialist activism, most notably in Belfast. In the 1960s, for example, the Republican Labour Party combined nationalist aspirations with socialist goals, the party's founder, Harry Diamond, having concluded that 'there is no room for pure Labour' (McAllister, 1977: 29). The very title of the Social Democratic and Labour Party attests to the importance placed on economic goals by the party's founders.

Within the Protestant community, there have been fewer opportunities to pursue economic goals because of the perceived need to preserve the unity of the majority and hence the union with Britain. Prior to the splits of the early 1970s, the Ulster Unionist Party went to great lengths to ensure that economic divisions were not politicised within the party, and that the economic demands of the Protestant working class were either ignored or diffused by transferring them to other parts of the unionist movement. Even after the Ulster Unionist Party began to split in the late 1960s, parties such as the Democratic Unionist Party and Vanguard – both of which had significant working-class support – differed from the Ulster Unionist Party mainly on the tactics they saw as most likely to preserve the union, not on issues of economic management (Bruce, 1994; Nelson, 1984).

The economic dimension has also figured in debates about the constitutional question. Discussions of Irish unity, even by republicans, have never been separated from considerations of how to maintain the

living standards of the Northern Irish population, since around one-quarter of the province's Gross Domestic Product (GDP) is accounted for by direct subvention from the British government (McGarry and O'Leary, 1995). The business community in Northern Ireland has also occasionally looked to particular constitutional solutions as a means not only of achieving political stability – and hence encouraging investment – but also as a means of increasing market opportunities and economic co-operation across boundaries. Business has been supportive of the European Union, which in the longer term might replace the British subvention. Not surprisingly, nationalist politicians such as John Hume have seen the EU as a model for reducing ethno-nationalist antagonism (Kennedy, 1994).

In terms of economic beliefs and partisanship, there are significant variations among supporters of the main political parties. Figure 3 shows the mean scores from a single measure combining the five economic belief items; the scale again runs from zero (economic conservatism) to 10 (economic radicalism). The parties whose supporters are the most economically conservative are the Ulster Unionists and the Alliance Party, at first glance a strange partnership, but explicable when viewed from the perspective of their shared sources of support within the province's mainly Protestant middle class. Indeed, when the Alliance figures are re-estimated for Protestant and Catholic party supporters, both have exactly the same score, 6.2. The most economically radical party within the Protestant community is the Democratic Unionist Party, led by Ian Paisley, which scores 7.1 on the scale. The DUP is only slightly less radical than the SDLP (7.2), though substantially less radical than Sinn Fein (7.7).

Despite the fact that economic considerations do not figure much, if at all, in party political competition, it is evident that the parties do attract supporters with differing views of economic management. Although these differences are not as great as those found in Britain, where the equivalent figures are 7.3 (Labour), 6.7 (Liberal-Democrats) and 5.4 (Conservatives), they still represent a discernible political division in distinguishing levels of party support in relation to this issue.

Figure 3

Economic beliefs and partisanship

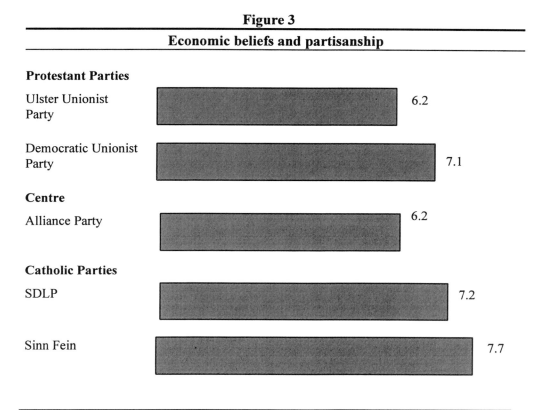

Figures are mean scores based on a combination of the five economic belief items in Table 1, and measured from 0 – 10.

Economic beliefs also play a modest role in distinguishing those who opt for the four major constitutional solutions to the Northern Ireland problem: continued union with Britain, Irish unity, joint sovereignty, and independence (Figure 4). The largest differences between the two Northern Ireland communities emerge on independence; as we might expect – since it is an extreme solution for nationalists – Catholics who support it are significantly more economically radical than their counterparts who support other solutions, with the exception of Irish unity. Catholics who support the union are the most economically conservative of their community. There are comparatively few differences between Protestants, while the British are more likely to follow Catholics than Protestants in linking economic beliefs to constitutional options.

Figure 4

Economic beliefs and constitutional preferences

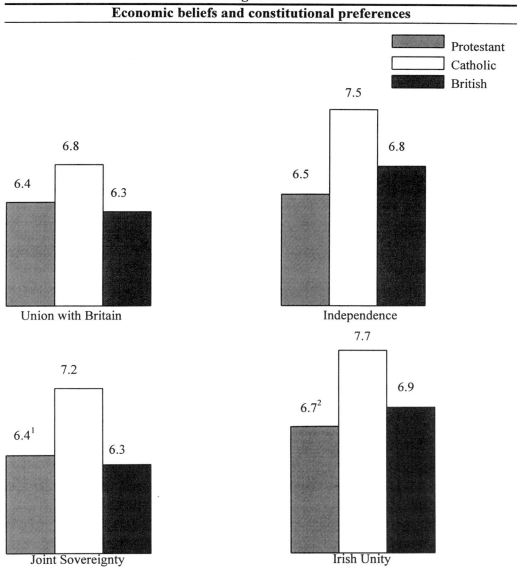

Figures are mean scores based on a combination of the five economic belief items in Table 1, and measured from 0-10.

[1] Statistically different from Catholics at $p < .05$.

[2] Fewer than 25 cases.

Although party politics in Northern Ireland has traditionally excluded economic considerations from their popular appeals, the results presented here show some residual link between economic beliefs and party support on the one hand, and on constitutional options on the other. While the divisions between economic conservatives and economic radicals do tend to follow the unionist-nationalist divide, it is notable that Democratic Unionists are more economically radical than Ulster Unionists, while Sinn Fein supporters are more radical than SDLP partisans. As their name and appeal suggests, Alliance supporters would probably move to support economically conservative parties in the event that the constitutional issue ever ceased to have the salience it has been accorded over the past century.

Conclusion

Political parties grow out of a need or opportunity to represent sections of the electorate and their success is contingent on their ability to mobilise that support. In contrast to Britain, where economic interests have developed as the primary basis for party support, religious differences based on constitutional issues have traditionally been considered the primary cleavage underlying political behaviour in Northern Ireland. Not only is Northern Ireland considered a prototypical example of a religiously-based political system, but it is this continuing religious division which sets the society apart from the rest of contemporary Europe. As McAllister and Wilson briefly explain: 'Among Western European democracies the Northern Ireland political system is the best example of a bi-polar conflict. The two religious communities face one another in a conflict that is both perpetual and zero-sum. Although the political parties eschew religious titles, virtually all are confessional in so far as they attract the exclusive support of one or other community' (1978: 207).

Despite this continuing political polarisation, the results presented here suggest that it is an oversimplification to describe Northern Ireland purely in terms of these religious differences. The reasons for this are threefold. First, it is socio-economic differences and not religious divisions which distinguish economic beliefs within this society. Although Protestants and Catholics also differ in their views in relation to these issues, at least as far as the question of economic management is concerned, it is inequalities in

access to socio-economic resources and not religious differences which emerge as the key characteristic in distinguishing attitudes. Second, a similar, if not more pronounced, pattern emerges in terms of the relationship between economic lifestyle and these economic considerations. As is also the case among their British counterparts, it is differences in access to 'popular capitalism' which again sharply divide the Northern Ireland population in terms of economic beliefs. This is not to deny the continuing importance of religious differences: as a group, Protestants are significantly more likely to favour a more conservative approach to the question of economic management than their more radical Catholic counterparts. However, in terms of their overall contribution, these religious differences are of secondary importance. Finally, the impact of these economic divisions continues even when political affiliation and constitutional preferences are considered. Despite the fact that these economic considerations figure little, if at all, in terms of party competition and debate, Northern Ireland parties do attract supporters with differing views of economic management.

As has long been the case in Britain, economic issues such as public ownership, the rights of workers and the redistribution of income combine to form an important political cleavage within Northern Ireland politics. While differences in these 'bread-and-butter' issues have been largely ignored within Northern Ireland, their political importance should not be under-estimated. For example, the results of this analysis suggest that economic issues represent a potential middle-ground for politicians within this society. Political leaders who wish to transcend the current religiously-based constitutional divisions within this society would be advised to concentrate on these economic issues. Not only do the latter represent a political cleavage that is potentially religiously non-aligned, but also an important untapped source of electoral support.

References

AUGHEY, A. 1989. *Under Siege: Ulster Unionism and the Anglo-Irish Agreement*, Belfast, Blackstaff.

BELL, D. 1990. *Acts of Union: Youth Culture and Sectarianism in Northern Ireland*, London, Macmillan.

BENSON, D.E. and SITES, P. 1992. 'Religious Orthodoxy in Northern Ireland: The Validation of Identities', *Sociological Analysis*, 53, 219-228.

BEW, P., GIBBON, P. and PATTERSON, H. 1979. *The State in Northern Ireland, 1921-72*, Manchester, Manchester University Press.

BEW, P., GIBBON, P. and PATTERSON, H. 1995. *Northern Ireland 1921-1994: Political Forces and Social Classes*, London, Serif.

BIRRELL, D. 1972. 'Relative Deprivation as a Factor in Conflict in Northern Ireland', *Sociological Review*, 20, 317-44.

BRUCE, S. 1986. *God Save Ulster! The Religion and Politics of Paisleyism*, Oxford, Oxford University Press.

BRUCE, S. 1994. *The Edge of the Union: the Ulster Loyalist Political Vision*, Oxford, Oxford University Press.

CORMACK, R. J. and OSBORNE, R. D. 1991. 'Disadvantage and Discrimination in Northern Ireland', in R. J. Cormack and R. D. Osborne (eds.), *Discrimination and Public Policy in Northern Ireland*, Oxford, Clarendon.

DALTON, R. J. 1996. *Citizen Politics in Western Democracies*, 2nd ed, New Jersey, Chatham House.

EVANS, G., HEATH, A. and LALLJEE, M. 1996. 'Measuring Left-Right and Libertarian-Authoritarian Values in the British Electorate', *British Journal of Sociology*, 47, 93-112.

FRANKLIN, M., MACKIE, T. T. and VALEN, H. (eds.), 1992. *Electoral Change: Responses to Evolving Social and Attitudinal Structures in Fifteen Countries*, Cambridge, Cambridge University Press.

GAFFIKIN, F. and MORRISSEY, M. 1987. 'Poverty and Politics in Northern Ireland', in P. Teague (ed.), *Beyond the Rhetoric: Politics, the Economy and Social Policy in Northern Ireland*, London, Lawrence and Wishart.

GAFFIKIN, F. and MORRISSEY, M. 1990. *Northern Ireland: The Thatcher Years*, London, Zed Books.

GARRETT, G. 1994. 'Popular Capitalism: The Electoral Legacy of Thatcherism', in A. Heath, R. Jowell, J. Curtice and B. Taylor (eds.), *Labour's Last Chance: The 1992 Election and Beyond*, Aldershot, Dartmouth.

GUELKE, A. 1994. 'The United States and the Northern Ireland Question', in B. Barton and P. J. Roche (eds.), *The Northern Ireland Question:*

Perspectives and Policies, Aldershot, Avebury.

HEATH, A., JOWELL, R. and CURTICE, J. 1985. *How Britain Votes*. Oxford, Pergamon.

HEATH, A., JOWELL, R., CURTICE, J. and EVANS, G. 1990. 'The Rise of the New Political Agenda?', *European Sociological Review*, 6, 31-48.

HEATH, A., JOWELL, R., CURTICE, J., EVANS, G., FIELD, J. and WITHERSPOON, S. 1991. *Understanding Political Change*, Oxford, Pergamon.

HEWITT, C. 1981. 'Catholic Grievances, Catholic Nationalism and Violence in Northern Ireland During the Civil Rights Period', *British Journal of Sociology*, 32, 362-80.

JAY, R. and WILFORD, R. 1991. 'An End To Discrimination? The Northern Ireland Fair Employment Act of 1989', *Irish Political Studies*, 6, 15-36.

KELLEY, J. and MCALLISTER, I. 1984. 'The Genesis of Conflict: Religion and Status Attainment in Ulster, 1968', *Sociology*, 18, 171–90.

KENNEDY, D. 1994. 'The European Union and the Northern Ireland Question', in B. Barton and P. J. Roche (eds.), *The Northern Ireland Question: Perspectives and Policies*, Aldershot, Avebury.

MACIVER, M. 1987. 'Ian Paisley and the Reformed Tradition', *Political Studies*, 35, 359-378.

MCALLISTER, I. 1977. *The Northern Ireland Social and Democratic Labour Party*, London, Macmillan.

MCALLISTER, I. 1983. 'Political Parties: Traditional and Modern', in John Darby (ed.), *Northern Ireland: The Background to the Conflict*, Belfast, Appletree.

MCALLISTER, I. and WILSON, B. 1978. 'Bi-Confessionalism in a Confessional Party System: The Northern Ireland Alliance Party', *Economic and Social Review*, 9, 207–25.

MCAULEY, J.W. 1994. *The Politics of Identity: A Loyalist Community in Belfast*, Aldershot: Avebury.

McCRUDDEN, C. 1983. 'The Experience of the Legal Enforcement of the Fair Employment (Northern Ireland) Act 1976', in R.J. Cormack and R.D. Osborne (eds.), *Religion, Education and Employment: Aspects of Equal Opportunity in Northern Ireland*, Belfast, Appletree.

MCGARRY, J. and O'LEARY, B. 1995. *Explaining Northern Ireland*, Oxford, Blackwell.

MOXON-BROWN, E. 1991. 'National Identity in Northern Ireland', in P. Stringer and G. Robinson (eds.), *Social Attitudes in Northern Ireland*, Belfast, Blackstaff.

NELSON, S. 1984. *Ulster's Uncertain Defenders*, Belfast, Blackstaff.

O'BRIEN, C.C. 1972. *States of Ireland*, London, Hutchinson.

O'DOWD, L., ROLSTON, B. and TOMLINSON, M. 1980. *Northern Ireland: Between Civil Rights and Civil War*, London, CSE Books.

ROSE, R. 1974. *Electoral Behavior*, New York, Free Press.

ROSE, R. and MCALLISTER, I. 1990. *The Loyalties of Voters*, London, Sage.

ROWTHORN, B. and WAYNE, N. 1988. *Northern Ireland: The Political Economy of Conflict*, Cambridge, Polity.

SANDERS, D. 1992. 'Why the Conservative Party Won – Again', in A. King et al. (eds.), *Britain at the Polls 1992*, New Jersey, Chatham House.

SARLVIK, B. and CREWE, I. 1992. 'Policy Alternatives and Party Choice in the 1979 Election', in D. Denver and G. Hands (eds.), *Issues & Controversies in British Electoral Behaviour*, London, Harvester Wheatsheaf.

SMITH, D. 1988. 'Policy and Research: Employment Discrimination in Northern Ireland', *Policy Studies*, 9, 41-59.

SMITH, D. and CHAMBERS, G. 1991. *Inequality in Northern Ireland*, Oxford, Clarendon.

STANDING ADVISORY COMMISSION ON HUMAN RIGHTS (SACHR). 1987. *Religious and Political Discrimination and Equality of Opportunity in Northern Ireland*, London, HMSO.

STUDLAR, D. T. and MCALLISTER, I. 1992. 'A Changing Political Agenda? The Structure of Political Attitudes in Britain, 1974-87', *International Journal of Public Opinion Research*, 4, 148-76.

WHYTE, J. 1990. *Interpreting Northern Ireland*, Oxford, Oxford University Press.

Appendix

Table A1
Factor analyses results

	Northern Ireland	Great Britain
1. Government should redistribute income from the better-off to those less well off.	.66	.72
2. Big business benefits owners at the expense of workers.	.82	.80
3. Ordinary working people do not get their fair share of the nation's wealth.	.85	.84
4. There is one law for the rich and one for the poor.	.83	.81
5. Management will always try to get the better of employees if it gets the chance.	.77	.76
Alpha reliability coefficient	.840	.840

Table A2
Definition, means and standard deviations for variables used in the analysis

Variable	Scoring	Northern Ireland		Great Britain	
		Mean	Standard deviation	Mean	Standard deviation
Gender	1=male 0=female	.44	.50	.46	.50
Marital status	1=married 0=other	.65	.48	.66	.47
Age	Years	45.21	17.13	46.26	17.81
Religion	1=Protestant 0=Catholic	.56	.50	.83	.38
Education:					
Tertiary	1=yes 0=no	.19	.40	.23	.42
Secondary	1=yes 0=no	.41	.49	.44	.50
No qualifications	Omitted category	.39	.49	.33	.47
Employment status	1=self-employed 0=employee	.13	.34	.13	.34
Work Status	1=supervisor 0=non-supervisor	.34	.47	.37	.48
Occupation	1=non-manual 0=manual	.50	.50	.55	.50
HHld income	Annual	16594.48	11067.33	17850.37	11098.33
Housing tenure	1=owner-occupier 0=other	.75	.43	.69	.46
Share ownership	1=owner 0=non-owner	.18	.38	.25	.43
Union membership	1=member 0=non-member	.24	.43	.22	.41
Right-Left scale	0 to 10	6.72	1.88	6.61	1.96

9

Work, Marriage and Family: A Time of Change?

Gillian Robinson and Norma Heaton

Introduction

Two of the major debates of the 1990s concern the linked issues of changing family roles and the relationship between work and family life. As women and, in particular, mothers enter the labour market in ever increasing numbers, are attitudes to children, marriage and work, inside as well as outside the home, changing too?

There have been several published analyses on this theme using information from Great Britain, making international comparisons including those with the Republic of Ireland. In Northern Ireland, previous analysis has tended solely to concentrate on the province, or to draw comparisons with Great Britain. It is unusual to see work drawing comparisons with Northern Ireland and the Republic but this will be our focus and we explore similarities and differences between attitudes in Northern Ireland and the Republic of Ireland using data on Family and Changing Gender Roles drawn from the International Social Survey Programme (ISSP) in 1994.

There is no doubt that both parts of Ireland have undergone enormous change, in both economic and social terms, in the last two decades. Some commentators, for example Ester et al. (1993) have argued that, as countries advance economically, so they converge in terms of value systems. This would include a move towards greater acceptance of women's economic independence and support for women who choose to move away from children and home as their primary focus. However, in a previous study on values and social change in the Republic of Ireland, Whelan (1994) suggests

that the idea of movement from an integrated, coherent starting point labelled 'tradition' to an equally integrated end-point called 'modernity' is too simplistic and that emerging patterns of family values in Ireland represent a 'pick and mix' approach blending a variety of traditional and modern value systems to form a distinct alternative. While the publicity surrounding the two referenda on divorce and abortion has tended to reinforce the notion of Ireland as a conservative country with a strong adherence to traditional family values, the conclusion from Whelan's study is that Irish values are not consistently more traditional than those of other European countries.

Where then does Northern Ireland lie in comparison? The assumption of most commentators seems to be that Northern Ireland is a little more 'progressive' than the rest of Ireland though lagging behind the views of those in more liberal Britain. As we show in this chapter, there is no simple answer. Rather, what emerges is an intriguing picture, North and South, of men and women adjusting their attitudes to cope with change, but not in a uniform way. The chapter begins by looking at gender roles and explores the level of support for the 'traditional' model of breadwinner husband and homemaker wife. It then examines attitudes towards women working at various stages of the family life cycle. From the public arena of paid employment the chapter moves back into the private world of the home to explore the domestic division of labour and attitudes to marriage, children and divorce.

The Irish Labour Markets

As Goodwin (1995) has noted, both parts of Ireland have a great deal in common with regard to their economy. These similarities include relatively high unemployment rates; a decline in manufacturing and an increase in employment in service industries; relatively low-skilled workforces; the increasing importance of women to the workforce; and finally a move towards flexibility and non-standard working.

The level of workforce participation of women in the Republic has been, and remains, at a lower level. For example, in 1991, the rate of economic activity for women in Northern Ireland was 61 per cent, compared to a figure of 50 per cent in the Republic. In the same year, women's share of employment stood at 43 per cent in Northern Ireland, some 10 percentage

points higher than in the Republic (Ackah and Heaton, forthcoming). However, women's participation in the labour market in the Republic is increasing rapidly: between 1989 and 1994, there was an increase in women's employment of 20 per cent, compared to an increase in men's employment of only 3 per cent in the same period (*Statistical Bulletin*, 1996). Mahon (1994) has suggested that one of the interesting features here is the increase in the number of married women as a percentage of the female labour force.

One of the striking areas of difference, though, is the availability of part-time work. Such work enables women to combine paid work with domestic and childcare responsibilities, but has been associated with low pay/low status industries. It is far more prevalent in Northern Ireland than in the Republic: in 1991, 34 per cent of women at work in Northern Ireland were part-time, compared to only 17 per cent in the Republic. As Robinson (1993) has noted, however, the number of regular part-time jobs has grown rapidly, starting from an admittedly low base. It might be expected that this will affect attitudes to women working at different times during the family life cycle, an issue discussed below.

Gender Roles

Given that women in both parts of Ireland are joining the workforce in ever increasing numbers, how do men and women feel about the potential for role conflict? Do 'traditional' attitudes persist? In answering this question, we have been able to draw on both the information from 1994 and also, in some instances, previously reported data. In particular, we use information from the 1991 Northern Ireland Survey (Davies and Downey, 1993), the 1988 ISSP (Scott et al., 1993) and the 1990 European Values Survey (Whelan, 1994) for comparative purposes.

Broadly speaking, Table 1 shows that in both parts of Ireland women are more likely than men to take an egalitarian stance, rejecting the view that work and family life are incompatible. Women in the Republic appear to be more traditional than those in Northern Ireland, particularly with regard to the effects of women working on family life.

Table 1

'Egalitarian' stances on the consequences of women working

	Men		Women	
	NI	**RoI**	**NI**	**RoI**
A working mother can establish just as warm and secure a relationship with her children as a mother who does not work. % agreeing	60	60	71	64
All in all, family life suffers when the woman has a full-time job. % disagreeing	45	38	52	40
A pre-school child is likely to suffer if his or her mother works. % disagreeing	42	40	48	45

However there is evidence that men in the Republic are becoming more egalitarian. For example, the proportion agreeing that 'a working mother can establish just as warm and secure a relationship with her children as a mother who does not work' has increased from 52 per cent in 1988 (Scott et al., 1993) to 60 per cent in the current survey. The women's responses, on the other hand, are virtually identical in the 1988, 1990 and 1994 surveys. For Northern Ireland, published comparative data only exists for the question on pre-school children, but here attitudes have swung a little away from the view that such children suffer if their mother works.

Analysis of similar information on Britain suggests that we might expect differences according to age. Scott (1990) found that, broadly, the younger one is, the more likely one is to reject the traditional views associated with women working. This is largely confirmed in the Irish data: for example, as Table 2 shows, the proportion of men and women disagreeing with the suggestion that 'family life suffers when the woman has a full-time job' falls steadily from the youngest to the oldest age group. We might also expect to find differences in attitude between those women who work and those who do not. This is confirmed to be the case in both Northern Ireland and the Republic, as Table 3 shows.

Table 2

**All in all, family life suffers when the woman has a full-time job
(% disagreeing)**

	Men		Women	
Age Group	NI	RoI	NI	RoI
18-29	59	52	65	61
30-39	53	51	56	48
40-49	49	48	53	44
50 and over	28	21	41	22

Table 3

**A pre-school child is likely to suffer if his or her mother works
(% disagreeing)**

	NI	RoI
Woman works:		
full-time	61	63
part-time	47	47
not in paid work	43	36

The next set of questions concern perceptions of gender roles. In response to the suggestion that 'a man's job is to earn...a woman's is to look after the home and family', Kiernan (1992), examining data for Great Britain, found that women were more likely to disagree, but not by much, and that there was no strong evidence that men and women were increasingly likely to reject the traditional model.

As Table 4 shows, in both Northern Ireland and the Republic, more women than men disagree with the proposition. Furthermore, there is evidence of change in the Republic, since the proportion of women disagreeing has risen from 50 per cent in 1988 to 58 per cent in 1994, while the proportion of men disagreeing has also increased, from 40 per cent to 48 per cent. If we group together these three questions containing the suggestion that 'a woman's place is in the home' men from Northern Ireland

appear less traditional than those from the Republic. The views of women from the two parts of Ireland are much more similar, though more women from Northern Ireland disagree that 'what most women really want is a home and children'.

Table 4

'Egalitarian' stances on gender-role ideology (% disagreeing)

	Men		Women	
	NI	RoI	NI	RoI
A man's job is to earn money; a woman's job is to look after the home and family	53	48	58	58
A job is all right but what most women really want is a home and children	43	29	47	38
Being a housewife is just as fulfilling as working for pay	27	21	31	29

Referring back to previous findings in Britain, Scott (1990) found that there was a clear age pattern with respect to the views of women, with older women more likely to endorse the view that 'what most women really want is a home and children'. In a similar vein, O'Connor (1995) in her examination of marriage and family in Ireland, argued that women's identification with and absorption into the family context, is most likely to be a characteristic of older women. As Table 5 shows, the situation is not so

Table 5

A job is all right but what most women want is a home and children (% disagreeing)

	Men		Women	
	NI	RoI	NI	RoI
Age Group:				
18-29	54	42	54	58
30-39	47	45	58	48
40-49	49	36	53	40
50 and over	29	13	34	20

clear-cut in Northern Ireland in particular where differences between young people and those in middle-age groups are not very dissimilar. However, there is quite a change in the views of those aged 50 and over.

One of the interesting issues raised is whether women are going out to work for self-fulfilment or out of economic necessity. This is explored in the next set of questions, concerning the importance of work (see Table 6). Overall, in both parts of Ireland, men and women are less likely to come down on the side of independence and more likely to agree that women have to work. There is strong support for the proposition that both men and women should contribute to the household income. Moreover, in the Republic at least there is evidence of rapid change in this area. Whelan (1994) reported that in 1990, 27 per cent of men and 32 per cent of women disagreed that both should be contributing; the 1994 data shows the proportions to have fallen to nine per cent of men and 16 per cent of women.

Table 6

'Egalitarian' stance on importance of work (% agreeing)

	Men		Women	
	NI	RoI	NI	RoI
Having a job is the best way for a woman to be an independent person	61	68	64	68
Both the man and woman should contribute to the household income	71	75	71	80
Most women have to work these days to support their families	79	82	85	88

Turning to men's roles at home and at work, Table 7 shows that on the issue of 'role reversal' – that is, where the man stays at home while the woman works – men are more likely than women to be uncomfortable. Furthermore, in Northern Ireland, more men than women agree that role reversal is not a good thing. The picture is similar in the Republic. What is also clear is that there is more concern in the Republic for the suggestion that family life may suffer if men concentrate too much on their work. However,

we do not know whether this reflects a perception in Northern Ireland that no harm arises if men work too hard, or a greater concern in the Republic for family life.

Table 7

Men at work and at home (% agreeing)				
	Men		Women	
	NI	RoI	NI	RoI
It is not good if the man stays home and cares for the children and the woman goes out to work	36	41	24	32
Family life often suffers because men concentrate too much on their work	58	75	55	73

To sum up, we have a picture of Ireland in which more women than men reject the view that work and family life are incompatible, with women in the Republic more likely than those in Northern Ireland to subscribe to traditional views. Age clearly makes a difference, with younger people more likely to reject traditional attitudes. However on the suggestion that 'a woman's place is in the home' men from the Republic appear less egalitarian than those from Northern Ireland, while the views of women in the two regions are quite similar. Age does not have the same impact in this area of study.

With regard to the importance of work, men and women in both parts of Ireland are more likely to agree that women have to work out of economic necessity, rather than by way of creating a sense of independence. Men and women in the Republic are more likely than their Northern Ireland counterparts to feel that both men and women should contribute to the household economy. This may go some way towards explaining the findings in the next section, on working women and the family life cycle.

Working Women and the Family Life Cycle

In Northern Ireland and the Republic, there is a clear relationship between the age of the youngest child in the home, and the economic activity of

women. The lower the age of the youngest dependent child under 16, the less likely it is that a woman will be economically active or in paid employment (Heaton et al., 1993; Callan and Farrell, 1992). We also know that a higher proportion of women in Northern Ireland are at work at each stage of the family life cycle, compared to those in the Republic (Ackah and Heaton, forthcoming).

Previous research on Northern Ireland data (Davies and Downey, 1993) found that a majority of both men and women believed that a woman's right to work was conditional on her first discharging her responsibilities to her children. For example, they found that, in 1991, the vast majority of people felt that after marriage and before children a woman should work full-time. However, paid work (even part-time) was not regarded as acceptable by about half the respondents when a woman had a child under five years old. Also, when children were of school age, the majority saw part-time work as appropriate. Similarly, the 1988 data for the Republic showed that just over half of the male and female respondents felt that women with pre-school children should not work (Scott et al., 1993)

Studies on British data have come to similar conclusions. For example, Scott et al. (1993) found that while British men and women were fairly egalitarian with respect to gender roles in the home, they back-peddled when questioned about women's roles outside the home, particularly with regard to women with pre-school children going out to work. The current attitudes of men and women in Northern Ireland and the Republic are shown in Table 8. There is clear approval for a woman working before she has children. Full-time work is seen as the norm, by both men and women. While this represents little change in Northern Ireland from the position reported previously, it does mark a shift in attitude in the Republic, where there has been an increase in the number of men and women in favour of full-time work. This has been accompanied by a fall in the number of women and men who believe that part-time work is preferable.

However, a majority of men and women in Northern Ireland continue to believe that a woman should stay at home if she has a child under school age. In contrast, women in the Republic are less wedded to this idea: a small majority feel a woman should work, though most approve of part-time work

Table 8
Attitudes towards women's work roles (%)

	Men		Women	
	NI	RoI	NI	RoI
Should women work...				
...after marrying and before there are children				
yes, full-time	84	80	92	89
yes, part-time	12	15	6	8
no, stay at home	5	6	2	3
...when there is a child under school age				
yes, full-time	8	13	7	10
yes, part-time	32	35	39	43
no, stay at home	60	52	55	47
...after the youngest starts school				
yes, full-time	21	26	22	26
yes, part-time	65	43	70	55
no, stay at home	14	31	9	19
...after the children leave home				
yes, full-time	73	73	78	75
yes, part-time	22	21	20	19
no, stay at home	6	6	2	6

rather than full-time. Here, the number of men and women, who think the mother of a pre-school child should stay at home, has fallen. In both Northern Ireland and the Republic there is little enthusiasm for full-time work for women at this particular stage of the family life cycle, though the figures are higher for the Republic.

Once all the children are at school, there is a higher level of approval from men and women for mothers working, accompanied by a sharp drop in the numbers who believe that such women should stay at home. Overall, both men and women in the Republic are slightly more likely to approve of full-time work for mothers of school age children, compared to those in Northern Ireland. However, paradoxically, the Republic also has a higher level of

approval than Northern Ireland for women staying at home. The largest differences between the Republic and Northern Ireland come in the question of part-time work. This is the choice which approximately two-thirds of men, and even more women, in Northern Ireland would make for mothers of school-age children. In the Republic, it is the choice of only 43 per cent of men and 55 per cent of women.

Finally, while there is enthusiasm for young married women to work, men and women are less convinced about women working full-time in later life, even after children have left home. There are no major differences between men and women here, nor between those living in Northern Ireland and the Republic.

It would be reasonable to assume that age might be a key factor in attitudes towards women's work roles. Indeed, Kiernan (1992) found that age was important here, with younger women less likely to feel that women with young children should stay at home. This was confirmed in the study by Scott et al. (1993) which suggested that 'age (or at any rate the stage in a person's life cycle) appears to be the most important predictor of attitudes towards working mothers'. As Table 9 shows, age is clearly a factor in Ireland. While 48 per cent of men aged under 30 in Northern Ireland believe that women with pre-school children should stay at home, this figure rises with age, so that for the over 50s the corresponding proportion is 73 per cent. For women in Northern Ireland, there is a similar age gradient. Only for the group of women under 30 years of age is a majority in favour of women working. For those in their 30s, the group most likely to have experience of combining work and domestic responsibilities, 52 per cent think that staying at home is preferable. In the 30-39 age group, more men than women in Northern Ireland think that full-time work is appropriate.

The responses from the men and women in the Republic are quite different. In every age group, there are fewer people in the Republic who think that women with pre-school children should stay at home. This holds true for men and women. Some of the differences are quite startling. Only a third of women in both the 30s and 40s age groups in the Republic believe that the 'stay at home' option is appropriate compared to over half in Northern Ireland. Once again, the most conservative views are found in the

Table 9
Should women work when there is a child under school age? (%)

	Men		Women	
	NI	RoI	NI	RoI
Age group				
18-29				
yes, full-time	9	18	11	24
yes, part-time	43	44	55	52
no, stay at home	48	38	35	24
30-39				
yes, full-time	15	16	9	18
yes, part-time	32	43	39	50
no, stay at home	53	41	52	32
40-49				
yes, full-time	8	22	8	6
yes, part-time	32	32	37	50
no, stay at home	61	47	56	32
50 and over				
yes, full-time	3	6	2	2
yes, part-time	24	27	28	31
no, stay at home	73	67	70	67

oldest age group. The option of full-time work, though, remains the choice of a small minority, with part-time work favoured by about half the women from the Republic in each group under 50 years. Age is not such an important deciding factor in relation to the question *should women work after the youngest child starts school?* Men and women in Northern Ireland strongly favour part-time work as the best option for women with school age children, whatever the age of the respondents. Men and women in the Republic also place part-time work as the most favoured option, but the figures here are much lower than those for Northern Ireland.

To sum up, on the crucial questions concerning mothers of young children staying at home, views in Northern Ireland remain unchanged: the majority of people believe that these mothers should not work. In contrast, the views of men and women in the Republic appear to have undergone considerable

change and now differ from those of their northern counterparts with young people, in particular, increasingly rejecting this notion. In view of earlier discussion on continued adherence in the Republic to traditional family values, we can only speculate on the underlying reasons. It may be associated with pragmatism. If economics dictate that both partners should contribute to the household economy, then so be it!

The Domestic Division of Labour

Having established attitudes towards gender roles and working women we move now to explore the division of labour within the home. As women's roles outside the home change, do we find corresponding changes in men's roles inside the home? British studies have shown a continued persistence of the homemaker role for women regardless of whether or not they have a paid job (Witherspoon, 1985, 1988; Kiernan, 1992). Kiernan (1992) noted that women are still primarily responsible for the laundry, cleaning and cooking while men tended to be exclusively responsible for the household repairs and little else. She also noted that shopping, dishwashing and financial matters are more likely to be shared. Moreover, she notes 'Changes over time in the sharing of individual household tasks...are barely perceptible' (Kiernan, 1992: 102). Likewise the Northern Ireland studies (Montgomery and Davies, 1991; Davies and Downey, 1993) found that it was overwhelmingly the women who did the repeated and routine work of the household with the exception of household repairs. Previous research in the Republic shows that, amongst men who did take responsibility for at least one domestic task, the proportion who were willing to cook, clean, shop or dress children was lower than in any other European Community country (O'Connor, 1995). O'Connor also reports results from a more recent survey (Market Research Bureau of Ireland, 1992) showing that, while the majority of housewives felt that these tasks should be equally shared between spouses, this ideal was not what actually happened.

The items included in the 1994 survey afford some opportunity for comparison. They covered traditional domestic jobs like the laundry, small household repairs, caring for sick family members, shopping for groceries and decisions on what to have for dinner. Table 10 shows that in 1994 women on both sides of the Irish border are still mostly responsible for

these household chores.   Laundry appears to be the last bastion of exclusively women's work within the home with a vast majority of women always or usually responsible for doing the washing and ironing in Northern Ireland and in the Republic. This holds true regardless of age of respondent.

Table 10

Responsibility for the household chores (%)		
	NI	RoI
Always/usually the woman		
Laundry	88	88
Cares for sick family members	53	52
Shops for groceries	57	67
Decides what to have for dinner	65	75
Always/usually the man		
Makes small repairs around the home	81	71

Caring for sick family members is more likely to be shared while the other three items show interesting differences between respondents in Northern Ireland and those in the Irish Republic. Women in the Irish Republic are more likely than their Northern Irish counterparts to do the grocery shopping and make the decision on what to have for dinner. Finally while minor domestic repairs remain the province of men in both Northern Ireland and the Irish Republic it appears that women in the Republic are more likely to take on these tasks than are women in Northern Ireland.

It has been suggested from earlier studies that in households where both partners work it is more likely for household tasks to be shared. Table 11 illustrates that this is indeed the case in Ireland in 1994 with women who are not in paid work much more likely than their working counterparts to be always or usually responsible for the household chores considered. However, regardless of employment status, women on both sides of the border bear the brunt of the household tasks considered. Women in the

Republic working full-time appear to fare slightly better than their counterparts in the North.

Table 11

Responsibility for household chores by employment status (women only) (%)

	Full-time		Part-time*		Not in paid work	
	NI	RoI	NI	RoI	NI	RoI
Laundry (always/usually woman)	81	73	91	82	89	93
Makes small repairs around the house (always/usually man)	77	62	82	61	74	69
Cares for sick family members (always/usually woman)	45	38	47	30	61	63
Shops for groceries (always/usually woman)	55	52	67	63	52	77
Decides what to have for dinner (always/usually woman)	58	56	74	52	73	89

*small base figures here for Republic, n=37

One of the most interesting features here is the position of women working part-time. In Northern Ireland, these women are far more likely to have responsibility for shopping for groceries than either those in full-time work or the home-makers. Similarly, for laundry or deciding what to have for dinner, the Northern Ireland women who work part-time are closer to the homemakers than those working full-time. In contrast, the women in the Republic who work part-time do appear to fall midway between those in full-time work and the homemakers. There is no readily apparent explanation for this difference, though the Northern Ireland situation is similar to that reported by Kiernan (1992) for Great Britain. Part-time work can of course refer to a wide range of working hours and patterns. What does seem to be

happening, though, is that Northern Ireland women are making up in domestic duties any time gained by working part-time.

In short the answer to the question posed at the beginning of this section is a resounding no – there does not appear to be any major change in men's roles within the home, with women on both sides of the Irish border continuing to bear the brunt of household chores (with the exception of domestic repairs). This holds true regardless of age of respondent and while women working full-time do seem to get a little more help from their partners than women who are not in paid work or those who work part-time, the differences are marginal.

Attitudes to Marriage and Children

We have already alluded to the fact that both parts of Ireland are considered to be more conservative and traditional than Britain or indeed other European countries. This is particularly true with respect to attitudes to marriage, divorce and sexual freedom. There is considerable literature on the role played by the Catholic church in maintaining opposition to sexual permissiveness (Hornsby-Smith and Whelan, 1994) and a continuing attachment to large families (Mahon, 1994). However, Breen et al. (1990) have argued that class inequalities, the gradual weakening of religious influence, and growing unemployment rates almost invariably imply increasing strains on conventional arrangements in these areas. Similarly, Whelan (1994: 61) suggests that the traditional sequencing of marriage, entry into sexual activity and procreation has been greatly disrupted, if not entirely abandoned.

Scott et al. (1993) using 1988 ISSP data found that 59 per cent of respondents in the Irish Republic advised marriage without living together first. This compared to 46 per cent in the USA, 37 per cent in Britain and 19 per cent in the former West Germany. The 1994 survey findings reveal somewhat different trends although the questions are somewhat different (see Appendix). Now it appears that just over half of men and women in the Republic of Ireland agree (see Table 12) that it is *all right for a couple to live together without intending to get married* and exactly the same proportion agree that it is *a good idea for a couple who intend to get married to live together first*. Moreover, while the Republic may have

been more traditional than many other countries in terms of attitudes towards cohabitation in 1988 (Scott et al., 1993), in 1994, in comparison with Northern Ireland, it is less traditional. Northern Irish respondents are more conservative with fewer men and women than in the Republic agreeing that it is all right for a couple to live together without intending to get married and many fewer agreeing that it is a good idea for a couple who intend to get married to live together.

Table 12
Attitudes towards cohabitation (% agreeing)

	Men		Women	
	NI	RoI	NI	RoI
It is all right for a couple to live together without intending to get married	46	51	42	51
It is a good idea for a couple who intend to get married to live together first	41	51	38	51

Kiernan (1992) reminds us that only a few decades ago living together was definitely something shocking while now, cohabitation without marriage is commonplace and the vast majority of young people regard sex before marriage as perfectly acceptable. Thus, it might be expected that there would be considerable age differences in attitudes towards these issues, with older people finding cohabitation less acceptable than younger people. Table 13 shows that indeed there are striking differences in attitudes to cohabitation across the age groups with many more people in the youngest age groups agreeing with the statements than in the oldest age group. There are minor differences between men and women within each country but for the most part it is women of all ages in Northern Ireland who hold the most conservative views.

Given that such a high percentage of people support cohabitation it is interesting to explore attitudes to marriage. First is there a perception that married people are happier than unmarried people? The 1988 data (Scott et al., 1993) showed that 46 per cent of Irish people agree that married people were happier. This figure has dropped over the intervening years to 33 per

cent. The figure is even lower in Northern Ireland at 28 per cent. It is perhaps unsurprising to find that women are consistently less convinced than men that marriage brings happiness in the light of the greater burden of work women share in a marriage (Scott et al., 1993). However, while Scott et al.

Table 13
Attitudes to cohabitation by age (% agreeing)

It is all right for a couple to live together without intending to get married

Age group	Men		Women	
	NI	RoI	NI	RoI
18-29	68	79	62	77
30-39	61	73	61	69
40-49	48	57	40	55
50 or over	18	24	16	26

It is a good idea for a couple who intend to get married to live together first

Age group	Men		Women	
	NI	RoI	NI	RoI
18-29	65	77	59	80
30-39	49	69	52	69
40-49	43	58	39	52
50 or over	16	25	13	27

(1993) found the gender gap to be the greatest in the Irish Republic – which they attributed to the more traditional family values there – this study shows a greater gender gap in Northern Ireland. So, in contrast and perhaps in contradiction to the findings above on cohabitation, for the most part it is people in the Republic who are more likely to agree that marriage brings happiness. Again, attitudes differ with age (see Table 14). The clear trend emerging is that the older one is, regardless of gender and location, the more likely one is to agree that married people are generally happier than unmarried people. Women in Northern Ireland who are under 50 years of age are the least convinced that marriage brings happiness.

In terms of traditional views on the main purposes of marriage there is little difference in opinion North and South that people who want children

Table 14
Married people are generally happier than unmarried people (% agreeing)

	NI	RoI
Men	35	38
Women	22	30
Total	28	33
Men		
18-29	16	26
30-39	38	34
40-49	32	39
50 or over	50	44
Women		
18-29	8	17
30-39	11	29
40-49	19	31
50 or over	40	35

ought to get married, with around 70 per cent agreeing (see Table 15). Again attitudes towards this item vary with age, with just under 50 per cent agreeing in the youngest age group for both men and women while 90 per cent or more agree in the oldest age group. Both men and women in the

Table 15
Attitudes to marriage (% agreeing)

	Men		Women	
	NI	RoI	NI	RoI
The main advantage of marriage is that it gives financial security	25	28	19	24
The main purpose of marriage these days is to have children	22	31	19	26
It is better to have a bad marriage than no marriage at all	4	8	3	6
People who want children ought to get married	70	72	71	72

South are more likely to see the main purpose of marriage these days to be to have children than are their counterparts in the North. However, again this figure has dropped from the 1988 figures recorded for the Republic: men, 34 per cent; women, 30 per cent (Scott et al., 1993). Only one-fifth to one-quarter agree that the main advantage of marriage is that it gives financial security, with women in the North least likely to agree. There are very low levels of support for the statement that it is better to have a bad marriage than no marriage at all although the figures are slightly higher in the Republic where divorce legislation is just about to be introduced following the recent referendum and subsequent court rulings.

So far then we have noted fairly high levels of support for cohabitation and low levels of acceptance that married people are happier than non-married people. Furthermore, amongst the youngest group of respondents both North and South there is not even majority acceptance of the notion that people who want children should marry. What then are the opinions on children and family size?

It is an indisputable fact that birth rates are falling in most, if not all, developed nations. The factors that are considered to have contributed to the fall are the increased cost of children, higher standards of education, knowledge of family planning methods and the increased participation of women in the labour force (Whelan and Fahey, 1994). However, the birth rate in Northern Ireland, at 15.9 per thousand population was, in 1992, the highest in the European Union, marginally ahead of the Republic (Equal Opportunities Commission for Northern Ireland, 1995). Respondents in Northern Ireland and the Republic were asked what they considered to be the ideal family size (see Table 16).

What we find is that people in the Republic are much more likely to prefer a larger family than are respondents in Northern Ireland. However, this preference has dropped significantly from the majority of 51 per cent recorded by Whelan and Fahey (1994) in 1990. At that time they compared the Republic with many European countries and found that only Northern Ireland came close to the Republic. It is the oldest groups in both the North and South who are most likely to think a larger family is the

Table 16
Ideal family size, by age group (%)

Age group	2 or less		4 or more	
	NI	RoI	NI	RoI
18-29	45	40	26	30
30-39	46	40	28	27
40-49	54	27	26	38
50 or over	35	23	40	53
Total	44	30	31	40

ideal. Looking at the gender comparisons within each country we can note opposite trends, with men in Northern Ireland more in favour of small families than are women. The opposite is true for the Republic where men are less in favour of small families.

Despite the fact that more people now prefer smaller families, the benefits of having children appear to be agreed between the two countries and between men and women with only minor differences recorded in Table 17. The vast majority of respondents believe watching children

Table 17
Attitudes to children (% agreeing)

	Men		Women	
	NI	RoI	NI	RoI
Watching children grow up is life's greatest joy	81	86	86	88
Having children interferes too much with the freedom of parents	9	10	7	10
People who have never had children lead empty lives	21	24	20	19

grow up is life's greatest joy while around one-fifth of respondents agree that people who have never had children lead empty lives.

Finally, we can consider views on the permanence of marriage. The divorce rate in Northern Ireland (3.3 per thousand couples) is much lower

than that for England and Wales, or Scotland. We cannot make direct comparisons with the Republic, but, according to O'Connor (1995), there has been a dramatic increase in the number of couples in Ireland experiencing marital breakdown: she quotes the most recent estimate as a figure of between 65,000 and 70,000 people, nearly twice the number who identified themselves as separated in the 1986 census. This emerged despite the absence of divorce in the Republic of Ireland during that period, together with the absence of effective mechanisms to ensure that maintenance is paid in cases of separation.

Unsurprisingly, then, in the light of this, both men and women in the Republic are more likely to think that couples should stay together (Table 18) than are people in Northern Ireland, and that divorce is not the best option.

Table 18

Attitudes towards separation and divorce (% agreeing)

	Men		Women	
	NI	RoI	NI	RoI
When there are children in the family, parents should stay together even if they don't get along	32	42	22	29
Even when there are no children a married couple should stay together even if they don't get along	11	12	9	8
Divorce is usually the best solution when a couple can't seem to work out their marriage problems	57	55	55	48

Given the fact that women were noted above to be less likely to agree that married people are happier, we find that women in Northern Ireland and in the Republic of Ireland are less likely to believe that couples should stay together for the sake of the children than are men. (When there are no children involved, a small minority believe a married couple should stay together, but there are no differences between North and South.) While women are less likely than men to agree that a couple should stay together, paradoxically they are also less likely to agree that divorce is usually the best

solution. In fact, women in the Republic are the only group where a majority are not in agreement that divorce is usually the best solution when a couple can't seem to work out their marriage problems.

Age, once again, strongly influences attitudes to these issues as Table 19 shows. With respect to couples staying together the trends are easily seen;

Table 19

	Men		Women	
	NI	RoI	NI	RoI
When there are children in the family, parents should stay together even if they don't get along				
18-29 years	14	23	7	14
30-39 years	26	28	12	18
40-49 years	28	34	19	25
50 or over	52	61	41	47
Even when there are no children a married couple should stay together even if they don't get along				
18-29 years	3	5	5	3
30-39 years	6	4	5	6
40-49 years	7	10	6	6
50 or over	23	20	15	14
Divorce is usually the best solution when a couple can't seem to work out their marriage problems				
18-29 years	52	64	47	61
30-39 years	48	67	57	58
40-49 years	64	66	57	55
50 or over	60	40	58	32

Attitudes to separation and divorce by age (% agreeing)

for men and women in both parts of Ireland the older they are the more likely they are to think that couples should stay together. It is those who are 50 or older who hold the strongest views by far on this issue. However when we look at responses to whether or not respondents think divorce is the best option, a complicated picture emerges. While we have already noted the

overall trend for people in the Republic to be less inclined to agree that divorce is the best option, Table 19 shows that this is primarily because of the views of the older respondents there. What we see is increasing support for divorce with age in Northern Ireland in comparison to the opposite for the Republic. This age differential for the Republic is easy to explain as one might expect younger people to be more in favour of divorce. The trend in Northern Ireland is perhaps explained by a 'religion effect': the Catholic population in Northern Ireland is younger. Conversely, quite a large proportion of the elderly are Protestant.

Conclusion

Attitudes in Ireland, North and South, are changing but not on all aspects of gender, marriage and family roles. Some of the trends we have detected are puzzling, if not downright contradictory.

Women are more likely than men to subscribe to the view that work and family life are compatible, though women in Northern Ireland are more likely than women in the Republic to take this view. The suggestion that a woman's place is in the home meets with a little more support from men in the Republic than those in Northern Ireland, while a majority of women in both parts of Ireland reject this idea.

However, when questioned about whether mothers of young children should stay at home, it is Northern Ireland which appears the more traditional. Certainly in the Republic, the views of both men and women have undergone considerable change, while the majority of people in Northern Ireland still believe that mothers of pre-school children should stay at home. Age is an important factor here, with young people more in favour of mothers working.

One of the important differences comes in attitudes to part-time work. This is overwhelmingly the choice which men and women in Northern Ireland would make for mothers of school-age children whereas in the Republic this option enjoys much less support. Turning to the division of labour within the home, once again the position of part-time women workers presents an interesting comparison. In Northern Ireland, part-time workers appear on average to have more domestic responsibilities than their counterparts in the Republic. There are of course similarities: women in both

parts of Ireland continue to bear the brunt of household tasks, regardless of employment status.

With regard to marriage and cohabitation, once again we find more change in the Republic. Now, Northern Ireland appears to be more conservative, with fewer men and women agreeing that it is all right for a couple to live together without getting married. When it comes to the purpose of marriage, though, there is little difference: the majority of people North and South believe that people who want children ought to get married. Those in the Republic are more likely to favour large families, but in both parts of Ireland it is older groups who think a larger family ideal.

The issue of divorce, so hotly debated in the Republic in recent times, produces some paradoxes. The majority of men in the Republic and Northern Ireland think that divorce is the best solution when a couple cannot work out marriage problems. The majority of women in the North also subscribe to this view, but are joined by fewer women from the Republic. Age is an issue here as older men and women in the Republic are much less likely to agree that divorce is the best option. In Northern Ireland, however, there is more support for divorce among older respondents probably due to the fact that a high proportion of the elderly population is Protestant.

We cannot conclude by stating unequivocally that Northern Ireland is more 'traditional' than the Republic, or vice versa. We have found contradictions in the attitudes of men and women in both parts of Ireland. Perhaps this should not be too surprising. Mahon (1994), for example has pointed to the fact that the participation of women in the labour force in Ireland is exceeded by that of developing countries like Singapore, while in contrast women's participation in second and third level education puts the Republic on a par with, if not ahead of, many European countries. Similarly, Whelan and Fahey (1994) have pointed out that the Republic's conservatism in some aspects of women's position in society must be set against Ireland's claim to have elected a feminist (Mary Robinson) as head of state.

In contrast, Northern Ireland can claim higher rates of labour force participation, and appears more 'modern' in a general consideration of women combining motherhood and working roles. However, women are under-represented in public life generally and there are no women elected

currently as Members of Parliament for the Northern Ireland seats at Westminster.

It may be misleading to talk of values and attitudes in the Republic and Northern Ireland as if there are no internal divisions. We have already alluded to religion as one possible explanation for seemingly contradictory attitudes in Northern Ireland. Similarly, class differences may be important. Attitudes to women may be influenced as professional, middle-class women establish themselves at work. It remains to be seen whether Northern Ireland and the Republic do indeed converge in term of values, or go their separate ways.

References

ACKAH, C. and HEATON, N. Forthcoming. 'Women's labour market participation in Northern Ireland: a re-examination of the "traditionalism" argument', *International Journal of Social Economics.*

BREEN, R., HANNA, D., ROTTMAN, D. and WHELAN, C. 1990. *Understanding Contemporary Ireland: State, class and development in the Republic of Ireland*, London, Macmillan.

CALLAN, T. and FARRELL, B. 1992. W*omen's participation in the Irish labour market*, National Economic and Social Council Report No. 91, Dublin.

DAVIES, C. and DOWNEY, A. 1993. 'Women's rights or responsibilities? Reconciling the demands of home and work', in P. Stringer, and G. Robinson (eds.), *Social Attitudes in Northern Ireland: The third report*, Belfast, Blackstaff Press.

EQUAL OPPORTUNITIES COMMISSION FOR NORTHERN IRELAND 1995. *Women and Men in Northern Ireland, Belfast,* EOCNI.

ESTER, P., HALMAN, L. and de MOOR, R. 1993. *The individualising society: Value changes in Europe and North America,* Tilburg, Tilburg University Press.

GOODWIN, J. 1995. 'Towards a Greater Understanding of Economy and Work in Ireland', *Work, Employment and Society*, 10 (2): 377-385.

HEATON, N., ROBINSON, G. and DAVIES, C. 1993. 'Gender matters in the Northern Ireland labour market', *Review of Employment Topics*, 1 (1): 67-90.

HORNSBY-SMITH, M. and WHELAN, C. 1994. 'Religious and Moral Values', in C. Whelan (ed.), *Values and Social Change in Ireland*, Dublin, Macmillan.

KIERNAN, K. 1992. 'Men and women at work and at home', in R. Jowell, L. Brook, G. Prior, and B. Taylor (eds.), *British Social Attitudes: the 9th report*, Aldershot, Dartmouth.

MAHON, E. 1994. 'Ireland: A private patriarchy?', *Environment and Planning*, 26: 1277-1296.

MARKET RESEARCH BUREAU OF IRELAND. 1992. *Mna na hEireann*, Dublin, MRBI.

MONTGOMERY, P. and DAVIES, C. 1991. 'A woman's place in Northern Ireland', in P. Stringer and G. Robinson (eds.), *Social Attitudes in Northern Ireland: 1990-91 edition*, Belfast, Blackstaff Press.

O'CONNOR, P. 1995. 'Understanding continuities and changes in Irish marriage: putting women centre stage', *Irish Journal of Sociology*, 5: 135-163.

ROBINSON, O. 1993. 'Part-time employment in the economies of Ireland', *Review of employment topics*, 1 (1): 143-160.

SCOTT, J. 1990. 'Woman and the family', in R. Jowell, L. Brook and B. Taylor (eds.), *British Social Attitudes: the 7th report*, Aldershot, Gower.

SCOTT, J., BRAUN, M. and ALWIN, D. 1993. 'The family way', in R. Jowell, L. Brook and L. Dowds (eds.), *International Social Attitudes: the 10th BSA Report*, Aldershot, Dartmouth.

STATISTICAL BULLETIN. 1996. Dublin, Central Statistical Office: Stationery Office.

WHELAN, C. (ed.) 1994. *Values and Social Change in Ireland*, Dublin, Gill and Macmillan.

WHELAN, C.T. and FAHEY, T. 1994. 'Marriage and the Family', in C. Whelan (ed.), *Values and Social Change in Ireland*, Dublin, Macmillan.

WITHERSPOON, S. 1985. 'Sex roles and gender issues', in R. Jowell, S. Witherspoon and L. Brook (eds.), *British Social Attitudes: the 1985 report*, Aldershot, Gower.

WITHERSPOON, S. 1988. 'Interim report: A woman's work', in R. Jowell, S. Witherspoon and L. Brook (eds.), *British Social Attitudes: the 5th Report*, Aldershot, Gower.

Appendix

Scott et al. (1993) were analysing the following 1988 question:
If you were advising a young woman, which of the following would you recommend?

> *to live alone, without a steady partner*
>
> *to live with a steady partner without marrying*
>
> *to live with a steady partner for a while and then marry*
>
> *to marry without living together first*
>
> *cant'choose.*

This compares to the questions asked in 1994:

> *It is alright for a couple to live together without intending to get married*
> (B204g) and:
>
> *It is a good idea for a couple who intend to get married to live together first*
> (B204h).

Appendix 1:
Technical Details of the Survey

Alan McClelland

Background to the Survey

The Northern Ireland Social Attitudes (NISA) survey was funded by the Nuffield Foundation and the Central Community Relations Unit for the third consecutive year in 1991. Subsequent funding for the NISA survey was secured for a further three years (1993–1995) with contributions from Government departments in Northern Ireland.

As in previous years, both the British Social Attitudes (BSA) survey and the NISA survey consisted of 'core' questions and of 'modules' on specific topic areas. As with the 1994 survey, two parallel versions of the questionnaire were fielded in Northern Ireland. Both versions of the questionnaire contained common core questions as well as topic modules specific to each version. Modules in the two Northern Ireland questionnaires were selected from the larger number that were used in the three versions of the British questionnaire. The one exception to this was a module dealing with issues specific to Northern Ireland which was included only in NISA. However, some of these Northern Ireland module questions were, for comparative purposes, also asked in Britain.

An advisory panel consisting of representatives from Social and Community Planning Research (SCPR), the Northern Ireland Statistics and Research Agency (NISRA), formerly the Policy Planning and Research Unit (PPRU) and the Central Community Relations Unit (CCRU) were responsible for constructing the basic content of the questionnaire used in Northern Ireland. The panel both planned the Northern Ireland module and advised on which modules from the British questionnaire might be most usefully incorporated into the Northern Ireland version.

Final responsibility for the construction and wording of the questionnaire remained with SCPR. Responsibility for sampling and fieldwork rested with the Central Survey Unit of NISRA.

Since 1993, NISA survey fieldwork has been completed by interviewers employing Computer Assisted Interviewing (CAI) (see Sweeney and McClelland, 1994).

Content of the Questionnaire

The basic schema of each of the Northern Ireland Social Attitudes questionnaires mirrored that of the British survey. Each had two components. The first consisted of the main questionnaire administered by interviewers, the second was a self-completion supplement which was filled in by respondents after the interview and was either collected by interviewers or returned by post.

Each year the questionnaire includes a number of core questions covering such areas as the economy and labour market participation, as well as a range of background and classificatory questions. It also contains questions (or modules) on attitudes to other issues. These are repeated less frequently, on a two or three year cycle, or at longer intervals.

The core modules, the Northern Ireland module and classification questions were asked of all respondents. In addition, half of respondents were asked the topic modules in version A of the questionnaire while the remainder were asked the topic modules in version B (see Table 1). The self-completion supplements consisted of the module designed for the International Social Survey Programme (ISSP) (for further details of the ISSP see Jowell et al., 1993), as well as items from all the modules which were suitable for that format.

Two versions of the self-completion questionnaire were used in association with the two versions of the main questionnaire administered by interviewers, with core questions asked in both versions and with each version concentrating on their specific topic modules.

Table 1

Contents of the 1995 Northern Ireland Social Attitudes survey questionnaire

Core questions *(Common to both versions of the questionnaire)*	Newspaper readership Government spending Labour market participation Religion Housing Classification
Topic Module Version A	Countryside/environment Welfare state Drugs ISSP module (National identity) - self-completion only
Topic Module Version B	Economic prospects Public spending Education International relations/Europe
Northern Ireland Module	Community relations Perceptions of religious prejudice Protestant-Catholic relations Segregation and integration Even-handedness of institutions Equal opportunities in employment Education/integrated schools Political partisanship Community/national identity Trust in government structures Party political identification

The Sample

As with the British Social Attitudes survey, the Northern Ireland Survey was designed to yield a representative sample of all adults aged 18 and over, living in private households (for further details of the BSA see Jowell et al., 1996).

The sample in Northern Ireland was drawn from the Valuation and Lands Agency (VLA) list, in contrast to that in Britain, which is based on the Postcode Address File (PAF) and involves a multi-stage sample design.

The list provided by the VLA is the most up-to-date listing of private households in Northern Ireland and is made available to CSU for research purposes.

This list was limited to private addresses and excluded people in institutions (but not those who live in private households at such institutions). Contained within the list, inevitably, were a proportion of 'non-viable' addresses which may have been, for example, derelict or vacant. The size of the allocated sample was adjusted to compensate for this wastage.

As the sampling frame was one of addresses, a further stage of sampling was required to select individual adults for interview. Consequently, weighting of the achieved sample was necessary to compensate for the effect of household size on the probability of an individual being selected as a respondent.

Sample Design and Selection of Addresses
Several factors common to Northern Ireland, including the generally low population density outside greater Belfast and its small geographical area, allow the use of an unclustered, simple random sample design. In addition, the extensive coverage of CSU's field force enables this sample design to be effectively used. The benefits gained from using a simple random sample include its effectiveness in generating representative samples of the population for surveys at any given sample size; and the greater precision of survey estimates compared to those of a clustered design.

The NISA sample was therefore a simple random sample of all private addresses contained on the VLA list. Addresses were selected from the computer-based copy of the VLA list using a routine for the generation of random numbers. Addresses selected for household surveys by CSU are excluded from further sampling for a period of two years.

Prior to drawing the sample, Northern Ireland as a whole was stratified into three geographical areas. This stratification, based on district council boundaries, consisted of Belfast – Belfast district council; East – most of the remaining district council areas east of the river Bann, excluding Moyle and Newry and Mourne; West – the remaining district council areas. Within each of these three areas, a simple random sample of addresses was

selected from the VLA list, with probability proportionate to the number of addresses in that stratified area. Figure 1 shows the distribution of addresses on the list, of selected addresses and the distribution of addresses at which interviews were achieved.

Figure 1

Geographical distribution of the sample

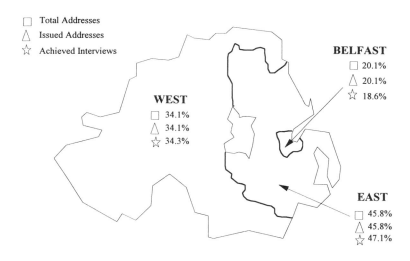

Selection of Individuals

The Valuation and Lands Agency list is a good up-to-date source of private addresses in Northern Ireland. The list does not, however, include information about the number of adults living at each address. Only one individual was to be selected at each address at which interviewers were successful in achieving initial co-operation. To achieve this, the interviewers entered anonymised details of all the adults in the household currently aged 18 or over into the laptop computer. From the list of eligible adults,

the computer selected one respondent through a Kish grid random selection procedure.

Weighting of the Achieved Sample

It is not possible, using the rating list, to select addresses in Northern Ireland with probability proportionate to the size of the household. To compensate for this potential source of bias, the data were weighted prior to analysis. The weighting adjusted for the fact that individuals living in larger households had a lower chance of being included in the sample than individuals living in smaller households. The data were weighted in relation to the number of eligible adults at that address, derived from the details of household structure recorded by the interviewers. In order to retain the actual number of interviews, the weighted sample was scaled back to the originally achieved sample size, yielding a total of 1,510 interviews and an average weight of 1 (see Table 2).

Table 2

Weighting of the sample

No. of adults 18 and over	Weight	Number	%	Scaled weight
1	1	467	30.9	0.5052
2	2	753	49.9	1.0104
3	3	186	12.3	1.5156
4	4	73	4.8	2.0207
5	5	20	1.3	2.5259
6	6	11	0.7	3.0311

Fieldwork

Prior to commencement of the fieldwork, advance letters were sent to each household selected in the sample. The letter informed the household that they had been selected for inclusion in the survey and contained a brief description of the nature of the survey.

The fieldwork was conducted by 62 interviewers from CSU's panel. They were fully briefed and familiarised with the survey procedures. The

first briefing session was held on 2 May 1995 with fieldwork beginning immediately afterwards. The main field period extended until 7 July 1995. A small proportion of interviews were carried out in the period between 7 July and 25 August 1995.

The survey was conducted as an SCPR survey, with all survey documents clearly identifying that research organisation. Interviewers however, carried and presented their normal CSU identity cards. To avoid any confusion on the part of respondents, interviewers also carried, and left with respondents, a letter of introduction from the research team at SCPR. The letter clearly identified the relationship between NISRA and SCPR in the context of the survey. Respondents were given the London telephone number of the Social Attitudes research team at SCPR as well as a Belfast telephone number, in case they had any queries or uncertainties about the survey or the interviewer. The Belfast telephone number was a direct telephone line manned by NISRA field-staff during office hours, and otherwise covered by an answering machine. Only a very small number of respondents used either method of contact.

Table 3
Response rate

	Number	%
Addresses issued	2400	
Vacant, derelict etc.	240	
In scope	2160	100
Interview achieved	1510	70
Interview not achieved	650	30
Refused	441	20
Non-contact	79	4
Unproductive interview	130	6

A total of 2,400 addresses were selected. They were assigned to interviewers using CSU's normal allocation procedures which ensure minimum travelling distances for each interviewer. The field work was supervised by CSU using the standard quality control methods employed

on all government surveys in Northern Ireland. Interviewers were required to make at least three calls at an address (normal procedure allows for additional calls to be made should the interviewer be passing the address while working in the area), before declaring it a non-contact and returning the allocation sheet to headquarters. The timing of the initial contact calls is left to the discretion of the interviewer, based on knowledge of the area, to maximise the likelihood of finding someone at home. Before declaring an address to be a non-contact, at least one call must have been made in the morning, afternoon and evening or weekend. Non-contact addresses were returned to headquarters and, if possible, re-issued before the end of the field period for, (up to) three more calls.

Figure 2
Summary of response to the survey

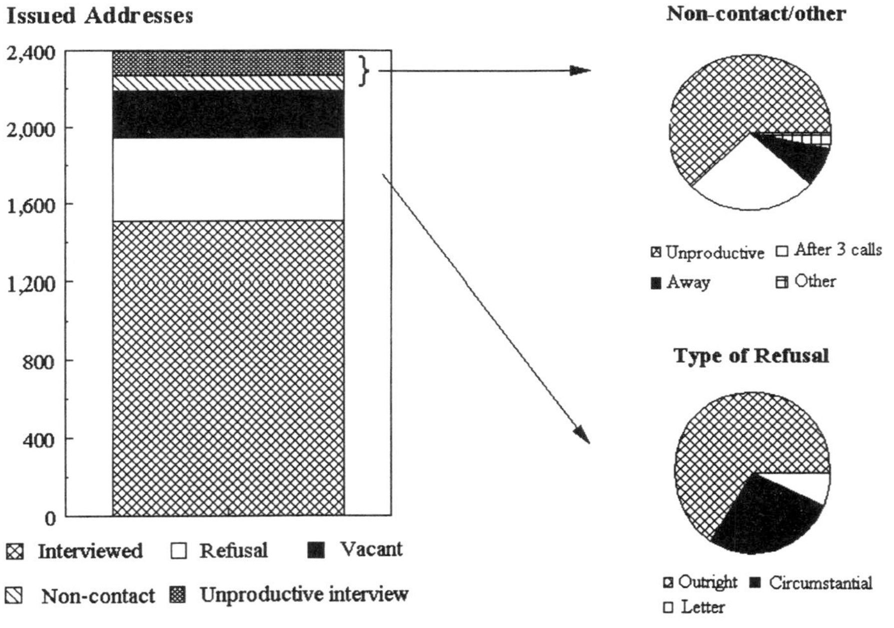

Field-staff at CSU monitored the return of work and quality assured the data which were returned on a weekly basis by the interviewers. Staff at CSU maintained telephone contact with all interviewers and dealt with any problems that arose in the field initially by this means.

An overall response rate of 70 per cent was achieved, based on the total number of issued addresses which were within the scope of the survey (that is, occupied, private addresses). Refusals were obtained at 20 per cent of eligible addresses (Table 3). At four per cent of addresses interviewers could not contact either the household or the selected respondent within the field period. Unproductive interviews were obtained at a further six per cent of addresses (Figure 2).

Self-Completion Questionnaire
At the end of the face-to-face interview, interviewers introduced the self-completion questionnaire. Where possible, the selected respondent completed the questionnaire while the interviewer was still in the house. If this was not possible, the questionnaire was either collected by the interviewer at a later date, or posted by the respondent to a Northern Ireland Post Office Box. The form was then forwarded, through CSU to SCPR.

The return of self-completion questionnaires was monitored by CSU field staff. Up to two reminder letters were sent at two weekly intervals after the initial interview. In all, 84 per cent of the self-completion questionnaires were returned (Table 4).

Table 4

Response rate for the self-completion questionnaires

	Number	%
Achieved interviews	1510	100
Self-completion returned	1263	84
Version A	657	
Version B	606	
Not returned	247	16

Data Processing and Coding

Disks containing interview information were returned by the field force on a weekly basis.   The information contained on the returned disks was transferred onto an office Field Management System on a weekly basis. This procedure meant that the progress of the fieldwork could be monitored on a week by week basis. After the completion of the fieldwork period, final checks were made on the information contained on the return disks prior to the datafiles being sent to SCPR for checking, coding and editing.   For the self-completion questionnaire, SCPR conducted all checking, editing, coding, keying and computer editing.

Analysis Variables

The analysis variables in the Northern Ireland dataset are the same as those in the British survey.   However, the questions on party identification use Northern Irish political parties.   A number of analysis variables were coded by SCPR from the current or last job held by the respondent (and spouse or partner).   Summary variables derived from these and some further derived variables are included in the dataset, as listed in Table 5.

Table 5
Analysis variables

Coded analysis variables	Standard Occupational Classification (1990)
	Employment status
	Socio-economic group (SEG)
	Registrar General's Social Class (I to V)
	Goldthorpe class schema
	Standard Industrial Classification (SIC, 1980)
Derived analysis variables	Age within sex
	Party political identification
	Current economic position
	Area
	Highest educational qualification
	Accommodation tenure
	Marital status

Sampling Errors

No sample is likely to reflect precisely the characteristics of the population it is drawn from, because of both sampling and non-sampling errors. An estimate of the amount of error due to the sampling process can be calculated.

For a simple random sample design, in which every member of the sampled population has an equal and independent chance of inclusion in the sample, the sampling error of any percentage, p, can be calculated by the formula:

$$s.e.(p) = \sqrt{p(100-p)/n}$$

where n is the number of respondents on which the percentage is based. The sample for the Northern Ireland Social Attitudes survey is drawn as a simple random sample, and thus this formula can be used to calculate the sampling error of any percentage estimate from the survey. A confidence interval for the population percentage can be calculated by the formula:

$$95 \text{ per cent confidence interval} = p \pm 1.96 \times s.e.(p)$$

If 100 similar, independent samples were chosen from the same population, 95 of them would be expected to yield an estimate for the percentage, p, within this confidence interval. The absence of design effects in the Northern Ireland survey, and therefore, of the need to calculate complex standard errors, means that the standard error and confidence intervals for percentage estimates from the survey are only slightly greater than for the British survey, despite the smaller sample size. It also means that standard statistical tests of significance (which assume random sampling) can be applied directly to the data.

A percentage estimate of 10 per cent (or 90 per cent) which is based on all respondents to the Northern Ireland survey has a standard error of 0.8 per cent and a 95 per cent confidence interval of ± 1.5 per cent. A percentage estimate of 50 per cent has a standard error of 1.3 and a 95 per cent confidence interval of ± 2.5 per cent. Sampling errors for proportions

based on sub-groups within the sample are somewhat larger than they would have been had the questions been asked of everyone.

Table A1 provides examples of the sampling errors and confidence intervals for typical percentage estimates from the Northern Ireland Social Attitudes survey.

Representativeness of the Sample

In any survey, there is a possibility of non-response bias. Non-response bias arises if the characteristics of non-respondents differ significantly from those of respondents, in such a way that they are reflected in the responses given in the survey. Accurate estimates of non-response bias can only be obtained by comparing characteristics of the achieved sample with the distribution of the same characteristics in the population at the time of sampling. Such comparisons are usually made to current Census of Population data.

It is not possible to estimate directly whether any non-response bias exists in the Northern Ireland Social Attitudes survey. However, tables (at the end of this appendix) compare the characteristics of both the households and individuals sampled with those sampled in the Continuous Household Survey (CHS) for the 1994-95 year (the survey year running from April 1994 to March 1995). The CHS has a much larger sample (over 3,000 households are interviewed) and uses the same simple random sample design. All adults aged 16 or over are interviewed. No weighting is required to compensate for the effect of household size on probability of selection. The CHS has been running for 10 years and produces consistent estimates from year to year.

Where available, figures from the 1991 Census of Population for Northern Ireland have been shown for comparison.

References

JOWELL, R., CURTICE, J., PARK, A., BROOK, L. and THOMSON, K 1996. *British Social Attitudes: the 13th report*, Aldershot, Dartmouth.

JOWELL, R., BROOK, L. and DOWDS, L. 1993. *International Social Attitudes: the 10th BSA report*, Aldershot, Dartmouth.

SWEENEY, K. and McCLELLAND, A. 1994. 'Technical details of the survey' in R. Breen, P. Devine and G. Robinson (eds.), *Social Attitudes in Northern Ireland: The Fourth Report*, Belfast, Appletree Press.

THE NORTHERN IRELAND CENSUS 1991: *Summary Report*, Belfast, HMSO.

Table A1
Standard errors and confidence limits

Classification variables, n=1510	% (p)	Standard error of p (%)	95% confidence interval +/-	95% confidence limits
Derived religion				
Protestant	58.3	1.3	2.5	55.8-60.8
Catholic	40.2	1.3	2.5	37.7-42.7
Other	2.3	0.4	0.7	1.5-3.1
(Tenure2) Housing Tenure*				
Owns	69.4	1.2	2.3	67.1-71.7
Rent from NIHE	24.5	1.1	2.2	22.3-26.7
Derived employment status				
Economically active	51.0	1.3	2.5	48.5-53.5
Unemployed	6.9	0.6	1.3	5.6-8.2
Attitudinal variables (all), n=1510				
(GPCHANGE) Consider it not difficult to change GP	68.8	1.2	2.3	66.5-71.1
Version B, n=744				
(ECGBCLSE) The UK should have closer links with the European Community	38.5	1.8	3.5	35.0-42.0
Employees only, n=627				
(INDREL) Not good relations between management and employees	15.4	1.4	2.8	12.6-18.2
Self-completion (A), n= 660				
(IMMIGRT1) Disagree that immigrants increase crime rates	36.7	1.9	3.7	33.0-40.4
Self-completion (B), n=621				
(TEACHPAY) Teachers are better paid now than 10 years ago	57.0	2.0	3.9	53.1-60.9

*Unweighted data

Table A2
Comparison of household characteristics

		NISA Survey 1995*	Continuous Household Survey 1994/5	Northern Ireland Census 1991
Tenure	Owner occupied	69	64	62
	Rented, NIHE	24	28	29
	Rented, other	6	8	8
	Rent free	1	1	1
Type of home	Detached	35	29	31
	Semi-detached	24	24	23
	Terraced	34	37	37
	Purpose-built flat	5	7	7
	Converted flat	2	1	2
	Other	-	2	-
Household income (£)	Less than 4000	10	13	
	4000 - 7999	24	25	
	8000 - 11999	14	14	
	12000 - 17999	14	14	
	18000 - 19999	4	4	
	20000 and over	23	19	
	Unknown	12	12	
Base = 100%		1510	3218	530,369

Household characteristics are based on unweighted data from the NISA survey

Table A3
Comparison of individual characteristics

		NISA Survey 1995	Continuous Household Survey 1994/5	Northern Ireland Census 1991
Sex	Male	44	47	48
	Female	56	53	52
Age	18-24	12	13	16
	25-34	19	20	21
	35-44	20	19	18
	45-54	18	16	15
	55-59	8	7	6
	60-64	6	6	6
	65 and over	16	20	18
Marital status	Single	22	24	28
	Married/cohabiting	65	61	59
	Widowed	8	9	9
	Divorced/separated	5	6	6
Economic activity	Working	51	49	49*
	Unemployed	7	6	9
	Inactive	42	41	42
	Refused/missing	-	4	-
Base = 100%		1,510	6,094	1,117,221**

*Based on total population aged 16 and over (base = 1,167,938)
**Persons aged 18 and over

Table A4
Stated religious denomination (%)

	NISA Survey 1995	Continuous Household Survey 1994/5	Northern Ireland Census 1991**
Protestant	52	57	50
Catholic	38	38	38
Non-Christian	-	-	-
No religion	10	3	4
Unwilling to say	7	1	2
Base = 100%	1510	5182	1577836
(Undefined CHS*)		(14%)	

*Religion remains undefined in the CHS for individuals who did not fully co-operate in the survey and were, therefore, not asked their denomination. The base for this percentage (6051) is the total number of adults aged 18 and over in the sampled households.
**Usually resident population (all ages)

Table A5
Redefined religious denomination (%)

Religious denomination* of persons aged 18 years and over	NISA Survey 1995	Continuous Household Survey 1994/5
Protestant	58	57
Catholic	40	39
Non-Christian	-	-
No religion	1	3
Unwilling to say	1	1
Base = 100%	1510	6051

* Religious denomination has been redefined in both surveys for those who stated 'No religion' or were unwilling to specify their denomination. In the NISA survey, denomination was calculated from the religion in which the respondent was brought up. In the CHS, denomination was redefined using the denomination specified by other members of the household.

Appendix 2:
Using Northern Ireland Social Attitudes Survey Data

All survey datasets are deposited and can be obtained from the ESRC Data Archive at Essex University. In addition, the survey years 1989-1991 are available as a fully documented *combined* dataset. Although the annual book covers many topics in depth, it cannot hope to provide time-series data for all questions included in that survey round; for that reason we would encourage interested parties to use the data directly.

The core of the survey is the community relations module which has been included in every survey round except for 1990 when a module on attitudes to crime and the police was fielded instead. The list on the following page shows the modules fielded in every survey year.

Topics covered* in Northern Ireland Social Attitudes surveys 1989-1995

TOPICS (excluding 'core' ones)	SURVEY YEAR					
	1989	1990	1991	1993	1994	1995
AIDS	✓					
Attitudes to work (ISSP)	✓					
Changing gender roles (ISSP)					✓	
Charitable giving			✓	✓		
Childcare					✓	✓
Civil liberties		✓			✓	
Community relations	✓		✓	✓	✓	✓
Countryside and the environment		✓		✓	✓	✓
Crime and the police		✓				
Diet and health	✓					
Drugs						✓
Economic prospects	✓	✓	✓	✓		✓
Education				✓		✓
Family networks						✓
Gender issues at the workplace			✓		✓	
Gender roles			✓		✓	
Global environmental issues (ISSP)				✓		
Health and lifestyle			✓			
Informal carers					✓	
National identity (ISSP)						✓
National Health Service	✓	✓	✓	✓	✓	✓
Political trust					✓	
Poverty	✓				✓	
Race and immigration					✓	
Religious beliefs (ISSP)			✓			
Role of government (ISSP)		✓				
Single parenthood and child support				✓	✓	✓
Sexual morality	✓	✓				
Social class	✓	✓			✓	
Taxation and public spending (long)						✓
Transport						✓
UK's relations with Europe/other countries	✓	✓	✓	✓	✓	✓
Welfare state				✓		✓

*Excluded are 'core topics' such as public spending, workplace issues and economic prospects, and standard classificatory items such as economic activity, newspaper readership, religious denomination and party identification, all of which are asked every year.

Appendix 3:
The Questionnaires

As explained in Appendix 1, two different versions of the NISA questionnaire (A and B) were fielded in 1995, each with its own self-completion supplement. In the following pages we reproduce first version A of the interview questionnaire in full, then those parts of version B that differ. The two versions of the self-completion questionnaire follow.

As the survey was carried out using Computer Assisted Interviewing (CAI), the two questionnaires reproduced here are derived from the Blaise program in which they were written. The keying codes have been removed and the percentage distribution of answers to each question inserted instead. The SPSS variable name is also included. Routing directions are given above each question and any routing instruction should be considered as staying in force until the next routing instruction. Percentages in the main questionnaire are based on the total sample (766 weighted in version A, 744 weighted in version B). In the self-completion questionnaire they are based on the forms returned (660 weighted in version A, 621 weighted in version B).

For further details on the questionnaires, readers are referred to Jowell et al. (1996).

References

JOWELL, R., CURTICE, J., PARK, A., BROOK, L. and THOMSON, K. 1996. *British Social Attitudes: the 13th report*, Dartmouth, Aldershot.

NORTHERN IRELAND SOCIAL ATTITUDES SURVEY 1995

VERSION A QUESTIONNAIRE

n = 1510

NEWSPAPER READERSHIP/POLITICS

ASK ALL

Q237 [ReadPap]
Do you normally read any daily morning newspaper at least 3 times a week?

%
57.6 Yes
42.4 No

IF 'yes' AT [ReadPap]

Q238 [WhPaper]
Which one do you normally read?
IF MORE THAN ONE ASK: Which one do you read most frequently?
ONE CODE ONLY

%
2.6 (Scottish) Daily Express
3.9 Daily Mail
10.8 Daily Mirror/Record
2.1 Daily Star
13.2 The Sun
0.7 Today
1.5 Daily Telegraph
0.2 Financial Times
0.6 The Guardian
0.4 The Independent
1.1 The Times
0.1 Morning Star
9.8 The News Letter
8.9 The Irish News
0.7 The Irish Times
0.4 Other Irish/Northern Irish/Scottish regional or local daily morning paper (WRITE IN)
0.1 Other (WRITE IN)
0.5 (More than one paper)

ASK ALL

Q243 [Politics]
How much interest do you generally have in what is going on in politics? ... READ OUT ...

%
6.9 ... a great deal,
15.8 quite a lot,
32.8 some,
29.9 not very much,
14.6 or, none at all?

PUBLIC SPENDING, WELFARE BENEFITS AND HEALTH CARE

n = 744

VERSION B: ASK ALL

Q248 [Spend1]
CARD
Here are some items of government spending. Which of them, if any, would be your highest priority for extra spending?
Please read through the whole list before deciding.
ENTER ONE CODE ONLY FOR HIGHEST PRIORITY

Q249 [Spend2]
CARD AGAIN
And which next?
ENTER ONE CODE ONLY FOR NEXT HIGHEST

	[Spend1]	[Spend2]
	%	%
Education	22.4	36.8
Defence	0.4	1.9
Health	57.7	23.0
Housing	4.6	10.1
Public transport	1.2	3.0
Roads	3.1	3.5
Police and prisons	0.4	2.0
Social security benefits	6.3	11.6
Help for industry	2.8	6.7
Overseas aid	0.8	0.8
(None of these)	-	0.3
(Don't Know)	0.3	0.4

Q250 [SocBen1]
CARD
Thinking now only of the government's spending on **social benefits** like those on the card.
Which, if any, of these would be your highest priority for **extra** spending?
ENTER ONE CODE ONLY FOR HIGHEST PRIORITY

Q251 [SocBen2]
CARD AGAIN
And which next?
ENTER ONE CODE ONLY FOR NEXT HIGHEST

	[SocBen1]	[SocBen2]
	%	%
Retirement pensions	40.7	23.0
Child benefits	12.8	19.6
Benefits for the unemployed	13.4	15.1
Benefits for disabled people	27.2	30.8
Benefits for single parents	4.7	9.5
(None of these)	0.9	1.2
(Don't Know)	0.3	0.7

ASK ALL

Q252 *[Dole]*
Opinions differ about the level of benefits for
unemployed people. Which of these **two** statements
comes closest to your own view ... **READ OUT** ...

%
50.5 ... benefits for unemployed people are **too low** and
cause hardship,

30.4 or, benefits for unemployed people are **too high** and
discourage them from finding jobs?

11.8 (Neither)
0.0 (Both: Unemployment Benefit causes hardship but
can't be higher or there would be no incentive to
work)

1.2 (Both: Unemployment Benefit causes hardship to some,
while others do well out of it)

0.2 (About right/in between)
2.9 Other answer **(WRITE IN)**
2.8 (Don't Know)

Q255 *[TaxSpend]*
CARD
Suppose the government had to choose between the
three options on this card. Which do you think it
should choose?

%
6.6 Reduce taxes and spend **less** on health, education
and social benefits

38.3 Keep taxes and spending on these services at the
same level as now

52.3 Increase taxes and spend **more** on health, education
and social benefits

1.7 (None)
1.1 (Don't Know)
0.0 (Refusal/NA)

Q256 *[NHSSat]*
CARD
All in all, how satisfied or dissatisfied would you
say you are with the way in which the NHS runs
nowadays?
Choose a phrase from this card.

Q257 *[GPSat]*
CARD AGAIN
From your own experience, or from what you have
heard, please say how satisfied or dissatisfied you
are with the way in which each of these parts of the
National Health Service runs nowadays.
First, local doctors or GPs?

Q258 *[DentSat]*
CARD AGAIN
(And how satisfied or dissatisfied are you with the
NHS as regards ...)
National Health Service dentists?

	[NHSSat]	*[GPSat]*	*[DentSat]*
	%	%	%
Very satisfied	7.8	36.7	23.6
Quite satisfied	40.0	46.1	49.5
Neither satisfied nor			
dissatisfied	17.3	7.6	12.8
Quite dissatisfied	21.4	6.5	8.1
Very dissatisfied	13.4	2.9	3.0
(Don't Know)	0.1	0.2	2.8

Q259 *[InPatSat]*
CARD AGAIN
(And how satisfied or dissatisfied are you with the
NHS as regards ...)
Being in hospital as an **in-patient**?

Q260 *[OutPaSat]*
CARD AGAIN
(And how satisfied or dissatisfied are you with the
NHS as regards ...)
Attending hospital as an **out-patient**?

	[InPatSat]	*[OutPaSat]*
	%	%
Very satisfied	24.3	14.8
Quite satisfied	42.8	47.1
Neither satisfied nor		
dissatisfied	11.9	13.3
Quite dissatisfied	9.7	14.9
Very dissatisfied	4.1	4.4
(Don't Know)	7.1	5.4

Q261 *[PrivMed]*
Are you covered by a private health insurance scheme,
that is an insurance scheme that allows you to get
private medical **treatment**?
ADD IF NECESSARY: For example, BUPA or PPP.

%
9.3 Yes
90.7 No

IF 'Yes' AT [PrivMed]
Q262 *[PrivPaid]*
Does your employer (or your partner's employer) pay
the majority of the cost of membership of this scheme?

%
3.4 Yes
5.9 No

Q263 **ASK ALL**
[NHSLimit]
It has been suggested that the National Health Service should be **available only to those with lower incomes**. This would mean that contributions and taxes could be lower and most people would then take out medical insurance or pay for health care. Do you support or oppose this idea?
IF 'SUPPORT' OR 'OPPOSE': A lot or a little?

%
6.8 Support a lot
15.0 Support a little
19.9 Oppose a little
56.4 Oppose a lot
1.9 (Don't Know)
0.0 (Refusal/NA)

Q264 [InPat1]
CARD
Now suppose you had to go into a local NHS hospital for observation and maybe an operation. From what you know or have heard, please say whether you think ... the hospital doctors would tell you all you feel you need to know?

Q265 [InPat2]
CARD AGAIN
(And please say whether you think ...)
... the hospital doctors would take seriously any views you may have on the sorts of treatment available?

Q266 [InPat3]
CARD AGAIN
(And please say whether you think ...)
... the operation would take place on the day it was booked for?

	[InPat1]	[InPat2]	[InPat3]
	%	%	%
Definitely would	17.7	10.3	11.5
Probably would	51.1	45.8	55.2
Probably would not	21.6	30.7	22.9
Definitely would not	7.7	8.7	5.8
(Don't Know)	1.9	4.5	4.6

Q267 [InPat4]
CARD AGAIN
(And please say whether you think ...)
... you would be allowed home only when you were really well enough to leave?

Q268 [InPat5]
CARD AGAIN
(And please say whether you think ...)
... the nurses would take seriously any complaints you may have?

Q269 [InPat6]
CARD AGAIN
(And please say whether you think ...)
... the hospital doctors would take seriously any complaints you may have?

	[InPat4]	[InPat5]	[InPat6]
	%	%	%
Definitely would	12.4	22.9	16.8
Probably would	36.9	59.9	59.7
Probably would not	34.4	12.9	16.1
Definitely would not	15.1	2.2	3.8
(Don't Know)	1.2	2.1	3.5

Q270 [InPat7]
CARD AGAIN
(And please say whether you think ...)
... there would be a particular nurse responsible for dealing with any problems you may have?

Q271 [OutPat1]
CARD AGAIN
Now suppose you had a back problem and your GP referred you to a hospital out-patients' department. From what you know or have heard, please say whether you think...
... you would get an appointment within three months?

Q272 [OutPat2]
CARD AGAIN
(And please say whether you think ...)
...when you arrived, the doctor would see you within half an hour of your appointment time?

	[InPat7]	[OutPat1]	[OutPat2]
	%	%	%
Definitely would	15.5	9.8	7.4
Probably would	41.1	36.3	33.5
Probably would not	28.4	30.9	35.7
Definitely would not	4.8	15.8	21.7
(Don't Know)	10.2	7.2	1.7

Q273 [OutPat3]
CARD AGAIN
(And please say whether you think ...)
...if you wanted to complain about the treatment you received, you would be able to without any fuss or bother?

5

6

225

Q274 **[WhchHosp]**
CARD AGAIN
Now suppose you needed to go into hospital for an operation. Do you think you would have a say about which hospital you went to?

	[OutPat3]	[WhchHosp]
	%	%
Definitely would	9.0	8.7
Probably would	45.1	28.0
Probably would not	28.4	38.8
Definitely would not	10.0	20.7
(Don't Know)	7.5	3.8

Q275 **[GPChange]**
Suppose you wanted to change your GP and go to a different practice, how difficult or easy do you think this would be to arrange? Would it be ...
READ OUT ...

%	
4.8	...very difficult,
17.4	fairly difficult,
34.9	not very difficult,
33.9	or, not at all difficult?
9.0	(Don't Know)

Q276 **[NHS5yrs]**
CARD
Please say how much better or worse you think each of these things has been getting **over the last five years** ...
... the general standard of health care on the **NHS**?

Q277 **[WtOp5yrs]**
CARD AGAIN
(Please say how much better or worse you think each of these things has been getting **over the last five years**)
... the time most people wait to get **operations** in NHS hospitals?

Q278 **[WtAp5Yrs]**
CARD AGAIN
(Please say how much better or worse you think each of these things has been getting **over the last five years**)
... the time most people wait to get **outpatients' appointments** in NHS hospitals?

	[NHS5yrs]	[WtOP5yrs]	[WtAp5yrs]
	%	%	%
Much better	2.7	1.0	0.8
Better	15.4	12.6	15.0
About the same	33.1	23.0	36.2
Worse	38.7	46.4	34.8
Much worse	9.2	12.1	7.4
(Don't Know)	0.9	4.9	5.8

Q279 **[WtCo5Yrs]**
CARD AGAIN
(Please say how much better or worse you think each of these things has been getting **over the last five years**)
... the time most people wait in **outpatients'** departments in NHS hospitals before a consultant sees them?

Q280 **[WtGP5Yrs]**
CARD AGAIN
(Please say how much better or worse you think each of these things has been getting **over the last five years**)
... the time most people wait at their **GP's surgery** before a doctor sees them?

	[WtCo5Yrs]	[WtGP5Yrs]
	%	%
Much better	1.0	2.9
Better	16.0	24.0
About the same	38.4	47.2
Worse	33.4	19.2
Much worse	6.0	4.8
(Don't Know)	5.1	1.8
(Refusal/NA)	0.1	0.0

Q281 **[SickPay1]**
CARD
Please say, from this card, who you think should be **mainly** responsible for ensuring that people who are off work because they are sick continue to get paid?

Q284 **[SickPay2]**
And if someone was off work sick for six months, who do you think should be **mainly** responsible for ensuring that they continue to get paid?

	[SickPay1]	[SickPay2]
	%	%
Mainly the government	37.2	62.9
Mainly the employer	23.7	12.8
Shared equally	36.6	20.1
(Should make private arrangement)	0.1	0.5
Some other arrangement **(WRITE IN)**	0.5	1.1
It depends	0.9	1.5
(Don't Know)	1.0	1.0

EMPLOYMENT

n = 1510

ASK ALL

Q291 *[REconAct]* **(Figures refer to first answer on the list)**
CARD
Which of these descriptions applies to what you were doing last week, that is, in the seven days ending last Sunday?
CODE ALL THAT APPLY
PROBE: Any others?

%
3.1   In full-time education (not paid for by employer, including on vacation)
0.7   On government training/employment programme (e.g. Employment Training, Youth Training, etc.)
50.1   In paid work (or away temporarily) for at least 10 hours in week
0.2   Waiting to take up paid work already accepted
5.6   Unemployed and registered at a benefit office
0.4   Unemployed, not registered, but actively looking for a job
0.9   Unemployed, wanting a job (of at least 10 hours per week) but not actively looking for a job
6.6   Permanently sick or disabled
15.0   Wholly retired from work
16.6   Looking after the home
0.9   (Doing something else) **(WRITE IN)**

ASK ALL IN PAID WORK (IF 'In paid work' AT [REconAct])   n = 756

Q292 *[REmploye]*
In your (main) job are you ... **READ OUT** ...
%
83.0   ... an employee,
17.0   or, self-employed?

ASK ALL EMPLOYEES (IF 'an employee'/DK AT [REmploye])   n = 627

Q293 *[EmploydT]*
For how long have you been continuously employed by your present employer?
ENTER NUMBER. THEN SPECIFY MONTHS OR YEARS
Median: 60 months

Q295 *[EstJbTim]*
In your present job, are you working ... **READ OUT** ...
RESPONDENT'S OWN DEFINITION
%
78.1   ... full-time,
21.9   or, part-time?

Q296 *[EJbHours]*
How many hours a week do you **normally** work in your (main) job?
IF RESPONDENT CANNOT ANSWER, ASK ABOUT LAST WEEK.
ROUND TO NEAREST HOUR.
CODE 95 FOR 95+
Median: 38

---

n = 627

Q297 *[EJbHrCat]* **(CALCULATED BY PROGRAM)**
HOURS WORKED - CATEGORISED
%
4.2   10-15 hours a week
11.6   16-23 hours a week
6.0   24-29 hours a week
78.2   30 or more hours a week
0.1   (Refusal/NA)

Q298 *[WageNow]*
How would you describe the wages or salary you are paid for the job you do - on the low side, reasonable, or on the high side?
IF LOW: Very low or a bit low?
%
10.2   Very low
25.5   A bit low
58.7   Reasonable
5.6   On the high side
-      Other answer **(WRITE IN)**

Q301 *[PayGap]*
CARD
Thinking of the **highest** and the **lowest** paid people at your place of work, how would you describe the **gap** between their pay, as far as you know? Please choose a phrase from this card.
%
24.5   Much too big a gap
27.6   Too big
40.0   About right
2.7   Too small
0.8   Much too small a gap
4.4   (Don't Know)

Q302 *[WageXpct]*
If you stay in this job, would you expect your wages or salary over the coming year to ... **READ OUT** ...
%
10.6   ... rise by **more** than the cost of living,
42.9   rise by the **same** as the cost of living,
33.8   rise by **less** than the cost of living,
10.8   or, not to rise at all?
1.2   (Will not stay in job)
0.6   (Don't Know)

IF 'Not rise at all' AT [WageXpct]
Q303 *[WageDown]*
Would you expect your wages or salary to stay the same, or in fact to go down?
%
9.8   Stay the same
1.0   Go down
0.1   (Don't Know)
0.6   (Refusal/NA)

Q304 ASK ALL EMPLOYEES (IF 'an employee' AT [REmploye])
[NumEmp]
Over the coming year do you expect your workplace to be ... READ OUT ...
%
19.3 ... increasing its number of employees,
22.9 reducing its number of employees,
55.6 or, will the number of employees stay about the same?
0.5 Other answer (WRITE IN)
1.7 (Don't Know)

Q307 [LeaveJob]
Thinking now about your own job. How likely or unlikely is it that you will leave this employer over the next year for any reason? Is it ... READ OUT ...
%
10.2 ... very likely,
9.2 quite likely,
30.5 not very likely,
49.5 or, not at all likely?
1.0 (Don't Know)

Q308 IF 'very likely' OR 'quite likely' AT [LeaveJob]
CARD
Why do you think you will leave? Please choose a phrase from this card or tell me what other reason there is.
CODE ALL THAT APPLY
%
0.6 Firm will close down [WhyGo1]
1.8 I will be declared redundant [WhyGo2]
0.7 I will reach normal retirement age [WhyGo3]
1.6 My contract of employment will expire [WhyGo4]
10.5 I will take early retirement [WhyGo5]
     I will decide to leave and work for another [WhyGo6]
     employer
2.2 I will decide to leave and work for myself, [WhyGo7]
     as self-employed
1.1 I will leave to look after home/children/relative [WhyGo10]
0.3 I will return to education [WhyGo11]
0.6 Other answer (WRITE IN) [WhyGo8]
1.0 (Don't know)

Q320 ASK ALL EMPLOYEES (IF 'an employee' AT [REmploye])
[ELookJob]
Suppose you lost your job for one reason or another – would you start looking for another job, would you wait for several months or longer before you started looking, or would you decide not to look for another job?
%
87.6 Start looking
4.8 Wait several months or longer
6.8 Decide not to look
0.6 (Don't Know)

Q321 IF 'Start looking' AT [ELookJob]
[EFindJob]
How long do you think it would take you to find an acceptable replacement job?
IF 'NEVER', PLEASE CODE 96
ENTER NUMBER, THEN SPECIFY MONTHS OR YEARS
Median: 2 months

11

Q323 IF 3 MONTHS OR MORE OR DK AT [EFindJob]
[ERetrain]
How willing do you think you would be in these circumstances to retrain for a different job ... READ OUT ...
%
33.0 ... very willing,
16.3 quite willing,
7.6 or – not very willing?
0.6 (Refusal/NA)

Q324 ASK ALL EMPLOYEES (IF 'an employee' AT [REmploye])
[EUnemp]
During the last **five years** – that is since May 1990 – have you been unemployed and seeking work for any period?
%
18.9 Yes
81.1 No

Q325 IF 'Yes' AT [EUnemp]
[EUnempT]
For how many **months** in total during the last five years?
ENTER NUMBER OF MONTHS
Median: 6 months

Q326 ASK ALL EMPLOYEES (IF 'an employee' AT [REmploye])
[WpUnions]
At your place of work are there unions, staff associations, or groups of unions recognised by the management for negotiating pay and conditions of employment?
IF YES, PROBE FOR UNION OR STAFF ASSOCIATION
IF 'BOTH', CODE '1'
%
55.2 Yes : trade union(s)
3.9 Yes : staff association
40.4 No, none
0.5 (Don't Know)

Q327 [TUShould]
CARD
Listed on the card are a number of things trade unions or staff associations can do. Which, if any, do you think is the **most important** thing they should try to do **at your workplace**?
UNIONS OR STAFF ASSOCIATIONS SHOULD TRY TO:
%
18.0 Improve working conditions
26.7 Improve pay
31.5 Protect existing jobs
4.9 Have more say over how work is done day-to-day
8.5 Have more say over management's long-term plans
4.4 Work for equal opportunities for women
0.5 Work for equal opportunities for ethnic minorities
4.0 Reduce pay differences at the workplace
1.0 (NONE OF THESE)
0.6 (Don't Know)

12

228

Q328 [IndRel]
In general how would you describe relations between management and other employees at your workplace
... READ OUT ...
%
34.3 ... very good,
50.0 quite good,
10.6 not very good,
4.8 or, not at all good?
0.3 (Don't Know)

Q329 [WorkRun]
And in general, would you say your workplace was
... READ OUT ...
%
29.2 ... very well managed,
55.9 quite well managed,
14.7 or, not well managed?
0.2 (Don't Know)

Q330 [EmpEarn]
Now for some more general questions about your work. For some people their job is simply something they do in order to earn a living. For others it means much more than that. On balance, is your present job ...
... READ OUT ...
%
36.0 ... just a means of earning a living,
63.9 or, does it mean much more to you than that?
0.1 (Don't Know)

IF 'just a means of earning a living' AT [EmpEarn]
Q331 [EmpLiv]
Is that because ... READ OUT ...
%
13.1 ... there are no better jobs around here,
8.9 you don't have the right skills to get a better job,
13.2 or, because you would feel the same about any job you had?
0.7 (Don't Know)
0.1 (Refusal/NA)

ASK ALL EMPLOYEES (IF 'an employee' AT [REmployee])
Q332 [EPrefJob]
If without having to work, you had what you would regard as a reasonable living income, do you think you would still prefer to have a paid job or wouldn't you bother?
%
74.2 Still prefer paid job
24.4 Wouldn't bother
0.7 Other answer (WRITE IN)
0.6 (Don't Know)

Q335 [EWkHrd]
CARD
Which of these statements best describes your feelings about your job? In my job :
%
7.8 I only work as hard as I have to
41.8 I work hard, but not so that it interferes with the rest of my life
50.4 I make a point of doing the best I can, even if it sometimes does interfere with the rest of my life

ASK ALL SELF-EMPLOYED (IF 'self-employed' AT [REmployee])
Q336 [SsrJbTim]
In your present job, are you working ... READ OUT ...
RESPONDENT'S OWN DEFINITION
%
89.4 ... full-time,
10.6 or, part-time?

Q337 [SJbHours]
How many hours a week do you normally work in your (main) job?
IF RESPONDENT CANNOT ANSWER, ASK ABOUT LAST WEEK.
ROUND TO NEAREST HOUR
CODE 95 FOR 95+
Median: 50

Q338 [SJbHrCat]
SELF-EMPLOYED HOURS WORKED - CATEGORISED
%
2.0 10-15 hours a week
5.5 16-23 hours a week
- 24-29 hours a week
92.5 30 or more hours a week

Q339 [SUnemp]
During the last five years - that is since May 1990 - have you been unemployed and seeking work for any period?
%
17.3 Yes
82.7 No

IF 'Yes' AT [SUnemp]
Q340 [SUnempT]
For how many months in total during the last five years (have you been unemployed) ?
ENTER NUMBER OF MONTHS
Median: 6 months

ASK ALL SELF-EMPLOYED (IF 'self-employed' AT [REmployee])
Q341 [SEmplee]
Have you, for any period in the last five years, worked as an employee as your main job rather than as self-employed?
%
16.9 Yes
83.1 No

IF 'Yes' AT [SEmplee]
Q342 [SEmpleeT]
In total for how many months during the last five years have you been an employee?
ENTER NUMBER OF MONTHS
Median: 24 months

Q343 **IF 'No' AT [SEmplee]**
[SEmplSer]
How seriously in the last five years have you considered getting a job as an **employee** ... **READ OUT** ...
%
5.1 ... very seriously,
2.7 quite seriously,
3.1 not very seriously,
72.2 or, not at all seriously?

ASK ALL SELF-EMPLOYED (IF 'self-employed' AT [REmployee])
Q344 [BusIOK]
Compared with **a year ago**, would you say your business is doing ... **READ OUT** ...
%
14.1 ... very well,
20.0 quite well,
50.2 about the same,
9.4 not very well,
2.7 or, not at all well?
2.7 (Business not in existence then)
0.8 (Refusal/NA)

Q345 [BusIFut]
And over **the coming year**, do you think your business will do ... **READ OUT** ...
%
23.9 ... better,
69.8 about the same,
4.7 or, worse than this year?
0.8 Other answer (**WRITE IN**)
0.8 (Refusal/NA)

Q348 [SPartnrs]
In your work or business, do you have any partners or other self-employed colleagues?
NOTE: DOES NOT INCLUDE EMPLOYEES
%
40.4 Yes, has partner(s)
59.6 No

Q349 [SNumEmp]
And in your work or business, do you have any employees, or not?
NOTE: FAMILY MEMBERS MAY BE EMPLOYEES ONLY IF THEY RECEIVE A REGULAR WAGE OR SALARY
%
40.4 Yes, has employee(s)
59.6 No

Q350 [SEmpEarn]
Now for some more general questions about you work. For some people their job is simply something they do in order to earn a living. For others it means much more than that. On balance, is your present job ... **READ OUT** ...
%
27.5 ... just a means of earning a living,
72.5 or, does it mean much more to you than that?

IF 'just a means of earning a living' AT [SEmpEarn]
Q351 [SEmpLiv]
Is that because ... **READ OUT** ...
%
5.9 ... there are no better jobs around here,
6.7 you don't have the right skills to get a better job,
14.1 or, because you would feel the same about **any** job you had?
0.8 (Refusal/NA)

ASK ALL SELF-EMPLOYED (IF 'self-employed' AT [REmployee])
Q352 [SPrefJob]
If without having to work, you had what you would regard as a reasonable living income, do you think you would still prefer to have a paid job or wouldn't you bother?
%
86.3 Still prefer paid job
12.9 Wouldn't bother
0.8 Other answer (**WRITE IN**)

Q355 [SWkHrd]
CARD
Which of these statements best describes your feelings about your job? In my job :
%
7.1 I only work as hard as I have to
31.4 I work hard, but not so that it interferes with the rest of my life
60.8 I make a point of doing the best I can, even if it sometimes does interfere with the rest of my life
0.8 (Don't Know)

ASK ALL LOOKING AFTER THE HOME (IF 'Looking after the home' AT [REconAct])
Q356 [EverJob]
Have you, during **the last five years**, ever had a full- or part-time job of 10 hours or more a week?
%
26.8 Yes
73.2 No

IF 'No' AT [EverJob]
Q357 [FtJobSer]
How seriously in the past five years have you considered getting a **full-time job** ? **PROMPT, IF NECESSARY**: Full-time is 30 or more hours a week ... **READ OUT** ...
%
2.6 ... Very seriously
3.6 Quite seriously
8.9 Not very seriously
58.1 Not at all seriously

17

IF 'not very seriously'//'not at all seriously' AT [FtJobSer]   n = 251

Q358 [PtJobSer]
How seriously, in the past five years, have you considered getting a **part-time** job ... **READ OUT** ...
%
1.2 ... very seriously,
4.6 quite seriously,
11.1 not very seriously,
50.0 or, not at all seriously?

ASK ALL UNEMPLOYED (IF 'Unemployed and registered at a benefit office'//'Unemployed, not registered at a benefit office'//'Unemployed, wanting a job but not actively looking for a job' AT [REconAct])   n = 105

Q359 [UUnempT]
In total how many months **in the last five years** - that is, since May 1990 - have you been unemployed and seeking work?
Median: 36 months

Q360 [CurUnemp]
How long has this **present** period of unemployment and seeking work lasted so far?
ENTER NUMBER THEN SPECIFY MONTHS OR YEARS
Median: 26 months

Q362 [JobQual]
How confident are you that you will find a job to match your qualifications ... **READ OUT** ...
%
7.7 ... very confident,
22.7 quite confident,
34.3 not very confident,
35.3 or, not at all confident?

Q363 [UFindJob]
Although it may be difficult to judge, how long **from now** do you think it will be before you find an acceptable job?
ENTER NUMBER THEN SPECIFY MONTHS OR YEARS
CODE 96 FOR NEVER
Median: 4 months

IF THREE MONTHS OR MORE/NEVER/DK AT [UFindJob]
Q365 [URetrain]
How willing do you think you would be in these circumstances to retrain for a different job ...
READ OUT ...
%
19.8 ... very willing,
20.8 quite willing,
15.0 or, not very willing?
0.5 (Don't Know)
24.2 (Refusal/NA)

ASK ALL UNEMPLOYED   n = 105

Q366 [ConMove]
Have you ever **actually** considered moving to a different area - an area other than the one you live in now - to try to find work?
%
25.1 Yes
74.9 No

Q367 [UJobChnc]
Do you think that there is a real chance nowadays that you will get a job in this area, or is there **no real chance** nowadays?
%
40.1 Real chance
58.0 No real chance
1.9 (Don't Know)

Q368 [UnemEarn]
For some people work is simply something they do in order to earn a living. For others it means much more than that. In general, do you think of work as ...
READ OUT ...
%
40.6 ... just a means of earning a living,
58.9 or, does it mean much more to you than that?
0.5 (Don't Know)

Q369 IF 'just a means of earning a living' AT [UnemEarn]
[Unempliv]
Is that because ... **READ OUT** ...
%
18.4 ... there are no good jobs around here,
9.7 you don't have the right skills to get a good job,
12.6 or, because you would feel the same about **any** job you had?
0.5 (Refusal/NA)

ASK ALL WHOLLY RETIRED (IF 'Wholly retired' AT [REconAct])   n = 226
Q370 [EmplPen]
Do you receive a pension from any past employer?
%
45.4 Yes
54.6 No

Q371 [MsCheck]
May I just check, are you ... **READ OUT** ...
%
54.4 ... married,
45.6 or, not married?

Q372 IF 'married' AT [MsCheck]
[SEmplPen]
Does your (**husband/wife**) receive a pension from any past employer?
%
14.3 Yes
39.6 No
0.4 (Refusal/NA)

18

ASK ALL WHOLLY RETIRED (IF 'Wholly retired' AT [REconAct])

Q373 *[PrPenGet]*
And do you receive a pension from any **private** arrangements you have made in the past, that is **apart** from the state pension or one arranged through an employer?

%
5.4 Yes
94.4 No
0.2 (Don't Know)

IF 'married' AT [MsCheck]

Q374 *[SPrPnGet]*
And does your **(husband/wife)** *(he/she)* receive a pension from any **private** arrangements *(he/she)* has made in the past, that is **apart** from the state pension or one arranged through an employer?

%
0.4 Yes
– No
53.9 Yes

ASK ALL WHOLLY RETIRED (IF 'Wholly retired' AT [REconAct])

Q375 *[RetAge]*
(Can I just check) are you over **(sixty-five/sixty)**?

%
92.4 Yes
7.6 No

IF 'Yes' AT [RetAge]

Q376 *[RPension]*
On the whole would you say the present **state** pension is on the low side, reasonable, or on the high side?

IF 'ON THE LOW SIDE': Very low or a bit low?

%
39.4 Very low
31.1 A bit low
21.3 Reasonable
– On the high side
0.7 (Don't Know)

Q377 *[RPenInYr]*
Do you expect your state pension in a year's time to purchase **more** than it does now, **less**, or about the **same**?

%
4.0 More
64.2 Less
23.0 About the same
1.1 (Don't Know)

ASK ALL WHOLLY RETIRED (IF 'Wholly retired' AT [REconAct])

Q378 *[RetirAg2]*
At what age did you retire from work?
NEVER WORKED, CODE: 00
Median: 60 years

ASK ALL ON GOVERNMENT PROGRAMME OR WAITING TO TAKE UP WORK (IF 'On government training scheme' OR 'Waiting to take up paid work' AT [REconAct])

Q379 *[WgUnemp]*
During the last five years – that is since May 1990 – have you been unemployed **and** seeking work for any period?

n
10 Yes
4 No

Q380 *[WgEarn]*
For some people work is simply something they do in order to earn a living. For others it means much more than that. In general, do you think of work as...
READ OUT ...

n
1 ... just a means of earning a living,
13 or, does it mean much more to you than that?

IF 'just a means of earning a living' AT [WgEarn]

Q381 *[WgLiv]*
Is that because ... **READ OUT** ...

n
1 ... there are no good jobs around here,
– you don't have the right skills to get a good job,
– or – because you would feel the same about **any** job you had?

COMMUNITY RELATIONS IN NORTHERN IRELAND

ASK ALL

Q382 *[PrejRC]*
Now I would like to ask some questions about religious prejudice against both Catholics and Protestants in Northern Ireland.
First thinking of **Catholics** – do you think there is a lot of prejudice against them in Northern Ireland nowadays, a little, or hardly any?

Q383 *[PrejProt]*
And now, thinking of **Protestants** – do you think there is a lot of prejudice against them in Northern Ireland nowadays, a little, or hardly any?

	[PrejRC]	[PrejProt]
	%	%
A lot	19.9	16.5
A little	49.2	51.3
Hardly any	28.6	29.6
(Don't Know)	2.0	2.3
(Refusal/NA)	0.3	0.3

Q384 *[SRrlPrej]*
% How would you describe yourself ...**READ OUT**...
0.5 ... as very prejudiced against people of other religions,
11.3 ... a little prejudiced,
88.0 ... or not prejudiced at all?
– Other **(WRITE IN)**
0.1 (Don't Know)
0.2 (Refusal/NA)

Q387 *[RIRelAgo]*
What about **relations** between Protestants and Catholics? Would you say they are **better** than they were 5 years ago, **worse**, or about the **same** now as then?
IF 'IT DEPENDS': On the whole...
%
56.2 Better
6.3 Worse
35.5 About the same
0.4 Other **(WRITE IN)**
1.4 (Don't Know)
0.3 (Refusal/NA)

Q390 *[RIRelFut]*
And what about in 5 years time? Do you think relations between Protestants and Catholics will be **better** than now, **worse** than now, or about the **same** as now?
IF 'IT DEPENDS': On the whole
%
62.8 Better than now
5.8 Worse than now
27.1 About the same
0.7 Other **(WRITE IN)**
3.3 (Don't Know)
0.3 (Refusal/NA)

Q393 *[RelgAlwy]*
Do you think that religion will **always** make a difference to the way people feel about each other in Northern Ireland?
%
82.2 Yes
14.6 No
1.3 Other **(WRITE IN)**
1.7 (Don't Know)
0.2 (Refusal/NA)

Q396 *[FrendRlg]*
CARD
About how many of your **friends** would you say are the same religion as you - that is, Protestant or Catholic? Please choose an answer from this card.
PROBE AS NECESSARY: As far as you know?

Q397 *[RelatRlg]*
CARD AGAIN
What about your **relatives**, including relatives by marriage? About how many are the same religion as you?

Q398 *[NeighRlg]*
CARD AGAIN
And what about your **neighbours**? About how many are the same religion as you ?
PROBE AS NECESSARY: As far as you know?

	[FrendRlg]	[RelatRlg]	[NeighRlg]
	%	%	%
All	13.6	42.7	31.1
Most	42.8	41.2	30.4
Half	31.7	9.8	20.2
Less than half	10.4	5.1	8.8
None	0.5	0.6	2.3
(Don't Know)	0.8	0.4	7.0
(Refusal/NA)	0.1	0.1	0.1

Q399 *[NHSRlgPj]*
CARD
For each of the next questions, please use this card to say whether you think **Catholics** are treated better than **Protestants** in Northern Ireland, or whether **Protestants** are treated better than **Catholics**, or whether both are treated equally.
First, the **National Health Service** in Northern Ireland. How does it treat Catholic and Protestant patients?

Q400 *[NIHRlgPj]*
CARD AGAIN
What about the **Northern Ireland Housing Executive** - how does it treat Catholics and Protestants who apply for a home?

Q401 *[DCRIgPj]*
CARD AGAIN
What about your **local district council** – how does it treat Catholics and Protestants who apply for jobs?

	[NHSRIgPj] %	[NIHRIgPj] %	[DCRIgPj] %
Catholics treated much better	1.1	2.9	1.5
Catholics treated a bit better	2.3	8.9	5.7
Both treated equally	89.1	63.3	54.4
Protestants treated a bit better	1.5	6.6	14.9
Protestants treated much better	0.4	1.0	3.5
(It depends/Can't say)	1.3	5.3	4.8
(Don't Know)	4.2	11.7	15.1
(Refusal/NA)	0.1	0.2	0.1

Q402 *[StrRIgPj]*
CARD AGAIN
And what about **central government** in Stormont – how does it treat Catholics and Protestants who apply for jobs?

Q403 *[GSURIgPj]*
CARD AGAIN
What about **government programmes for the unemployed** – how do they treat Catholics and Protestants who apply for places?

Q404 *[FECRIgPj]*
CARD AGAIN
And what about the **Fair Employment Commission** – how does it treat Catholics and Protestants?

	[StrRIgPj] %	[GSURIgPj] %	[FECRIgPj] %
Catholics treated much better	2.4	1.7	4.2
Catholics treated a bit better	8.6	5.6	11.3
Both treated equally	53.9	73.3	70.6
Protestants treated a bit better	12.3	3.2	2.2
Protestants treated much better	2.7	0.7	0.0
(It depends/Can't say)	3.6	2.5	2.4
(Don't Know)	16.4	12.7	9.0
(Refusal/NA)	0.1	0.1	0.3

Q405 *[RUCRIgPj]*
CARD AGAIN
And the **RUC** – how do they treat Catholic and Protestant members of the public?

Q406 *[ArmRIgPj]*
CARD AGAIN
What about the **army** – how do they treat Catholic and Protestant members of the public?

Q407 *[RIRRIgPj]*
CARD AGAIN
And the **Royal Irish Regiment** – how do they treat Catholic and Protestant members of the public?

	[RUCRIgPj] %	[ArmRIgPj] %	[RIRRIgPj] %
Catholics treated much better	0.9	0.2	0.1
Catholics treated a bit better	2.1	1.0	0.7
Both treated equally	58.3	56.7	47.2
Protestants treated a bit better	20.4	18.9	19.9
Protestants treated much better	8.7	9.3	14.4
(It depends/Can't say)	3.3	5.4	6.0
(Don't Know)	6.1	8.1	11.5
(Refusal/NA)	0.3	0.3	0.2

Q408 *[NTrRIgPj]*
CARD AGAIN
And the **courts** – how do they treat Catholics and Protestants accused of committing **non-terrorist** offences?

Q409 *[TerRIgPj]*
CARD AGAIN
And how do the **courts** treat Catholics and Protestants accused of committing **terrorist** offences?

	[NTrRIgPj] %	[TerRIgPj] %
Catholics treated much better	0.1	1.1
Catholics treated a bit better	1.2	3.5
Both treated equally	84.5	72.1
Protestants treated a bit better	3.4	9.8
Protestants treated much better	1.0	3.3
(It depends/Can't say)	1.9	2.8
(Don't Know)	7.8	7.2
(Refusal/NA)	0.1	0.2

Q410 *[MxRlgNgh]*
If you had a choice, would you prefer to live in a
neighbourhood with people of **only** your own religion,
or in a **mixed-religion** neighbourhood?
PROBE IF NECESSARY: Say if you **were** moving ...

%
18.3 Own religion only
78.2 Mixed-religion neighbourhood
3.2 (Don't Know)
0.2 (Refusal/NA)

Q411 *[MxRlgWrk]*
And if you were working and had to change your job,
would you prefer a workplace with people of **only** your
own religion, or a **mixed-religion** workplace?
PROBE IF NECESSARY: Say if you **did** have a job.

%
6.4 Own religion only
91.1 Mixed-religion workplace
2.2 (Don't Know)
0.3 (Refusal/NA)

Q412 *[OwnMxSch]*
And if you were deciding where to send your children
to school, would you prefer a school with children of
only your own religion, or a **mixed-religion** school?
PROBE IF NECESSARY: Say if you **did** have school-age
children

%
35.8 Own religion only
60.7 Mixed-religion school
3.3 (Don't Know)
0.2 (Refusal/NA)

Q413 *[JbRlgCh1]*
Thinking now about employment...
On the whole, do you think the Protestants and
Catholics in Northern Ireland who apply for the same
jobs have the **same** chance of getting a job or are
their chances of getting a job different?
IF 'IT DEPENDS' PROMPT: On the whole ...

%
54.9 Same chance
40.4 Different chance
4.5 (Don't Know)
0.2 (Refusal/NA)

IF 'Different chance'/DK AT [JbRlgCh1]
Q414 *[JbRlgCh2]*
Which group is **more** likely to get a job – Protestants
or Catholics?
IF 'IT DEPENDS' PROMPT: On the whole ...

%
22.7 Protestants
12.3 Catholics
9.7 (Don't Know)
0.4 (Refusal/NA)

Q415 *[JobRlgCh]*
Are *(Protestants/Catholics)* **much** more likely or just
a **bit** more likely to get a job?

%
9.7 Much more
25.2 Bit more
9.8 (Don't Know)
(Refusal/NA)

ASK ALL
Q416 *[JobRlgSh]*
And do you think Protestants and Catholics in Northern
Ireland who apply for the same jobs **should** have the
same chance of getting a job or should Protestants
have a better chance, or should Catholics have a
better chance?

%
98.1 Same chance
0.5 Protestants better
0.4 Catholics better
0.8 (Don't Know)
0.1 (Refusal/NA)

Q417 *[ProtJob]*
Now I'm going to ask **separately** about employment
chances of Protestants and Catholics.
Some people think that many employers are **more** likely
to give jobs to Protestants than to Catholics.
Do you think this happens ...**READ OUT**...
(IF 'IT DEPENDS': In general, what would you say?)

%
14.2 ... a lot,
51.4 a little,
29.4 or, hardly at all?
4.7 (Don't Know)
0.3 (Refusal/NA)

Q418 *[YrProtJob]*
IF 'a lot' OR 'a little' AT [ProtJob]
Why do you think this happens? –
Do you think it is **mainly** because employers discriminate
against Catholics or **mainly** because Catholics are not as
well qualified as Protestants?
IF 'BOTH', PROBE BEFORE CODING

%
54.9 Mainly because employers discriminate
4.2 Mainly because Catholics aren't qualified
1.8 Both **(AFTER PROBE)**
5.2 (Don't Know)
(Refusal/NA)

ASK ALL
Q419 *[RCJob]*
Some people think that many employers are **more** likely
to give jobs to Catholics than to Protestants.
Do you think this happens ...**READ OUT**...
(IF 'IT DEPENDS': In general, what would you say?)

%
9.5 ... a lot,
50.3 a little,
34.7 or, hardly at all?
5.2 (Don't Know)
0.3 (Refusal/NA)

235

25

26

Q420 **IF 'a lot' or 'a little' AT [RCJob]**
[YRCJob]
Why do you think this happens? -
Do you think it is **mainly** because employers discriminate against Protestants or **mainly** because Protestants are not as well qualified as Catholics?
IF 'BOTH', PROBE BEFORE CODING

%
51.2 Mainly because employers discriminate
2.7 Mainly because Protestants aren't qualified
4.2 Both **(AFTER PROBE)**
1.5 (Don't Know)
5.6 (Refusal/NA)

ASK ALL

Q421 [ChRlGRsp]
CARD
Do you think the government and public bodies should or should not ...
... do more to teach Catholic and Protestant children greater respect for each other?

Q422 [IntegHse]
CARD AGAIN
(Do you think the government and public bodies should or should not ...)
... do more to create integrated housing?

	[ChRlGRsp]	[IntegHSe]
	%	%
Definitely should	71.4	51.4
Probably should	21.9	36.5
Probably should not	3.3	8.2
Definitely should not	1.5	1.4
(Don't Know)	1.6	2.3
(Refusal/NA)	0.3	0.2

Q423 [BtrComRl]
CARD AGAIN
(Do you think the government and public bodies should or should not ...)
... do more to create better community relations generally?

Q424 [IntegWrk]
CARD AGAIN
(Do you think the government and public bodies should or should not ...)
... do more to create integrated workplaces?

	[BtrComRl]	[IntegWrk]
	%	%
Definitely should	66.1	60.4
Probably should	29.5	32.4
Probably should not	2.7	4.8
Definitely should not	0.1	0.8
(Don't Know)	1.3	1.4
(Refusal/NA)	0.2	0.3

27

[GovMxSch]
Thinking now about **mixed** or **integrated** schooling, that is, schools with fairly large numbers of both Catholic and Protestant children:
Do you think the government should **encourage** mixed schooling, **discourage** mixed schooling or leave things as they are?

%
66.4 Encourage it
2.3 Discourage it
30.4 Leave things as they are
0.7 (Don't Know)
0.2 (Refusal/NA)

Q426 [GBImpNI]
CARD
For each of the following, please say how active you think each should be in trying to improve relations between the communities in Northern Ireland.
Firstly, the British government?

Q427 [IRImpNI]
CARD AGAIN
... the government of the Irish Republic?

	[GBImpNI]	[IRImpNI]
	%	%
Much more active than now	48.5	33.9
A little more active than now	29.1	25.6
About the same as now	16.3	18.1
A little less active than now	2.6	8.0
Much less active than now	1.1	11.6
(Don't Know)	2.0	2.7
(Refusal/NA)	0.3	0.3

Q428 [UImpNI]
CARD AGAIN
... Unionist politicians?

Q429 [NatImpNI]
CARD AGAIN
... Nationalist politicians?

	[UImpNI]	[NatImpNI]
	%	%
Much more active than now	51.5	45.7
A little more active than now	25.6	25.1
About the same as now	14.8	17.1
A little less active than now	4.1	5.4
Much less active than now	1.4	3.5
(Don't Know)	2.4	3.0
(Refusal/NA)	0.2	0.2

Q430 [NISupPty]
Generally speaking, do you think of yourself as a supporter of any one political party?

%
31.6 Yes
67.8 No
0.2 (Don't Know)
0.4 (Refusal/NA)

28

Q432 **IF 'No'/DK AT [NISupPty]**
[NIClsPty]
Do you think of yourself as a little closer to one
political party than to the others?

%
24.1 Yes
43.7 No
0.6 (Refusal/NA)

Q435 [NIPtyID1]
IF 'Yes' AT [NISupPty] OR AT [NIClsPty]: Which one?
IF 'No'/DK AT [NIClsPty]: If there were a general
election tomorrow, which political party do you think
you would be most likely to support?

%
5.3 Conservative
7.2 Labour
0.7 Liberal Democrat
8.1 Alliance (Northern Ireland)
8.5 DUP/Democratic Unionist Party
22.3 OUP/Official Unionist
1.4 Other Unionist party
2.2 Sinn Fein
19.1 SDLP
0.8 Workers Party
1.1 Campaign for Equal Citizenship
0.7 Green Party
    Other party (WRITE IN)
    Other answer (WRITE IN)
18.0 None
1.9 (Don't Know)
2.0 (Refusal/NA)

Q441 **IF 'Conservative', 'Labour', OR 'Liberal Democrat'**
AT [NIPtyID1]
[NIPtyID3]
If there were a general election in which only
Northern Ireland parties were standing, which one
do you think you would be most likely to support?
CODE ONE ONLY

%
2.3 Alliance (Northern Ireland)
0.9 DUP/Democratic Unionist Party
3.0 OUP/Official Unionist
0.7 Other Unionist party
2.1 SDLP
0.2 Sinn Fein
0.1 Workers Party
0.1 Campaign for Equal Citizenship
0.4 Green Party
0.5 Other party (WRITE IN)
0.5 Other answer (WRITE IN)
1.9 None
0.6 (Don't Know)
4.2 (Refusal/NA)

Q446 **IF NORTHERN IRELAND PARTY MENTIONED AT**
[NIPtyID1] OR AT [NIPtyID3]
[NIIDStrn]
Would you call yourself very strong ... (name of
Northern Ireland party) ... fairly strong, or not
very strong?

%
5.7 Very strong (name of Northern Ireland party)
24.0 Fairly strong
43.6 Not very strong

Q447 **ASK ALL**
[NINatID]
CARD
Which of these **best** describes the way you usually
think of yourself?

%
42.5 British
27.7 Irish
7.5 Ulster
20.5 Northern Irish
0.5 British Irish
1.1 Other (WRITE IN)
0.1 (Don't Know)
0.0 (Refusal/NA)

Q450 [BrtIRSde]
When there is an argument between Britain and the
Republic of Ireland, do you generally find yourself on
the side of the British or of the Irish government?
IF 'IT DEPENDS': On the whole ...

%
48.3 Generally British government
14.7 Generally Irish government
21.3 It depends **(AFTER PROBE)**
14.8 Neither
0.5 (Don't Know)
0.4 (Refusal/NA)

Q451 [UntdIRel]
At any time in the next 20 years, do you think it
is likely or unlikely that there will be a united
Ireland?
PROBE: Very likely/unlikely or **quite likely/unlikely**

%
9.4 Very likely
31.3 Quite likely
28.4 Quite unlikely
24.2 Very unlikely
3.1 (Even chance)
3.5 (Don't Know)
0.1 (Refusal/NA)

Q452 [GovIntNI]
CARD
Under direct rule from Britain, as now, how much do
you generally trust **British governments** of **any** party
to act in the best interests of Northern Ireland?
PROBE IF NECESSARY

Left page

n = 1510

Q453 [StrIntNI]
CARD AGAIN
If there was self-rule, how much do you think you
would generally trust a **Stormont government** to act in
the best interests of Northern Ireland?
PROBE IF NECESSARY

Q454 [IreIntNI]
CARD AGAIN
And if there was a united Ireland, how much do you
think you would generally trust an **Irish government**
to act in the best interests of Northern Ireland?
PROBE IF NECESSARY

	[GovIntNI]	[StrIntNI]	[IreIntNI]
	%	%	%
Just about always	3.1	9.8	3.4
Most of the time	20.3	39.9	24.1
Only some of the time	45.7	28.9	33.2
Rarely	19.2	9.4	16.8
Never	10.4	8.5	18.1
(Don't Know)	1.1	3.2	4.1
(Refusal/NA)	0.2	0.3	0.2

Right page

n = 766

ENVIRONMENT AND TRANSPORT (VERSION A)

VERSION A: ASK ALL

Q458 [CthtNew1]
CARD
Now a few questions about the countryside.
Which, if any, of the things on this card do you think
is the **greatest threat** to the countryside?
If you think none of them is a threat, please say so.
CODE ONE ONLY

IF ANSWER GIVEN AT [CthtNew1]

Q461 [CthtNew2]
CARD AGAIN
And which do you think is the **next greatest threat**
(to the countryside)?
CODE ONE ONLY

	[CthtNew1]	[CthtNew2]
	%	%
Litter and fly-tipping of rubbish	27.8	23.5
New housing and urban sprawl	9.8	8.6
Superstores and out-of-town shopping centres	2.3	3.4
Building new roads and motorways	3.3	6.5
Industrial development like factories, quarries and power stations	9.4	13.7
Land and air pollution, or discharges into rivers and lakes	40.6	28.0
Changes to traditional ways of farming and of using farmland	2.9	5.5
Changes to the ordinary natural appearance of the countryside, including plants and wildlife	2.1	7.0
The number of tourists and visitors in the countryside	0.3	0.5
Other answer (WRITE IN)	0.4	0.5
(None of these)	0.7	1.5
(Don't Know)	0.3	0.3
(Refusal/NA)	–	0.3

VERSION A: ASK ALL

Q464 [Crowded1]
CARD
Beauty spots and other popular places in the
countryside often get crowded. Suppose one of these
was visited so much that enjoying its peace and quiet
was being spoiled. Using this card, are you in
favour of or against ...
... cutting down or closing car parks near the site?

Q465 [Crowded2]
CARD AGAIN
(To limit the number of visitors, are you in favour of
or against ...)
... stopping anyone at all from visiting it at
particular times each year?

Q466 [Crowded3]
CARD AGAIN
(To limit the number of visitors, are you in favour
of or against ...)
... making visitors pay and using the extra money to
help protect it?

	[Crowded1]	[Crowded2]	[Crowded3]
	%	%	%
Strongly in favour	8.3	6.7	16.4
In favour	38.5	32.2	57.9
Neither in favour nor against	19.9	15.9	17.6
Against	27.1	37.4	15.0
Strongly against	5.5	7.0	2.4
(Don't Know)	0.7	0.9	0.7

Q467 [Crowded4]
CARD AGAIN
(To limit the number of visitors, are you in favour
of or against ...)
... issuing free permits in advance so people will
have to plan their visits?

Q468 [Crowded5]
CARD AGAIN
(To limit the number of visitors, are you in favour
of or against ...)
... cutting down on advertising and promoting it?

Q469 [Crowded6]
CARD AGAIN
(To limit the number of visitors, are you in favour
of or against ...)
... advertising and promoting other popular places in
the countryside instead?

	[Crowded4]	[Crowded5]	[Crowded6]
	%	%	%
Strongly in favour	5.7	2.8	6.6
In favour	34.9	33.0	54.7
Neither in favour nor against	13.4	23.0	21.0
Against	39.7	36.7	15.1
Strongly against	5.2	3.1	1.0
(Don't Know)	1.0	1.5	1.6

Q470 [TrafPrb6]
CARD
Now thinking about traffic and transport problems,
how serious a problem is ...
... congestion on motorways?

Q471 [TrafPrb7]
CARD AGAIN
(And how serious a problem is ...)
... increased traffic on country roads and lanes?

Q472 [TrafPrb8]
CARD AGAIN
(And how serious a problem is ...)
... traffic congestion at popular places in the
countryside?

	[TrafPrb6]	[TrafPrb7]	[TrafPrb8]
	%	%	%
A very serious problem	20.1	15.8	10.6
A serious problem	34.9	45.9	47.2
Not a very serious problem	38.6	33.4	36.1
Not a problem at all	3.8	1.6	2.8
(Don't Know)	2.6	3.2	3.2

Q473 [TrfPrb9]
CARD AGAIN
(And how serious a problem is ...)
... traffic congestion in towns and cities?

Q474 [TrfPrb10]
CARD AGAIN
(And how serious a problem are ...)
... exhaust fumes from traffic in towns and cities?

Q475 [TrfPrb11]
CARD AGAIN
(And how serious a problem is ...)
... noise from traffic in towns and cities?

	[TrafPrb9]	[TrafPrb10]	[TrafPrb11]
	%	%	%
A very serious problem	34.3	44.6	20.6
A serious problem	51.1	41.3	47.3
Not a very serious problem	13.4	11.7	28.5
Not a problem at all	0.3	1.0	2.2
(Don't Know)	0.9	1.4	1.5

Q476 [TransCar]
Do you, or does anyone in your household, own or
have the regular use of a car or a van?
**IF 'YES' PROBE FOR WHETHER RESPONDENT, OR OTHER
PERSON(S) ONLY, OR BOTH**

%	
27.8	Yes, respondent only
18.3	Yes, other(s) only
35.3	Yes, both
18.6	No

Q477 [NumbCars]
**IF 'Yes, respondent only', 'Yes, other(s) only' OR
'Yes, both' AT [TransCar]**
How many vehicles in all?

%	
47.9	One
24.6	Two
6.9	Three
1.9	Four
0.1	Five or more

Q478 [CompCar]
Is this vehicle (Are any of these vehicles) provided by an employer or run as a business expense?

	%
No	69.1
Yes, one (of them)	10.7
Yes, two (of them)	0.8
Yes, three or more (of them)	0.8

IF 'Yes, respondent only' OR 'Yes, both' AT [TransCar]
Q479 [MotMembR]
Do you yourself belong to any motoring association?
IF 'Yes' PROBE FOR WHICH

	%
Automobile Association (AA)	7.4
The Royal Automobile Club (RAC)	3.4
(AA and RAC)	0.1
Other motoring organisation (WRITE IN)	0.5
No	51.9

IF 'No' AT [MotMembR] OR 'Yes, other(s) only' AT [TransCar]
Q482 [MotMemHH]
Does any member of your household belong to any motoring association?
IF 'Yes' PROBE FOR WHICH

	%
Automobile Association (AA)	4.2
The Royal Automobile Club (RAC)	2.8
Other motoring organisation (WRITE IN)	0.5
No	62.4
(Don't Know)	0.4

IF 'Yes, respondent only' OR 'Yes, both' AT [TransCar]
Q485 [NCarIncv]
If for some reason you could no longer have the use of a car (or a van), would you find it really inconvenient ... READ OUT ...

	%
... more or less every day of your life,	43.6
several times a week,	10.8
several times a month,	1.8
only occasionally,	4.5
or - would you never really find it inconvenient?	2.3

IF EVER INCONVENIENT AT [NCarIncv]
Q486 [NeedCar1]
I am going to read out some reasons people give as to why they really need a car (or a van). For each, please say whether it applies or does not apply to you.
First, you live too far from a station or bus-stop.

Q487 [NeedCar2]
Does this apply ....
... Bus or train does not run often enough.

Q488 [NeedCar3]
And does this apply ....
... No convenient bus or train route to where you need to go.

Q489 [NeedCar4]
And does this apply ....
... Cost of bus or train travel is too high.

	[NeedCar1]	[NeedCar2]	[NeedCar3]	[NeedCar4]
	%	%	%	%
Yes, applies	22.1	27.8	32.9	20.3
No, does not apply	38.7	31.7	27.8	36.0
(Don't Know)	-	1.3	0.1	4.5

Q490 [NCarPTr]
Now, suppose that public transport in your area were better or less expensive. Do you think you would then use a car (or a van) as much as now, or might you use it less?
IF 'LESS': Would that be much less or a bit less?

	%
Use it as much as now	38.6
Use it a bit less	16.8
Use it much less	5.3

VERSION A: ASK ALL
Q491 [Drive]
May I just check, do you drive a car at all these days?

	%
Yes	68.6
No	31.4

IF 'Yes' AT [Drive]
Q492 [Travel1]
CARD
How often nowadays do you usually travel ....
... by car as a driver?

VERSION A: ASK ALL
Q493 [Travel2]
CARD AGAIN
(And how often do you usually ...)
... travel by car as a passenger?

Q494 [Travel3]
CARD AGAIN
(And how often do you usually ...)
... travel by local bus?

	[Travel1]	[Travel2]	[Travel3]
	%	%	%
Every day or nearly every day	52.5	13.6	3.3
2-5 days a week	12.7	27.6	8.6
Once a week	1.5	18.8	9.1
Less often but at least once a month	0.8	13.9	9.9
Less often than that	0.5	11.4	14.8
Never nowadays	0.6	14.8	54.3

Q495 [Travel4]
CARD AGAIN
(And how often do you usually ...)
... travel by train?

Q496 [Travel6]
CARD AGAIN
(And how often do you **usually** ...)
... travel by bicycle?

Q497 [Travel9]
CARD AGAIN
(And how often do you **usually** ...)
... go somewhere on foot at least 15 minutes' walk away?

	[Travel4]	[Travel5]	[Travel6]
	%	%	%
Every day or nearly every day	-	1.5	24.9
2-5 days a week	0.6	2.4	20.0
Once a week	0.8	3.0	16.5
Less often but at least once a month	2.8	1.6	9.5
Less often than that	16.2	5.8	8.7
Never nowadays	79.6	85.7	20.4

WELFARE (VERSION A)

VERSION A: ASK ALL

[UB1Poor]
Q502 Now some questions about welfare benefits. Think of a 25-year-old unemployed woman living alone. Her only income comes from state benefits. Would you say that she ... **READ OUT** ...

[MumPoor]
Q503 What about an unemployed single mother with a young child. Their only income comes from state benefits. Would you say they ... **READ OUT** ...

	[UB1Poor]	[MumPoor]
	%	%
... has/have more than enough to live on,	1.1	1.5
has/have enough to live on,	21.8	21.2
is/are hard up,	55.6	48.8
or, is/are really poor?	13.6	21.0
(Don't Know)	8.0	7.5

Q504 [UB1On47]
Now thinking again of that 25-year-old unemployed woman living alone. After rent, her income is £47 a week. Would you say that she ... **READ OUT** ...

Q505 [MumOn78]
And thinking again about that unemployed single mother with a young child. After rent, their income is £78 a week. Would you say they ... **READ OUT** ...

	[UB1On47]	[MumOn78]
	%	%
... has/have more than enough to live on,	1.2	2.7
has/have enough to live on,	21.8	30.9
is/are hard up,	56.4	47.7
or, is/are really poor?	19.6	17.0
(Don't Know)	1.0	1.6

Q506 [PenWhoSh]
CARD
Please say, from this card, who you think should be **mainly** responsible for ensuring that people have an adequate retirement pension.

	%
Mainly the government	54.4
Mainly employers	10.9
Shared equally	30.9
Some other arrangement	2.8
(Don't Know)	1.0

Q507 *[MstUnemp]*
Suppose two people working for a large firm each became unemployed through no fault of their own. One had a very high income, one had a very low income. Do you think that the very high earner should be entitled to ... **READ OUT** ...

%
13.9 ...more unemployment benefit than the very low earner,
73.4 the same amount,
10.2 less benefit,
1.0 or, no unemployment benefit at all?
0.1 Other answer **(WRITE IN)**
1.5 (Don't Know)

Q510 *[MstRetir]*
Now suppose a very high earner and a very low earner in a large firm retired. Do you think the very high earner should be entitled to ... **READ OUT** ...

%
14.4 ...a bigger **state** retirement pension than the very low earner,
74.5 the same amount,
7.7 a lower **state** pension,
1.8 or, no **state** pension at all?
0.4 Other answer **(WRITE IN)**
1.2 (Don't Know)

Q513 *[MstChild]*
Now what about child benefit. Should very high earners be entitled to ... **READ OUT** ...

%
1.3 ...more child benefit than very low earners,
56.4 the same amount,
22.3 less,
18.9 or, no child benefit at all?
0.1 (It depends)
0.3 Other answer **(WRITE IN)**
0.8 (Don't Know)

Q516 *[MtUnmar1]*
Imagine an unmarried couple who split up. They have a child at primary school who remains with the mother. Do you think that the father should always be made to make maintenance payments to support the child?

%
87.6 Yes
11.4 No
1.0 (Don't Know)

Q517 *[MtUnmar2]*
If he **does** make maintenance payments for the child, should the amount depend on his income, or not?

%
90.2 Yes
9.1 No
0.7 (Don't Know)

Q518 *[MtUnmar3]*
Do you think the amount of maintenance should depend on the **mother's** income, or not?

%
66.2 Yes
32.5 No
1.5 (Don't Know)

Q519 *[MtUnmar4]*
Suppose the mother now marries someone else. Should the child's natural father go on paying maintenance for the child, should he stop, or should it depend on the step-father's income?

%
39.5 Continue
20.0 Stop
38.6 Depends
1.9 (Don't Know)

Q520 *[WorseOff]*
CARD
Please look at this card and say, as far as money is concerned, what you think happens when a marriage breaks up.

%
25.3 The woman nearly always comes off worse than the man
22.5 The woman usually comes off worse
19.9 The woman and the man usually come off about the same
17.5 The man usually comes off worse
4.6 The man nearly always comes off worse than the woman
5.7 (Varies/depends)
0.6 Other answer **(WRITE IN)**
3.8 (Don't Know)

DRUGS (VERSION A)

VERSION A: ASK ALL

Q527 *[HerUsNow]*
Now, I'd like to ask you some questions about illegal
drug-use in Northern Ireland.
First, thinking about the drug **heroin** ... Do you
think there are **more** people taking heroin in Northern
Ireland now than there were 5 years ago, **less**, or
about the **same** number?

- 82.9 More now
- 1.3 Less now
- 8.3 About the same number
- 0.1 Other answer **(WRITE IN)**
- 7.4 (Don't Know)

Q530 *[HerCrime]*
CARD
How much do you agree or disagree that ...
... heroin is a cause of crime and violence?

Q531 *[HeroinOK]*
CARD AGAIN
(How much do you agree or disagree that ....)
... heroin isn't nearly as damaging to users as some
people think?

Q532 *[HerLegAd]*
CARD AGAIN
(How much do you agree or disagree that ....) if you
legalise heroin many more people will become addicts?

	[HerCrime]	[HeroinOK]	[HerLegAd]
	%	%	%
Strongly agree	52.7	2.2	30.2
Agree	34.1	5.4	40.1
Neither agree nor disagree	6.1	5.2	9.2
Disagree	4.5	40.4	15.5
Strongly disagree	0.1	38.7	0.9
(Don't Know)	2.4	8.1	4.0

Q533 *[HerUsePr]*
CARD AGAIN
(How much do you agree or disagree that ....) people
should **not** be prosecuted for possessing small amounts
of heroin for their own use?

Q534 *[HerSelPr]*
(How much do you agree or disagree that ...) people
who **sell** heroin should always be prosecuted?

	[HerUsePr]	[HerSelPr]
	%	%
Strongly agree	1.7	78.7
Agree	9.7	15.4
Neither agree nor disagree	4.3	1.1
Disagree	42.3	0.7
Strongly disagree	39.6	3.1
(Don't Know)	2.4	1.0

Q535 *[HerLegal]*
CARD
Which of these statements comes closest to your own
view?

- %
- 0.8 Taking heroin should be legal, without restrictions
- 7.4 Taking heroin should be legal, but it should only
  be available from licensed shops
- 90.6 Taking heroin should remain illegal
- 1.1 (Don't Know)

Q536 *[CanUsNow]*
Now thinking about the drug **cannabis**. Do you think
there are **more** people taking cannabis in Northern
Ireland now than there were 5 years ago, **less**, or
about the **same** number?

- %
- 82.4 More now
- 0.4 Less now
- 9.9 About the same number
- 0.1 Other answer **(WRITE IN)**
- 7.2 (Don't Know)

Q539 *[CanUsFut]*
Do you think there will be **more**, **less**, or about the
same number of people taking cannabis in Northern
Ireland in 5 years' time compared with now?

- %
- 79.0 More now
- 2.6 Less
- 12.2 About the same number
- 6.3 (Don't Know)

Q540 *[CanYoung]*
Do you think cannabis is mainly used just by young
people nowadays?

- %
- 47.8 Yes
- 42.2 No
- 10.0 (Don't Know)

Q541 *[CanSelf]*
And have you yourself **ever tried** cannabis?

- %
- 9.7 Yes
- 90.0 No
- 0.2 (Don't Know)
- 0.1 (Refusal/NA)

Q542 **IF 'Yes' AT [CanSelf]**
[CanFreq]
Have you tried it often, occasionally, hardly ever
or only once?
%
0.3 Often
2.1 Occasionally
3.6 Hardly ever
3.6 Only once
-    Other answer **(WRITE IN)**
0.3 (Refusal/NA)

VERSION A: ASK ALL

Q545 [CanCrime]
CARD
How much do you agree or disagree that ...
... cannabis is a cause of crime and violence?

Q546 [CannabOK]
CARD AGAIN
(How much do you agree or disagree ...)
... cannabis isn't nearly as damaging as some people
think?

Q547 [CanLegAd]
CARD AGAIN
(How much do you agree or disagree that ...)
... if you legalise cannabis many more people will
become addicts?

	[CanCrime]	[CannabOK]	[CanLegAd]
	%	%	%
Strongly agree	30.7	2.0	23.5
Agree	37.6	21.0	41.5
Neither agree nor disagree	8.0	9.7	7.7
Disagree	17.5	40.7	20.1
Strongly disagree	1.7	18.2	2.4
(Don't Know)	4.4	8.4	4.7
(Refusal/NA)	-	0.1	0.2

Q548 [CanUsePr]
CARD AGAIN
(How much do you agree or disagree that ...) people
should **not** be prosecuted for possessing small amounts
of cannabis for their own use?

Q549 [CanSelPr]
CARD AGAIN
(How much do you agree or disagree that ...) people
who **sell** cannabis should always be prosecuted?

	[CanUsePr]	[CanSelPr]
	%	%
Strongly agree	3.0	59.5
Agree	19.8	30.5
Neither agree nor disagree	4.3	3.4
Disagree	45.4	2.9
Strongly disagree	25.5	2.8
(Don't Know)	2.0	0.9

43

Q550 [CanLegal]
CARD
Which of these statements comes closest to your own
view?
%
2.0 Taking cannabis should be legal, without
     restrictions
17.5 Taking cannabis should be legal, but it should only
     be available from licensed shops
78.8 Taking cannabis should remain illegal
1.6 (Don't Know)

44

244

HOUSING

ASK ALL

Q687 *[HomeType]*
Now a few questions on housing.
INTERVIEWER CODE FROM OBSERVATION AND CHECK WITH RESPONDENT
Would I be right in describing this accommodation as a ... **READ OUT ONE YOU THINK APPLIES**

%
39.9 ... detached house or bungalow,
24.0 ... semi-detached house or bungalow,
31.4 ... terraced house,
3.3 ... self-contained, purpose-built flat/maisonette (inc. in tenement block),
1.1 ... self-contained converted flat/maisonette,
0.2 ... room(s), not self-contained.
0.0 Other answer **(WRITE IN)**

Q691 *[HomeEst]*
May I just check, is your home part of a housing estate?
NOTE: MAY BE PUBLIC OR PRIVATE, BUT IT IS THE RESPONDENT'S VIEW WE WANT
%
41.5 Yes, part of estate
58.5 No

Q692 *[Tenure1]*
Does your household own or rent this accommodation?
PROBE IF OWNS: Outright or on a mortgage?
PROBE IF RENTS: From whom?
%
34.1 **OWNS:** Own (leasehold/freehold) outright
40.7 **OWNS:** Buying (leasehold/freehold) on mortgage
19.8 **RENTS:** Housing Executive
0.7 **RENTS:** Housing Association
0.2 **RENTS:** Property company
0.3 **RENTS:** Employer
0.4 **RENTS:** Other organisation
2.0 **RENTS:** Relative
0.0 **RENTS:** Other individual
0.0 **RENTS:** Housing Trust
0.4 Rent free, squatting, etc.
0.1 (Don't Know)

RELIGION AND ETHNIC ORIGIN

ASK ALL

Q699 *[Religion]*
Do you regard yourself as belonging to any particular religion?
IF YES: Which?
CODE ONE ONLY - DO NOT PROMPT
%
10.1 No religion
2.9 Christian - no denomination
37.5 Roman Catholic
15.3 Church of Ireland/Anglican
1.5 Baptist
4.3 Methodist
23.9 Presbyterian/Church of Scotland
0.1 Other Christian
0.0 Hindu
– Jewish
– Islam/Muslim
– Sikh
– Buddhist
0.1 Other non-Christian
0.5 Free Presbyterian
0.7 Brethren
0.4 United Reform Church (URC)/Congregational
1.9 Other Protestant
0.1 (Don't Know)
0.5 (Refusal/NA)

Q707 **IF NOT REFUSAL AT** *[Religion]*
[FamRelig]
In what religion, if any, were you brought up?
PROBE IF NECESSARY: What was your family's religion?
CODE ONE ONLY - DO NOT PROMPT
%
1.0 No religion
0.7 Christian - no denomination
40.6 Roman Catholic
19.6 Church of Ireland/Anglican
1.0 Baptist
4.6 Methodist
28.8 Presbyterian/Church of Scotland
– Other Christian
0.0 Hindu
0.2 Free Presbyterian
1.0 Brethren
0.3 United Reform Church (URC)/Congregational
1.6 Other Protestant
0.1 (Don't Know)
0.1 (Refusal/NA)

n = 1510

IF GIVING A RELIGION AT [Religion] OR AT [FamRelig]

Q715 *[ChAttend]*
Apart from such special occasions as weddings, funerals and baptisms, how often nowadays do you attend services or meetings connected with your religion?

%	**PROBE AS NECESSARY.**
46.2	Once a week or more
7.4	Less often but at least once in two weeks
10.6	Less often but at least once a month
9.2	Less often but at least twice a year
3.1	Less often but at least once a year
3.4	Less often
18.3	Never or practically never
0.4	Varies too much to say
0.6	(Refusal/NA)

ASK ALL

Q716 *[RaceOrig]*
CARD
To which of these groups do you consider you belong?

%	**CODE ONE ONLY**
-	**BLACK**: of African or Caribbean or other origin
0.0	**ASIAN**: of Indian origin
-	**ASIAN**: of Pakistani origin
-	**ASIAN**: of Bangladeshi origin
-	**ASIAN**: of Chinese origin
-	**ASIAN**: of other origin **(WRITE IN)**
99.7	**WHITE**
0.2	**MIXED ORIGIN (WRITE IN)**
0.1	(Refusal/NA)

47

n = 1510

CLASSIFICATION

ASK ALL

Q103 *[NumAdult]*
INTERVIEWER: YOU ARE GOING TO ASK ABOUT ALL THE ADULTS AGED 18 OR OVER IN THE HOUSEHOLD. STARTING WITH THE HOH, LIST ALL ADULTS IN DESCENDING ORDER OF AGE. Including yourself, how many adults are there in your household, that is, people aged 18 and over whose main residence this is and who are catered for by the same person as yourself or share living accommodation with you?

%	**ENTER NUMBER OF PERSONS AGED 18 AND OVER**
15.6	1 person
50.4	2 persons
18.7	3 persons
9.8	4 persons
3.3	5 persons
2.2	6 persons

Q175 *[NumChild]*
And how many people are there in your household aged **under 18** (INCLUDING CHILDREN)?

%	
55.6	None
15.9	1 child
16.3	2 children
7.9	3 children
2.9	4 children
1.2	5 children
0.1	6 children
0.2	7 children

dv *[Househld]*

%	NUMBER OF PERSONS IN HOUSEHOLD INCLUDING RESPONDENT.
11.9	1 person
25.7	2 persons
20.2	3 persons
19.8	4 persons
11.2	5 persons
6.5	6 persons
2.8	7 persons
1.3	8 persons
0.3	9 persons
0.3	10 persons

dv *[RMarStat]*

%	RESPONDENT'S MARITAL STATUS
62.4	Married
2.4	Cohabiting
20.4	Single, no children
1.6	Single parent
8.2	Widowed
1.9	Divorced
3.2	Separated

48

n = 1510

dv [RSex]
RESPONDENT'S SEX
%
44.2 Male
55.8 Female

dv [RAge]
RESPONDENT'S AGE
Median: 44 years

dv [RResp]
WHETHER RESPONDENT HAS LEGAL RESPONSIBILITY FOR THE
ACCOMMODATION (INCLUDING JOINT OR SHARE RESPONSIBILITY)
%
79.5 Legally responsible
20.5 Not legally responsible

Q743 [SlfMxSch]
Did you ever attend a mixed or integrated school,
that is, a school with fairly large numbers of **both**
Catholic **and** Protestant children?
IF YES: In Northern Ireland or somewhere else?
%
15.6 Yes, in Northern Ireland
4.0 Yes, somewhere else
80.4 No, did not

Q744 [OthChild]
Apart from people you have already mentioned who live
in your household, have you any (other) children,
including stepchildren, who grew up in your household?
'CHILDREN' MEANS THOSE THEN AGED UNDER 18, AND
INCLUDES THOSE NO LONGER LIVING.
%
29.3 Yes
70.6 No
0.1 (Refusal/NA)

IF THERE ARE CHILDREN UNDER 18 IN THE HOUSEHOLD OR
ANSWERED 'Yes' AT [OthChild]
Q745 [ChdMxSch]
And have any of your children ever attended a mixed
or integrated school, with fairly large numbers of
both Catholics and Protestants attending?
IF YES: In Northern Ireland or somewhere else?
%
12.3 Yes, in Northern Ireland
1.6 Yes, somewhere else
52.8 No, did not
0.0 (Don't Know)

ASK ALL
Q746 [DutyResp]
Who is the person **mainly** responsible for general
domestic duties in this household?
%
49.9 Respondent mainly
34.2 Someone else mainly
15.9 Duties shared equally

n = 1510

IF 'Someone else mainly' OR 'Duties shared
equally' AT [DutyResp]
PLEASE SPECIFY THIS PERSON'S/THESE PEOPLE'S
RELATIONSHIP TO RESPONDENT
%
Q747
28.6 Wife/female partner of respondent [DutyWife]
10.4 Mother/mother-in-law of respondent [DutyMum]
4.1 Husband/male partner of respondent [DutyHusb]
4.2 Other female in household [DutyFem]
3.2 Other male in household [DutyMale]
2.2 Other answer [DutyOthr]

IF THERE ARE CHILDREN UNDER 18 IN THE HOUSEHOLD at
[NumChild]
Q749 [ChldResp]
Who is the person mainly responsible for the general
care of the child(ren) here?
%
21.6 Respondent mainly
14.9 Someone else mainly
7.9 Care shared equally

IF 'Someone else mainly' OR 'Care shared equally'
AT [ChldResp]
PLEASE SPECIFY THIS PERSON'S/THESE PEOPLE'S
RELATIONSHIP TO RESPONDENT
%
Q750
14.3 Wife/female partner of respondent [ChldWife]
5.1 Mother/mother-in-law of respondent [ChldMum]
2.7 Husband/male partner of respondent [ChldHusb]
0.8 Other female in household [ChldFem]
0.4 Other male in household [ChldMale]
0.1 Other answer [ChldOthr]

ASK ALL
Q752 [TEA]
How old were you when you completed your continuous
full-time education?
PROBE IF NECESSARY
%
34.8 15 or under
27.8 16
11.7 17
9.4 18
13.7 19 or over
0.5 Still at school
2.0 Still at college or university
- Other answer (WRITE IN)

Q755 [SchQual]
CARD
Have you passed any of the examinations on this card?
%
49.6 Yes
50.3 No
0.1 (Don't Know)

Q756
IF 'Yes' AT [SchQual]
Which ones? PROBE: Any others?
CODE ALL THAT APPLY

%
11.6 CSE Grades 2-5   [EdQual1]
      GCSE Grades D-G

41.2 CSE-Grade 1   [EdQual2]
      GCE 'O'level
      GCSE - Grades A-C
      School certificate
      Scottish (SCE) Ordinary
      Scottish School-leaving Certificate lower grade
      SUPE Ordinary
      Northern Ireland Junior Certificate

18.6 GCE 'A' level/'S' level   [EdQual3]
      Higher school certificate
      Matriculation
      Scottish SCE/SLC/SUPE at Higher grade
      Northern Ireland Senior Certificate

 0.6 Overseas school leaving exam or certificate [EdQual4]

 0.1 (Refusal)
      (Don't know)

ASK ALL
Q757
[PSchQual]
CARD
And have you passed any of the exams or got any of
the qualifications on **this** card?

%
48.3 Yes
51.7 No

Q758 IF 'Yes' AT [PSchQual]
Which ones? PROBE: Any others?
CODE ALL THAT APPLY

%
 6.6 Recognised trade apprenticeship **completed**   [EdQual5]
15.6 RSA/other clerical, commercial qualification   [EdQual6]
 8.5 City & Guilds Certificate - Craft/Intermediate/   [EdQual7]
      Ordinary/ Part I
 4.5 City & Guilds Certificate - Advanced/Final/   [EdQual8]
      Part II or Part III
 1.2 City & Guilds Certificate - Full technological   [EdQual9]
 3.8 BEC/TEC General/Ordinary National Certificate [EdQual10]
      (ONC) or Diploma (OND)
 2.9 BEC/TEC Higher/Higher National Certificate   [EdQual11]
      (HNC) or Diploma (HND)
 4.6 Teacher training qualification   [EdQual12]
 3.5 Nursing qualification   [EdQual13]
 2.5 Other technical or business qualification/   [EdQual14]
      certificate
 8.6 University or CNAA degree or diploma   [EdQual15]
 4.7 Other recognised academic or vocational   [EdQual16]
      qualification (**WRITE IN**)

Q762
IF NOT 'In paid work' OR 'Waiting to take up
paid work' AT [REconAct]
[JobChk]
May I just check, have you **ever** had a job?

%
44.7 Yes
 5.1 No, never

ASK ALL WHO HAVE EVER WORKED (IF 'In paid work'
OR 'Waiting to take up paid work' AT [REconAct]
OR 'Yes' AT [JobChk])
Q763
[RTitle] (NOT ON THE DATA FILE)
IF 'In paid work' AT [REconAct]: Now I want to ask
you about your present job. What is your job?
PROBE IF NECESSARY: What is the name or title of the job?
IF 'Waiting to take up paid work' AT [REconAct]: Now
I want to ask you about your future job. What is
your job?
PROBE IF NECESSARY: What is the name or title of the job?
IF NOT IN PAID WORK (OR WAITING TO TAKE UP PAID WORK)
BUT EVER HAD JOB IN THE PAST (IF 'Yes' AT [JobChk]):
Now I want to ask you about your last job. What was
your job?
PROBE IF NECESSARY: What was the name or title of the job?
Open question (Maximum of 50 characters)

Q764
[RTypeWk] (NOT ON THE DATA FILE)
What kind of work *(do/will/did)* you do most of the time?
IF RELEVANT: What materials/machinery *(do/will/did)*
you use?
Open question (Maximum of 50 characters)

Q765
[RTrain] (NOT ON THE DATA FILE)
What training or qualifications *(are/were)* needed for
that job?
Open question (Maximum of 50 characters)

Q766
[RSuper2]
(Do/Will/Did) you directly supervise or *(are you/will*
you be/were you) directly responsible for the work of
any other people?

%
33.9 Yes
65.9 No
 0.2 (Refusal/NA)

Q767 IF 'Yes' AT [RSuper2]
[RMany]
How many?
Median: 6

ASK ALL WHO HAVE EVER WORKED (IF 'In paid work' OR 'Waiting to take up paid work' AT [REconAct] OR 'Yes' AT [JobChckl]

Q768 [RSupMan]
Can I just check, (are you/will you be/were you) a
... **READ OUT** ...
%
17.0 ...manager,
15.4 ...foreman or supervisor,
67.3 or not?
0.2 (Refusal/NA)

Q769 [REmplyee]
Can I just check: (are you/will you be/were you)
... **READ OUT** ...
%
86.8 ... an employee
13.0 or, self-employed?
0.1 (Don't Know)
0.1 (Refusal/NA)

IF 'an employee' AT [REmplyee]
Q770 [Premises]
(Is/Was) where you (work/will work/worked) your employer's **only** premises, or (are/were) there other premises elsewhere?
%
29.2 Employer's only premises
57.2 Employer has other premises elsewhere
0.3 (Refusal/NA)

ASK ALL WHO HAVE EVER WORKED (IF 'In paid work' OR 'Waiting to take up paid work' AT [REconAct] OR 'Yes' AT [JobChckl]
Q771 [REmpMake] **(NOT ON THE DATA FILE)**
What (does/did) your employer/you make or do at the place where you usually (work/will work/worked) (from)?
Open question (Maximum of 50 characters)

Q772 [REmpWork]
Including yourself, how many people (are/were) employed at the place where you usually (work/will work/worked) (from)?
IF SELF-EMPLOYED: (Do/Will/Did) you have any employees?
IF YES: PROBE FOR CORRECT PRECODE
%
4.1 None
22.0 Under 10
18.4 10-24
22.6 25-99
19.9 100-499
12.0 500 or more
0.8 (Don't Know)
0.2 (Refusal/NA)

Q773 [RPartFul]
(Is/Was) the job ... **READ OUT** ...
%
81.6 ...full-time (30+ HOURS)
18.2 or, part-time (10-29 HOURS)?
0.1 (Don't Know)
0.1 (Refusal/NA)

ASK ALL
Q788 [UnionSA]
Are you **now** a member of a trade union or staff association?
CODE FIRST TO APPLY
%
20.8 Yes, trade union
3.2 Yes, staff association
75.7 No
0.1 (Don't Know)
0.1 (Refusal/NA)

IF 'No' AT [UnionSA]
Q789 [TUSAEver]
Have you **ever** been a member of a trade union or staff association?
CODE FIRST TO APPLY
%
25.1 Yes, trade union
1.7 Yes, staff association
48.8 No
0.1 (Don't Know)
0.2 (Refusal/NA)

ASK IF MARRIED OR COHABITING
Q793 [SEconAct] **(Figures refer to the first answer on the list)**
CARD
Which of these descriptions applies to what your (husband/wife/partner) was doing last week, that is the seven days ending last Sunday?
PROBE: Any others?
CODE ALL THAT APPLY
%
1.0 In full-time education (not paid for by employer, including on vacation)
0.1 On government training/employment programme (e.g. Employment Training, Youth Training, etc.)
56.4 In paid work (or away temporarily) for at least 10 hours in week
0.1 Waiting to take up paid work already accepted
4.6 Unemployed and registered at a benefit office
0.4 Unemployed, **not** registered, but actively looking for a job
0.3 Unemployed, wanting a job (of at least 10 hours a week) but **not** actively looking for a job
6.8 Permanently sick or disabled
11.7 Wholly retired from work
18.1 Looking after the home
0.5 (Doing something else) **(WRITE IN)**

IF SPOUSE/PARTNER IS NOT IN WORK (IF 'In full-time education', 'On government training scheme', 'Unemployed', 'Permanently sick', 'Wholly retired', 'Looking after home', 'Doing something else' AT [SEconAct])

Q794 [SLastJob]
How long ago did your (husband/wife/partner) last have a paid job (other than the government programme you mentioned) of at least 10 hours a week?

%
4.7 Within past 12 months
9.3 Over 1, up to 5 years ago
10.0 Over 5, up to 10 years ago
9.4 Over 10, up to 20 years ago
5.3 Over 20 years ago
4.5 Never had a paid job of 10+ hours a week
0.1 (Don't Know)

ASK ALL WHOSE SPOUSE/PARTNER HAS EVER WORKED (IF 'In paid work' OR 'Waiting to take up paid work' AT [SEconAct] OR 'Within past 12 months'/'Over 1, up to 5 years ago'/'Over 5, up to 10 years ago'/'Over 10, up to 20 years ago'/'Over 20 years ago' AT [SLastJob])

Q795 [STitle] (NOT ON THE DATA FILE)
IF SPOUSE/PARTNER 'In paid work' AT [SEconAct]: Now I want to ask you about your husband's/wife's/partner's present job. What is (his/her) job?
PROBE IF NECESSARY: What is the name or title of that job?
IF SPOUSE/PARTNER 'Waiting to take up paid work' AT [SEconAct]: Now I want to ask you about your (husband's/wife's/partner's) future job. What is (his/her) job?
PROBE IF NECESSARY: What is the name or title of that job?
IF NOT IN PAID WORK (OR WAITING TO TAKE UP PAID WORK) BUT HAS EVER WORKED IN THE PAST (IF 'Within past 12 months'/'Over 1, up to 5 years ago'/'Over 5, up to 10 years ago'/'Over 10, up to 20 years ago'/'Over 20 years ago' AT [SLastJob]): Now I want to ask you about your (husband's/wife's/partner's) last job. What was (his/her) job?
PROBE IF NECESSARY: What was the name or title of that job?
Open question (Maximum of 50 characters)

Q796 [STypeWk] (NOT ON THE DATA FILE)
What kind of work (does/will/did) (he/she) do most of the time?
IF RELEVANT: What materials/machinery (does/will/did) (he/she) use?
Open question (Maximum of 50 characters)

Q797 [STrain] (NOT ON THE DATA FILE)
What training or qualifications (are/were) needed for that job?
Open question (Maximum of 50 characters)

Q798 [SSuper2]
(Does/Will/Did) (he/she) directly supervise or (is/will/was) (he/she) (be) directly responsible for the work of any other people?
%
34.5 Yes
64.7 No
0.3 (Don't Know)
0.5 (Refusal/NA)

IF 'Yes' AT [SSuper2]
Q799 [SMany]
How many?
Median: 5

ASK ALL WHOSE SPOUSE/PARTNER HAS EVER WORKED (IF 'In paid work' OR 'Waiting to take up paid work' AT [SEconAct] OR 'Within past 12 months'/'Over 1, up to 5 years ago'/'Over 5, up to 10 years ago'/'Over 10, up to 20 years ago'/'Over 20 years ago' AT [SLastJob])

Q800 [SSupMan]
Can I just check, (is/will/was) (he/she) (be) a ...
READ OUT ...
21.3 ...manager,
15.0 ...foreman or supervisor,
63.3 or not?
0.4 (Refusal/NA)

Q801 [SEmploye]
Can I just check: (is/will/was) (he/she) (be) ...
READ OUT ...
83.8 ... an employee
15.8 or, self-employed?
0.3 (Refusal/NA)

Q802 [SEmpMake] (NOT ON THE DATA FILE)
What (does/did) (his/her) employer (IF SELF-EMPLOYED: (he/she)) make or do at the place where (he/she) usually (works/will work/worked) (from)?
Open question (Maximum of 50 characters)

Q803 [SEmpWork]
Including (himself/herself), how many people (are/were) employed at the place where (he/she) usually works/will work/worked) (from)?
IF SELF-EMPLOYED: (Does/Will/Did) (he/she) have any employees?
IF YES: PROBE FOR CORRECT PRECODE
%
3.3 None
25.1 Under 10
16.1 10-24
21.9 25-99
19.5 100-499
11.6 500 or more
2.2 (Don't Know)
0.3 (Refusal/NA)

Q804 [SPartFul]
(Is/Was) the job ... **READ OUT** ...
%
82.9 ..full-time (30+ HOURS)
16.8 or, part-time (10-29 HOURS)?
0.3 (Refusal/NA)

IF MARRIED OR COHABITING

Q819 [ReligSam]
Is your (husband/wife/partner) the same religion as you?
PROBE IF NECESSARY
%
89.7 Yes, same religion
8.4 No, not same religion
1.7 No religion at all
0.2 (Refusal/NA)

ASK ALL

Q820 [CarOwn]
Do you, or does anyone else in your household, own or have the regular use of a car or a van?
%
78.0 Yes
22.0 No
0.0 (Refusal/NA)

Q821 [AnyBNew]
CARD
Do you or does your (husband/wife/partner) receive any of the **state** benefits on this card at present?
%
36.9 Yes
62.7 No
0.1 (Don't Know)
0.3 (Refusal/NA)

IF 'Yes' AT [AnyBNew]
Q822 Which ones?
Any others?
CODE ALL THAT APPLY
%
2.1 Unemployment benefit [BenftN1]
15.6 Income support [BenftN2]
3.2 One-parent benefit [BenftN3]
3.3 Family credit [BenftN4]
8.6 Housing benefit (rent-rebate) [BenftN5]
1.8 Statutory sick pay/sickness benefit [BenftN6]
10.0 Invalidity benefit [BenftN7]
2.7 Disability living allowance [BenftN8]
3.4 Widow's pension [BenftN10]
1.3 Severe disablement allowance [BenftN13]
0.6 Attendance allowance [BenftN14]
0.1 Other state benefit(s) (**PLEASE SAY WHAT**) [BenftN11]
0.4 (Don't know)
0.4 (Refusal)

ASK ALL
Q837 [Disab]
Do you have any long-standing health problems or disabilities which limit what you can do at work, at home or in your leisure time?
INTERVIEWER: 'LONG-STANDING' MEANS HAD PROBLEM FOR 3 YEARS OR MORE OR EXPECT PROBLEM TO LAST FOR 3 YEARS OR MORE
%
22.5 Yes
77.2 No
0.3 (Refusal/NA)

Q838 [EvrLivGB]
Have you **ever** lived in mainland Britain for more than a year?
%
16.9 Yes
83.0 No
0.1 (Refusal/NA)

Q839 [EvrLivER]
And have you **ever** lived in the Republic of Ireland for more than a year?
%
4.1 Yes
95.8 No
0.0 (Refusal/NA)

Q840 [UniNatID]
Generally speaking, do you think of yourself as a unionist, a nationalist or neither?
%
41.1 Unionist
19.3 Nationalist
39.1 Neither
0.1 (Don't Know)
0.5 (Refusal/NA)

IF 'Unionist' OR 'Nationalist' AT [UniNatID]
Q841 [UniNatSt]
Would you call yourself a very strong (unionist/nationalist), fairly strong, or not very strong?
%
7.0 Very strong
26.8 Fairly strong
26.5 Not very strong
0.6 (Refusal/NA)

ASK ALL
Q842 [HhIncome]
CARD
Which of the letters on this card represents the total income of your household from **all** sources **before** tax? Please just tell me the letter.
NOTE: INCLUDES INCOME FROM BENEFITS, SAVINGS, ETC.

ASK ALL RESPONDENTS WHO ARE WORKING (IF 'In
paid work' AT [REconAct])

Q843 [REarn]
CARD AGAIN
Which of the letters on this card represents your **own**
gross or total **earnings**, before deduction of income
tax and national insurance?

n = 1510

	[HhIncome] %	[REarn] %
Less that £3,999	5.7	4.9
£4,000 - £5,999	10.4	5.4
£6,000 - £7,999	8.5	9.0
£8,000 - £9,999	7.0	5.7
£10,000 - £11,999	6.2	5.1
£12,000 - £14,999	7.5	4.5
£15,000 - £17,999	7.2	3.9
£18,000 - £19,999	4.8	1.7
£20,000 - £22,999	4.6	2.2
£23,000 - £25,999	5.1	1.6
£26,000 - £28,999	3.5	0.8
£29,000 - £31,999	3.8	0.5
£32,000 - £34,999	2.0	0.5
£35,000 - £37,999	1.7	0.2
£38,000 - £40,999	1.2	0.2
£41,000 or more	5.2	1.4
(Don't Know)	11.4	0.9
(Refusal/NA)	4.2	1.7

ASK ALL
Q844 [OwnShare]
Do you (or your (husband/wife/partner)) own any
shares quoted on the Stock Exchange, including unit
trusts?

%
17.6 Yes
81.9 No
0.1 (Don't Know)
0.5 (Refusal/NA)

VERSION B QUESTIONNAIRE

n = 744

ECONOMIC PROSPECTS (VERSION B)

VERSION B: ASK ALL
Q555 [Prices]
Now I would like to ask you about two economic
problems - **inflation** and **unemployment**.
First, **inflation**: in a year from now, do you expect
prices generally to have gone up, to have stayed the
same, or to have gone down?
IF GONE UP OR GONE DOWN: By a lot or a little?

Q556 [Unemp]
Second, **unemployment**: in a year from now, do you
expect unemployment to have gone up, to have stayed
the same, or to have gone down?
IF GONE UP OR GONE DOWN: By a lot or a little?

	[Prices] %	[Unemp] %
To have gone up by a lot	32.9	8.4
To have gone up by a little	56.0	23.0
To have stayed the same	7.8	32.3
To have gone down by a little	2.1	32.3
To have gone down by a lot	0.1	2.4
(Don't Know)	1.0	1.5

Q557 [UnempInfl]
If the government **had** to choose between keeping
down inflation or keeping down unemployment, to
which do you think it should give highest priority?
%
30.1 Keeping down inflation
68.6 Keeping down unemployment
0.3 (Both equally)
1.0 (Don't Know)

Q560 [Concern]
Which do you think is of the most concern to **you
and your family ... READ OUT ...**
%
55.7 ... inflation,
43.5 or, unemployment?
0.4 (Both equally)
0.1 (Neither a threat)
0.3 (Don't Know)

Q563 [Industry]
Looking ahead over the next year, do you think the
UK's general industrial performance will improve,
stay much the same, or decline?
IF IMPROVE OR DECLINE: By a lot or a little?
%
2.9 Improve a lot
24.7 Improve a little
54.6 Stay much the same
10.3 Decline a little
2.6 Decline a lot
5.0 (Don't Know)

Q564 *[IncomGap]*
Thinking of income levels generally in the UK today,
would you say that the **gap** between those with high
incomes and those with low incomes is ... **READ OUT** ...

%
87.1 ... too large,
8.6 about right,
2.1 or, too small?
2.2 (Don't Know)

Q565 *[TaxHi]*
CARD
Generally, how would you describe **levels of taxation?**
Firstly, for those with **high** incomes? Please choose
a phrase from this card.

Q566 *[TaxMid]*
CARD AGAIN
Next for those with **middle** incomes? Please choose a
phrase from this card.

Q567 *[TaxLow]*
CARD AGAIN
Next for those with **low** incomes? Please choose a
phrase from this card.

	[TaxHi]	*[TaxMid]*	*[TaxLow]*
	%	%	%
Much too high	3.5	3.6	28.5
Too high	9.9	35.1	52.9
About right	31.2	52.0	14.4
Too low	39.5	5.4	1.1
Much too low	12.6	0.7	-
(Don't Know)	3.4	3.2	3.1

Q568 *[SRInc]*
Among which group would you place yourself ... **READ
OUT** ...

%
3.7 ... high income,
44.3 middle income,
50.3 or, low income?
1.5 (Don't Know)

Q569 *[HIncDiff]*
CARD
Which of the phrases on this card would you say comes
closest to your feelings about your household's
income these days?

%
27.7 Living comfortably on present income
47.8 Coping on present income
17.9 Finding it difficult on present income
6.4 Finding it very difficult on present income
0.1 Other answer **(WRITE IN)**
0.1 (Don't Know)

Q572 *[HIncPast]*
Looking back over the **last year** or so, would you say
your household's income has ... **READ OUT** ...

%
49.6 ... fallen behind prices,
43.7 kept up with prices,
6.3 or, gone up by more than prices?
0.5 (Don't Know)

Q573 *[HIncXpct]*
And looking forward to the **year ahead**, do you expect
your household's income will ... **READ OUT** ...

%
44.6 ... fall behind prices,
45.4 keep up with prices,
8.5 or, go up by more than prices?
1.5 (Don't Know)

61

62

253

TAXATION/PUBLIC SPENDING (VERSION B)

n = 744

VERSION B: ASK ALL

Q578 [SizeTax]
CARD
About how much do you think that an extra one penny in the pound on the basic rate of income tax would cost your household?
IF RESPONDENT DOES NOT KNOW, ENCOURAGE THEM TO GIVE AN ESTIMATE
IF THEY CAN'T, CODE 'DON'T KNOW'

Q579 [SizeVAT]
CARD AGAIN
About how much do you think that a one percentage point increase in the rate of VAT (that is, from 17½ percent to 18½ percent) would cost your household?
IF RESPONDENT DOES NOT KNOW, ENCOURAGE THEM TO GIVE AN ESTIMATE
IF THEY CAN'T, CODE 'DON'T KNOW'

		[SizeTax]	[SizeVat]
		%	%
A	Nothing	16.6	1.6
B	<£1 per week - <£50 per year	11.3	11.8
C	£1-2 per week - £50-£100 per year	18.4	18.1
D	£2-3 per week - £100-£150 per year	13.9	18.6
E	>£3 per week - >£150 per year	18.0	29.2
	(Don't Know)	21.5	20.7
	(Refusal/NA)	0.3	0.1

Q580 [SpdPre1]
Now some questions about government spending and the taxes to pay for it. Suppose that if spending goes up, then taxes have to be raised to pay for it. If it goes down, taxes can be cut.

ASK RANDOM HALF OF RESPONDENTS (SERIAL NUMBERS NOT DIVISIBLE BY 4)   n = 388

Q582 [SpdPre2A]
HAND OVER THE GREEN ANSWER SHEET.
Here are seven areas of government spending.
POINT TO THE SEVEN SPENDING AREAS.
Suppose that the government had to choose between these three options ... READ OUT ... increasing spending and putting up income tax rates by one penny in the pound, keeping spending and income tax about the same as now, and cutting spending and taking one penny in the pound off the rate of income tax.
POINT TO THREE TAX/SPENDING OPTIONS.

Q584 [SpdPre3]
For each of these seven areas of government spending, which option do you think would be best for the country as a whole?
Please tick one box on each line. If you change your mind as you go through, just cross your old answer out. Please tell me when you are ready.

Q585 [H1hSpdC1]
Now I'd just like to make a note of your answers.
RETRIEVE GREEN ANSWER SHEET FROM RESPONDENT.
(Which of these would be best for the country as a whole?)
HEALTH:

n = 388

Q586 [PolSpdC1]
(Which of these would be best for the country as a whole?)
POLICE:

Q587 [EdcpdC1]
(Which of these would be best for the country as a whole?)
EDUCATION:

	[H1hSpdC1]	[PolSpdC1]	[EdcSpdC1]
	%	%	%
Increase spending and taxes	65.2	11.6	61.9
Keep spending and taxes the same	26.3	55.4	29.9
Cut spending and taxes	4.9	28.6	3.9
(None of these)	0.5	1.0	1.0
(Don't Know)	3.1	3.4	3.6

Q588 [DfcSpdC1]
(Which of these would be best for the country as a whole?)
DEFENCE:

Q589 [EnvSpdC1]
(Which of these would be best for the country as a whole?)
THE ENVIRONMENT:

	[DfcSpdC1]	[EnvSpdC1]
	%	%
Increase spending and taxes	7.7	28.6
Keep spending and taxes the same	42.5	54.6
Cut spending and taxes	43.8	12.4
(None of these)	1.3	1.0
(Don't Know)	4.6	3.4

Q590 [PTrSpdC1]
(Which of these would be best for the country as a whole?)
PUBLIC TRANSPORT:

Q591 [CulSpdC1]
(Which of these would be best for the country as a whole?)
CULTURE AND THE ARTS:

	[PTrSpdC1]	[CulSpdC1]
	%	%
Increase spending and taxes	21.9	6.7
Keep spending and taxes the same	61.1	52.6
Cut spending and taxes	13.4	35.1
(None of these)	0.3	2.1
(Don't Know)	3.4	3.6

Q599 [SpdPre4]
HAND OVER GREY ANSWER SHEET.
Now I want to ask you which options you think would be best for **you and your household**. Again suppose that, for each of the seven areas of government spending, the government had to choose between these three options.
POINT TO THE THREE TAX/SPENDING OPTIONS.
Please tick **one** box per line.
If you change your mind as you go through, just cross your old answer out.

Q600 [HlhSpdR1]
Now I'd just like to make a note of your answers.
RETRIEVE GREY ANSWER SHEET FROM RESPONDENT.
(Which of these would be best for **you and your household**?)
HEALTH:

Q601 [PolSpdR1]
(Which of these would be best for **you and your household**?)
POLICE:

Q602 [EdcSpdR1]
(Which of these would be best for **you and your household**?)
EDUCATION:

	[HlhSpdR1]	[PolSpdR1]	[EdcSpdR1]
	%	%	%
Increase spending and taxes	62.4	11.9	47.7
Keep spending and taxes the same	28.9	54.6	39.2
Cut spending and taxes	5.2	28.9	8.8
(None of these)	1.3	1.5	1.5
(Don't Know)	2.3	2.8	2.8
(NA)	-	0.3	-

Q603 [DfcSpdR1]
(Which of these would be best for **you and your household**?)
DEFENCE:

Q604 [EnvSpdR1]
(Which of these would be best for **you and your household**?)
THE ENVIRONMENT:

	[DfcSpdR1]	[EnvSpdR1]
	%	%
Increase spending and taxes	7.0	25.5
Keep spending and taxes the same	39.4	53.3
Cut spending and taxes	48.0	16.5
(None of these)	2.3	1.3
(Don't Know)	3.4	3.3

Q605 [PtrSpdR1]
(Which of these would be best for **you and your household**?)
PUBLIC TRANSPORT:

Q606 [CulSpdR1]
(Which of these would be best for **you and your household**?)
CULTURE AND THE ARTS:

	[PtrSpdR1]	[CulSpdR1]
	%	%
Increase spending and taxes	18.6	7.7
Keep spending and taxes the same	52.1	46.4
Cut spending and taxes	25.8	40.2
(None of these)	0.5	2.6
(Don't Know)	3.3	3.1

ASK RANDOM HALF OF RESPONDENTS (SERIAL NUMBERS DIVISIBLE BY 4)

Q583 [SpdPre2B]
HAND OVER THE GOLD ANSWER SHEET.
Here are seven areas of government spending.
POINT TO THE SEVEN SPENDING AREAS.
Suppose that the government had to choose between these three options ... **READ OUT** ... increasing spending and raising taxes for **every adult** in the United Kingdom by £35 a year, keeping spending and taxes about the same as now, or cutting spending and reducing tax for every adult in the United Kingdom by £35 a year.
POINT TO THE THREE TAX/SPENDING OPTIONS.

Q584 [SpdPre3]
For each of these seven areas of government spending, which option do you think would be best for the **country as a whole**?
Please tick **one** box on each line. If you change your mind as you go through, just cross your old answer out. Please tell me when you are ready.

Q592 [HlhSpdC2]
Now I'd just like to make a note of your answers.
RETRIEVE GOLD ANSWER SHEET FROM RESPONDENT.
(Which of these would be best for **the country as a whole**?)
HEALTH:

Q593 [PolSpdC2]
(Which of these would be best for **the country as a whole**?)
POLICE:

Q594 [EdcSpdC2]
(Which of these would be best for **the country as a whole**?)
EDUCATION:

	[HlhSpdC2]	[PolSpdC2]	[EdcSpdC2]
	%	%	%
Increase spending and taxes	63.2	14.0	6.2
Keep spending and taxes the same	23.6	51.1	28.9
Cut spending and taxes	8.7	30.6	5.1
(None of these)	1.1	0.8	0.6
(Don't Know)	2.8	2.8	2.8
(Refusal/NA)	0.6	0.8	0.6

Q595 [DfcSpdC2]
(Which of these would be best for **the country as a whole**?)
DEFENCE:

Q596 [EnvSpdC2]
(Which of these would be best for **the country as a whole**?)
THE ENVIRONMENT:

	[DfcSpdC2]	[EnvSpdC2]
	%	%
Increase spending and taxes	5.1	30.1
Keep spending and taxes the same	39.0	55.3
Cut spending and taxes	52.0	10.7
(None of these)	0.6	0.6
(Don't Know)	3.1	3.1
(Refusal/NA)	0.6	0.6

Q597 [PTrSpdC2]
(Which of these would be best for **the country as a whole**?)
PUBLIC TRANSPORT:

Q598 [CulSpdC2]
(Which of these would be best for **the country as a whole**?)
CULTURE AND THE ARTS:

	[PTrSpdC2]	[CulSpdC2]
	%	%
Increase spending and taxes	25.0	8.4
Keep spending and taxes the same	59.6	49.7
Cut spending and taxes	11.0	37.4
(None of these)	0.8	0.8
(Don't Know)	3.1	3.4
(Refusal/NA)	0.6	0.6

Q599 [SpdPre4]
HAND OVER MAUVE ANSWER SHEET.
Now I want to ask you which options you think would be best for **you and your household**. Again suppose that, for each of the seven areas of government spending, the government had to choose between these three options.
POINT TO THE THREE TAX/SPENDING OPTIONS.
Please tick **one** box per line.
If you change your mind as you go through, just cross your old answer out.

Q607 [HlhSpdR2]
Now I'd just like to make a note of your answers.
RETRIEVE MAUVE ANSWER SHEET FROM RESPONDENT.
(Which of these would be best for **you and your household**?)
HEALTH:

Q608 [PolSpdR2]
(Which of these would be best for **you and your household**?)
POLICE:

Q609 [EdcSpdR2]
(Which of these would be best for **you and your household**?)
EDUCATION:

	[HlhSpdR2]	[PolSpdR2]	[EdcSpdR2]
	%	%	%
Increase spending and taxes	64.3	14.3	53.1
Keep spending and taxes the same	22.8	46.6	31.7
Cut spending and taxes	8.1	33.7	9.6
(None of these)	1.1	1.7	1.7
(Don't Know)	3.1	3.1	3.1
(Refusal/NA)	0.6	0.8	0.8

Q610 [DfcSpdR2]
(Which of these would be best for **you and your household**?)
DEFENCE:

Q611 [EnvSpdR2]
(Which of these would be best for **you and your household**?)
THE ENVIRONMENT:

	[DfcSpdR2]	[EnvSpdR2]
	%	%
Increase spending and taxes	4.5	25.0
Keep spending and taxes the same	39.3	53.4
Cut spending and taxes	50.6	16.9
(None of these)	1.4	1.1
(Don't Know)	3.4	3.1
(Refusal/NA)	0.8	0.8

Q612 [PTrSpdR2]
(Which of these would be best for **you and your household**?)
PUBLIC TRANSPORT:

Q613 [CulSpdR2]
(Which of these would be best for **you and your household**?)
CULTURE AND THE ARTS:

	[PTrSpdR2]	[CulSpdR2]
	%	%
Increase spending and taxes	21.3	8.1
Keep spending and taxes the same	52.8	43.3
Cut spending and taxes	20.8	42.7
(None of these)	1.1	1.4
(Don't Know)	3.4	3.7
(Refusal/NA)	0.6	0.8

VERSION B: ASK ALL

Q614 *[GvChTaxP]*
CARD
Suppose the government **did** decide to increase taxes to pay for extra spending, and suppose it had just three options ... **READ OUT** ...
... to put up income tax for **all taxpayers**, by 1p in the pound to 26p
OR
... to put income tax up **only for higher taxpayers**, but by 5p in the pound, to 45p
OR
... to raise **VAT** by one percent to 18% per cent on all taxable goods and services.

Q615 *[GvChTax1]*
CARD AGAIN
If these were the only options for the government, which **one** do you think that it should choose?

Q618 *[GvChTax2]*
CARD AGAIN
And which one do you think should be the government's second choice?

	[GvChTax1]	[GvChTax2]
	%	%
A penny in the pound for all taxpayers	27.5	49.5
Five pence in the pound for higher taxpayers	61.1	24.1
Raise VAT by one percent	7.2	20.9
Other answer (WRITE IN)	0.4	0.7
(Don't Know)	3.7	1.0
(Refusal/NA)	0.1	3.8

Q621 *[FamBTax]*
CARD AGAIN
Which one of these three would leave you and your family **best off?**

Q624 *[FamWTax]*
CARD AGAIN
And which one do you think would leave you and your family **worst off?**

	[FamBTax]	[FamWTax]
	%	%
A penny in the pound for all taxpayers	23.2	18.7
Five pence in the pound for higher taxpayers	63.1	9.0
Raise VAT by one percent	7.5	67.5
(Respondent not taxpayer)	0.1	0.1
Other answer (WRITE IN)	1.0	0.1
(Don't Know)	4.9	4.5
(Refusal/NA)	0.1	0.1

EDUCATION (VERSION B)

VERSION B: ASK ALL

Q630 *[EdSpend1]*
CARD
Now some questions about education. Which of the groups on this card, if any, would be your highest priority for **extra** government spending on education?
ONE CODE ONLY FOR HIGHEST PRIORITY

Q631 *[EdSpend2]*
CARD AGAIN
And which is your next highest priority?
ONE CODE ONLY FOR NEXT HIGHEST

	[EdSpend1]	[EdSpend2]
	%	%
Nursery or pre-school children	15.0	13.5
Primary school children	18.0	22.0
Secondary and grammar school children	20.1	23.9
Less able children with special needs	31.1	24.5
Students at colleges or universities	14.3	13.9
(None of these)	0.5	0.7
(Don't Know)	0.9	1.4
(Refusal/NA)	0.1	0.1

Q632 *[PrimImp1]*
CARD
Here are a number of things that some people think would improve education in our schools. Which do you think would be the **most** useful one for improving the education of children in **primary** schools – aged 5-11 years? Please look at the whole list before deciding.
CODE ONE ONLY

Q635 *[PrimImp2]*
CARD AGAIN
And which do you think would be the **next** most useful one for children in **primary** schools?
CODE ONE ONLY

	[PrimImp1]	[PrimImp2]
	%	%
More information available about individual schools	1.1	1.4
More links between parents and schools	8.6	13.9
More resources for buildings, books and equipment	16.2	21.7
Better quality teachers	10.4	11.8
Smaller class sizes	44.0	23.5
More emphasis on exams and tests	1.9	4.8
More emphasis on developing the child's skills and interests	15.8	20.7
Other (WRITE IN)	0.1	0.2
(Don't Know)	1.8	1.9
(Refusal/NA)	0.1	0.1

257

Q638 [SecImp1]
CARD
And which do you think would be the **most** useful thing for improving the education of children in **secondary and grammar** schools – aged 11-18 years?
CODE ONE ONLY

Q641 [SecImp2]
CARD AGAIN
And which do you think would be the **next** most useful one for children in **secondary and grammar** schools?
CODE ONE ONLY

	[SecImp1]	[SecImp2]
	%	%
More information available about individual schools	1.1	3.1
More links between parents and schools	8.6	7.9
More resources for buildings, books and equipment	21.5	15.4
Better quality teachers	11.1	9.3
Smaller class sizes	19.6	14.5
More emphasis on exams and tests	6.9	6.8
More emphasis on developing the child's skills and interests	14.6	20.9
More training and preparation for jobs	13.5	19.0
Other **(WRITE IN)**	0.7	-
(Don't Know)	2.2	2.8
(Refusal/NA)	0.1	0.1

Q644 [Advise16]
Suppose you were advising a 16 year old about their future. Would you say they should ... **READ OUT** ...

	%
... stay on in full-time education to get their GCE 'A' levels,	62.8
or, study full-time to get vocational, rather than academic, qualifications,	11.6
or, leave school and get training through a job?	6.3
(Varies/depends on the person)	18.3
(Don't Know)	0.8
(Refusal/NA)	0.1

Q645 [VoctVAcad]
In the long-run, which do you think gives people more opportunities and choice in life ... **READ OUT** ...

	%
... having good practical skills and training,	34.6
or, having good academic results?	40.7
(Mixture/depends)	23.6
(Don't Know)	1.0
(Refusal/NA)	0.1

Q646 [SegEdBoy]
If you had to advise an 11 year old **boy** on what sort of school he should go to, would you suggest a single-sex or a mixed-sex school?

	%
Single-sex	15.8
Mixed-sex	75.0
(No preference)	7.5
(It depends)	0.8
(Don't Know)	0.7
(Refusal/NA)	0.1

IF 'Single-sex' AT [SegEdBoy]
Q647 [SingleBo]
Is this because ... **READ OUT** ...

	%
...you think boys do better at their school work at single sex schools,	11.4
boys are happier to be with other boys at that age	4.3
or, for some other reason? **(WRITE IN)**	0.1
(Refusal/NA)	0.8

IF 'Mixed-sex' AT [SegEdBoy]
Q650 [MixedBoy]
Is this because ... **READ OUT** ...

	%
...you think boys do better at their school work at mixed sex schools,	4.7
boys and girls should learn to mix with each other,	69.2
or, for some other reason? **(WRITE IN)**	1.2
(Refusal/NA)	0.8

VERSION B: ASK ALL
Q653 [SegEdGr1]
And what if you had to advise an 11 year old **girl** on what sort of school she should go to? Would you suggest a single-sex or a mixed-sex school?

	%
Single-sex	19.7
Mixed-sex	71.5
(No preference)	7.2
(It depends)	0.8
(Don't Know)	0.7
(Refusal/NA)	0.1

IF 'Single-sex' AT [SegEdGrl]
Q654 [SingleGr]
Is this because ... **READ OUT** ...

	%
...you think girls do better at their school work at single sex schools,	14.6
girls are happier to be with other girls at that age	4.6
or, for some other reason? **(WRITE IN)**	0.5
(Refusal/NA)	0.8

IF 'Mixed-sex' AT [SegEdGrl]
Q657 [MixedGrl]
Is this because ... **READ OUT** ...

	%
...you think girls do better at their school work at mixed sex schools,	4.1
boys and girls should mix with each other,	66.4
or, for some other reason? **(WRITE IN)**	0.9
(Refusal/NA)	0.8

VERSION B: ASK ALL

Q660 *[HEdOpp]*
Do you feel that opportunities for young people in the UK to go on to **higher education** - to a university or college - should be increased or reduced, or are they at about the right level now?
IF INCREASED OR REDUCED: a lot or a little?

%
19.1 Increased a lot
23.0 Increased a little
51.7 About right
0.3   Reduced a little
2.9   Reduced a lot
2.9   (Don't Know)
0.1   (Refusal/NA)

Q661 *[HEFees]*
At present, Northern Ireland university students get their **teaching** fees paid by their Education and Library Board.
Do you think that students should .. **READ OUT** ...

%
15.1 ... pay something towards their own teaching fees,
83.1 or, should Education and Library Boards continue to pay the whole amount?
1.8   (Don't Know)
0.1   (Refusal/NA)

Q662 *[HEGrant]*
And, at present, some full-time UK university students get grants to help cover their **living** costs. Getting a grant depends upon the student's circumstances and those of their family. Do you think that ... **READ OUT** ...

%
41.3 ...**all** students should get grants to help cover their living costs,
54.1 some students should get grants to help cover their living costs, as now,
1.8   or, that no grants should be given to help cover students' living costs?
1.6   (It depends)
0.1   (Don't Know)
1.1   (Refusal/NA)

Q663 *[HELoan]*
Many full-time university students are now taking out government loans to help cover their living costs. They have to start repaying these loans when they begin working. Generally speaking, do you think that ... **READ OUT** ...

%
18.1 ...students **should** be expected to take out loans to help cover their living costs,
74.2 or, students **should not** be expected to take out loans to help cover living costs?
6.0   (It depends)
1.6   (Don't Know)
0.1   (Refusal/NA)

EUROPE (VERSION B)

VERSION B: ASK ALL

Q667 *[ECGBClse]*
Now a few questions about the UK's relationships with the European Union (sometimes still called the European Community).
As a member state, would you say that the UK's relationship with the European Union should be ... **READ OUT** ...

%
38.5 ... closer,
13.1 less close,
37.5 or, is it about right?
10.9 (Don't Know)
0.1   (Refusal/NA)

Q668 *[ECLnkInf]*
Do you think that closer links with the European Union would give the UK ... **READ OUT** ...

%
40.6 ...**more** influence in the world,
10.1 **less** influence in the world,
40.0 or, would it make no difference?
9.2   (Don't Know)
0.1   (Refusal/NA)

Q669 *[ECLnkStr]*
And would closer links with the European Union make the UK ... **READ OUT** ...

%
47.4 ...**stronger** economically,
10.8 **weaker** economically,
31.7 or, would it make no difference?
10.1 (Don't Know)
0.1   (Refusal/NA)

Q670 *[NIreland]*
Do you think the long-term policy for Northern Ireland should be for it ... **READ OUT** ...

%
63.9 ... to remain part of the United Kingdom,
27.0 or, to reunify with the rest of Ireland?
1.2   (Independent state)
1.8   (Up to Irish to decide)
5.0   Other answer **(WRITE IN)**
0.8   (Don't Know)
      (Refusal/NA)

Q673 *[DecFutNI]*
And who do you think should have the right to decide what the long-term future of Northern Ireland should be? Should it be ... **READ OUT** ...

%
63.9 ... the people in Northern Ireland on their own,
22.3 or, the people of Ireland, both north and south,
10.1 or, the people both in N.I. and in Britain?
1.7   (The people in Britain and Ireland north and south)
0.2   Other answer **(WRITE IN)**
1.7   (Don't Know)
0.1   (Refusal/NA)

Q676 [TroopOut]
Some people think that government policy towards Northern Ireland should include a complete withdrawal of British troops. Would you personally **support** or **oppose** such a policy?
IF 'SUPPORT' OR 'OPPOSE', PROBE: Strongly or a little?
%
16.3 Support strongly
24.1 Support a little
28.3 Oppose strongly
24.3 Oppose a little
0.3 (Withdraw in long term)
2.6 Other answer **(WRITE IN)**
3.7 (Don't Know)
0.2 (Refusal/NA)

Q679 [Nation]
On the whole, do you think the UK's interests are better served by .. **READ OUT** ...
%
46.9 ... closer links with Western Europe,
19.4 or, closer links with America?
20.9 (Both equally)
4.1 (Neither)
8.6 (Don't Know)
0.1 (Refusal/NA)

Q680 [UniteEC]
Which of these comes closer to your views ... **READ OUT** ...
%
45.3 ... the UK should do all it can to unite fully with the European Union,
40.6 or, the UK should do all it can to protect its independence from the European Union?
14.1 (Don't Know)
0.1 (Refusal/NA)

Q681 [ECPolicy]
CARD
Do you think the UK's long-term policy should be ... **READ OUT** ...
CODE ONE ONLY
%
6.5 ... to leave the European Union,
16.8 to stay in the EU and try to **reduce** its powers,
25.2 to leave things as they are,
29.3 to stay in the EU and try to **increase** its powers,
11.2 or, to work for the formation of a single European government?
10.9 (Don't Know)
0.1 (Refusal/NA)

Q682 [EcuView]
CARD
And here are three statements about the future of the pound in the European Union. Which **one** comes closest to your view?
CODE ONE ONLY
%
21.5 **Replace** the pound by a single currency
17.1 Use **both** the pound and a new European currency in the UK
54.2 Keep the pound as the **only** currency for the UK
7.1 (Don't Know)
0.1 (Refusal/NA)

n = 660

Head Office: 35 NORTHAMPTON SQUARE, LONDON EC1V 0AX
Tel: 0171-250 1866 Fax: 0171-250 1524

Field and DP Office: 100 KINGS ROAD, BRENTWOOD, ESSEX CM14 4LX
Tel: 01277 200600 Fax: 01277 214117

A

P.1430

NORTHERN IRELAND SOCIAL ATTITUDES 1995

Spring 1995

SELF-COMPLETION QUESTIONNAIRE

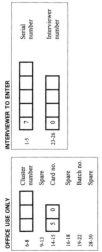

OFFICE USE ONLY | INTERVIEWER TO ENTER

Cluster number — Serial number
Spare
Card no. — Interviewer number
Spare
Batch no.
Spare

To the selected respondent:

Thank you very much for agreeing to take part in this important study - the sixth in this annual series. The study consists of this self-completion questionnaire, and the interview you have already completed. The results of the survey are published in a book each autumn; some of the questions are also being asked in twenty-two other countries, as part of an international survey.

Completing the questionnaire:

The questions inside cover a wide range of subjects, but each one can be answered simply by placing a tick (✓) or a number in one or more of the boxes. No special knowledge is required: we are confident that everyone will be able to take part, not just those with strong views or particular viewpoints. The questionnaire should not take very long to complete, and we hope you will find it interesting and enjoyable. Only you should fill it in, and not anyone else at your address. The answers you give will be treated as confidential and anonymous.

Returning the questionnaire:

Your interviewer will arrange with you the most convenient way of returning the questionnaire. If the interviewer has arranged to call back for it, please fill it in and keep it safely until then. If not, please complete it and post it back in the pre-paid, addressed envelope, AS SOON AS YOU POSSIBLY CAN.

THANK YOU AGAIN FOR YOUR HELP.

Social and Community Planning Research is an independent social research institute registered as a charitable trust. Its projects are funded by government departments, local authorities, universities and foundations to provide information on social issues in the UK. This survey series is funded mainly by one of the Sainsbury Family Charitable Trusts, with contributions also from other grant-giving bodies and government departments. Please contact us if you would like further information.

To begin, we have some questions about where you live: your neighbourhood or village; your town or city, your county, and so on. (By "neighbourhood" we mean the part of the town/city you live in. If you live in a village, we take this as your "neighbourhood").

A2.01 How close do you feel to ….
PLEASE TICK ONE BOX ON EACH LINE

		Very close	Close	Not very close	Not close at all	Can't choose/ Doesn't apply to me	(NA)
a.	…your neighbourhood (or village)? *[CLOSNGBH]*	% 24.1	46.7	20.5	3.7	2.1	2.8
b.	…your town or city? *[CLOSTOWN]*	% 13.7	47.5	23.7	5.1	4.2	5.7
c.	…your county? *[CLOSCNTY]*	% 12.9	45.1	24.8	5.8	3.8	7.6
d.	…Northern Ireland? *[CLOSNI]*	% 22.4	46.7	15.7	4.5	3.8	6.8
e.	…Europe? *[CLOSEURP]*	% 1.8	10.9	37.0	32.5	10.7	7.1

A2.02 If you could improve your work or living conditions, how willing or unwilling would you be to ….
PLEASE TICK ONE BOX ON EACH LINE

		Very willing	Fairly willing	Neither willing nor unwilling	Fairly unwilling	Very unwilling	Can't choose/ Doesn't apply to me	(NA)
a.	… move to another neighbourhood (or village)? *[MOVENGBH]*	% 14.8	26.5	13.4	14.2	21.9	7.5	1.8
b.	… move to another town or city within this county? *[MOVETOWN]*	% 9.2	22.4	13.9	17.2	27.0	6.4	3.8
c.	… move to another county? *[MOVECNTY]*	% 6.0	14.3	13.0	17.6	37.9	7.0	4.2
d.	… move outside Northern Ireland? *[MOVENI]*	% 7.4	8.7	9.1	16.5	46.9	7.3	4.1
e.	… move outside Europe? *[MOVEEURP]*	% 4.3	4.5	7.8	11.6	56.9	10.6	4.3

A2.03 *[UKUNITED]*
Which of these two statements comes closer to your own view?
PLEASE TICK ONE BOX ONLY

%

It is essential that the United Kingdom remains one nation   48.5

OR

Parts of the United Kingdom should be allowed to become fully separate nations if they choose to   33.5

Can't choose   16.5

(NA)   1.5

A2.04 How much do you agree or disagree with the following statements?
PLEASE TICK **ONE** BOX ON EACH LINE

n = 660

	Strongly agree	Agree	Neither agree nor disagree	Disagree	Strongly disagree	Can't choose	(NA)
[NATCITZN] a. I would rather be a citizen of the UK than of any other country in the world	% 25.5	28.4	26.0	8.3	3.4	4.8	3.6
[NATASHMD] b. There are some things about the UK today that make me feel ashamed of the UK	% 11.4	41.9	20.4	14.3	2.1	6.7	3.1
[NATLIKE] c. The world would be a better place if people from other countries were more like people from the UK	% 4.1	21.1	34.5	23.6	6.2	6.7	3.8
[NATBEST] d. Generally speaking the UK is a better country than most other countries	% 9.6	36.2	27.7	14.4	3.3	5.1	3.7

A2.05 How proud are you of the UK in each of the following?
PLEASE TICK **ONE** BOX ON EACH LINE

	Very proud	Somewhat proud	Not very proud	Not proud at all	Can't choose	(NA)
[NATPRID1] a. The way democracy works	% 6.7	37.1	26.5	9.9	16.6	3.1
[NATPRID2] b. Its political influence in the world	% 5.3	31.6	30.8	10.9	17.2	4.2
[NATPRID3] c. Its economic achievements	% 4.0	31.5	31.3	12.7	15.4	5.1
[NATPRID4] d. Its social security system	% 8.6	35.8	29.1	13.5	8.9	4.1
[NATPRID5] e. Its scientific and technological achievements	% 15.2	44.6	12.4	6.2	16.5	5.2
[NATPRID6] f. Its achievements in sports	% 16.3	44.9	18.0	5.7	11.5	3.5
[NATPRID7] g. Its achievements in the arts and literature	% 13.1	42.3	15.3	6.0	19.4	4.0
[NATPRID8] h. Its armed forces	% 27.6	29.6	12.6	13.8	12.5	3.8
[NATPRID9] i. Its history	% 21.7	33.5	15.1	12.6	14.2	3.0
[NATPRID10] j. Its fair and equal treatment of all groups in society	% 9.1	29.9	31.0	15.5	11.7	2.8

A2.06 Now we would like to ask a few questions about relations between the UK and other countries.
How much do you agree or disagree with the following statements?
PLEASE TICK **ONE** BOX ON EACH LINE

n = 660

	Strongly agree	Agree	Neither agree nor disagree	Disagree	Strongly disagree	Can't choose	(NA)
[FORGREL1] a. The UK should limit the import of foreign products in order to protect its national economy	% 17.9	44.2	15.5	9.3	2.4	8.0	2.8
[FORGREL2] b. For certain problems, like environmental pollution, international bodies should have the right to enforce solutions	% 19.0	48.8	11.3	9.0	1.2	8.2	2.5
[FORGREL3] c. Schools should make much more effort to teach foreign languages properly	% 26.7	46.6	15.6	4.2	0.4	3.8	2.7
[FORGREL4] d. The UK should follow its own interests, even if this leads to conflicts with other nations	% 11.3	29.8	22.7	22.6	3.8	7.3	2.6
[FORGREL5] e. Foreigners should not be allowed to buy land in the UK	% 7.8	20.6	27.8	29.0	5.1	7.3	2.5
[FORGREL6] f. Television should give preference to films and programmes made in the UK	% 6.7	22.4	28.4	27.5	6.1	6.3	2.5

A2.07 Now we would like to ask a few questions about minorities in Northern Ireland.
How much do you agree or disagree with the following statements?
PLEASE TICK **ONE** BOX ON EACH LINE

	Strongly agree	Agree	Neither agree nor disagree	Disagree	Strongly disagree	Can't choose	(NA)
[SHARTRAD] a. It is impossible for people who do not share the customs and traditions of Northern Ireland to become fully part of it	% 7.4	28.5	18.8	31.3	4.4	6.7	2.8
[ETHNCAID] b. Ethnic minorities should be given government assistance to preserve their customs and traditions	% 4.9	23.4	25.3	27.6	6.8	9.3	2.6

A2.08 [ETHNCVW] Some people say that it is better for a country if different racial and ethnic groups maintain their distinct customs and traditions. Others say that it is better if these groups adapt and blend into the larger society. Which of these views comes closer to your own?
PLEASE TICK **ONE** BOX ONLY

%

It is better for society if groups maintain their distinct customs and traditions 21.8

It is better if groups adapt and blend into the larger society 52.5

Can't choose 22.9

(NA) 2.8

There are different opinions about immigrants from other countries living in the UK. (By 'immigrants' we mean people who come to settle in the UK.)

A2.09 How much do you agree or disagree with each of the following statements?

PLEASE TICK ONE BOX ON EACH LINE

		Strongly agree	Agree	Neither agree nor disagree	Disagree	Strongly disagree	Can't choose	(NA)
	[IMMIGRT1]							
a.	Immigrants increase crime rates	% 5.7	15.8	29.2	31.5	5.2	9.7	2.8
	[IMMIGRT2]							
b.	Immigrants are generally good for the UK's economy	% 1.1	18.8	40.2	23.7	2.1	10.9	3.2
	[IMMIGRT3]							
c.	Immigrants take jobs away from people who were born in the UK	% 11.6	39.8	21.4	16.5	2.2	5.7	2.8
	[IMMIGRT4]							
d.	Immigrants make the UK more open to new ideas and cultures	% 3.8	41.8	29.6	10.2	2.8	9.7	2.2

[IMMNUMB]

A2.10 Do you think the number of immigrants to the UK nowadays should be ...

PLEASE TICK ONE BOX ONLY

	%
... increased a lot,	1.1
increased a little,	4.7
remain the same as it is,	36.8
reduced a little,	22.3
or reduced a lot?	21.5
Can't choose	11.9
(NA)	1.7

[REFSTAY]

A2.11 How much do you agree or disagree that refugees who have suffered political repression in their own country should be allowed to stay in the UK?

PLEASE TICK ONE BOX ONLY

	%
Strongly agree	10.9
Agree	41.7
Neither agree nor disagree	27.3
Disagree	9.3
Strongly disagree	2.4
Can't choose	6.7
(NA)	1.7

[LIVECHLD]

A2.12 Where did you spend most of your childhood, that is, until you turned 17?

PLEASE TICK ONE BOX ONLY

	%
In this town (city, village), but in this county	57.4
In a different town (city, village), but within the UK	27.6
In a different county, but in this county	11.6
Outside the UK	1.8
(NA)	1.7

[LIVEAREA]

A2.13 How long have you lived in the town (city, village), where you live now?

PLEASE FILL IN NUMBER OF YEARS OR TICK BOX IF LESS THAN ONE YEAR

Median: 25 years

(NA) 2.8%

[LIVEABRD]

A2.14 About how long altogether have you lived in other countries? (By 'other countries' we mean outside the UK)

PLEASE TICK ONE BOX ONLY

	%
Never lived in other countries	80.1
Less than 1 year in all	5.4
1 to 4 years in all	7.0
5 years or longer	5.7
(NA)	1.9

A2.15a What language(s) do you speak at home?

PLEASE FILL IN

At home I speak: ....

b. What language(s) do you speak well?

PLEASE FILL IN ....

n = 660

A2.16a *[CITIZEN]*
Are you a citizen of the UK?

	%
Yes	95.3
No	1.7
(NA)	3.0

b. *[CITZPAR]*
At the time of your birth, were both, one, or neither of your parents citizens of the UK?
PLEASE TICK ONE BOX ONLY

	%
Both were citizens of the UK	93.8
Only father was a citizen of the UK	0.8
Only mother was a citizen of the UK	0.8
Neither parent was a citizen of the UK	2.1
(NA)	2.6

And now a few questions about the European Union (sometimes still called the European Community).
[EUKNOW]
A2.17 How much have you heard or read about the European Union?
PLEASE TICK ONE BOX ONLY

	%
A lot	13.5
Quite a bit	24.8
Not much	42.0
Nothing at all	18.0
(NA)	1.8

A2.18 *[UKBENEU]*
Generally speaking, would you say that the UK benefits or does not benefit from being a member of the European Union?
PLEASE TICK ONE BOX ONLY

	%
Benefits	44.2
Does not benefit	16.9
Have never heard of the European Union	3.3
Can't choose	33.6
(NA)	2.0

n = 660

A2.19 *[EUUNITE]*
Which of the following statements comes closer to your own view?
PLEASE TICK ONE BOX ONLY

	%
The UK should do all it can to unite fully with the European Union	33.7
OR	
The UK should do all it can to protect its independence from the European Union	26.0
Can't choose	38.4
(NA)	1.9

A2.20 *[IMMEXCLU]*
How much do you agree or disagree with the following statement?

"The UK should take stronger measures to exclude illegal immigrants."

PLEASE TICK ONE BOX ONLY

	%
Strongly agree	30.9
Agree	30.9
Neither agree nor disagree	18.8
Disagree	6.8
Strongly disagree	2.1
Can't choose	8.7
(NA)	1.9

A2.21 From what you know or have heard, please tick a box for each of the items below to show whether you think the National Health Service in your area is, on the whole, satisfactory or in need of improvement.

PLEASE TICK ONE BOX ON EACH LINE

		In need of a lot of improvement	In need of some improvement	Satisfactory	Very good	(DK)	(NA)
a.	GPs' appointment systems [HSAREA1]	12.6	31.2	39.7	14.2	0.3	2.0
	[HSAREA2]						
b.	Amount of time GP gives to each patient [HSAREA3]	8.7	21.1	55.0	12.6	0.3	2.3
c.	Being able to choose which GP to see [HSAREA4]	8.3	17.5	53.4	18.2	0.3	2.3
d.	Quality of medical treatment by GPs [HSAREA5]	5.4	16.5	51.7	23.9	0.3	2.2
e.	Hospital waiting lists for non-emergency operations [HSAREA6]	28.3	43.0	20.4	2.7	1.1	4.4
f.	Waiting time before getting appointments with hospital consultants [HSAREA7]	33.8	42.9	18.0	2.2	0.5	2.5
g.	General condition of hospital buildings [HSAREA9]	12.2	35.2	42.9	6.3	0.5	2.9
h.	Staffing level of nurses in hospitals [HSAREA10]	31.1	39.9	21.8	4.0	0.5	2.8
i.	Staffing level of doctors in hospitals [HSAREA11]	30.7	39.1	23.4	3.4	0.5	3.0
j.	Quality of medical treatment in hospitals [HSAREA12]	5.7	26.3	48.5	16.2	0.2	3.0
k.	Quality of nursing care in hospitals [HSAREA13]	3.6	20.2	44.4	28.9	0.2	2.7
l.	Waiting areas in accident and emergency departments in hospitals [HSAREA14]	14.8	35.5	39.9	6.2	0.9	2.7
m.	Waiting areas for out-patients in hospitals [HSAREA15]	13.9	35.5	41.1	5.7	0.5	3.4
n.	Waiting areas at GPs' surgeries [HSAREA16]	7.2	21.7	52.0	16.2	0.6	2.4
o.	Time spent waiting in out-patient departments [HSAREA17]	18.0	47.2	30.0	1.9	0.5	2.3
p.	Time spent waiting in accident and emergency departments before being seen by a doctor [HSAREA18]	26.6	41.7	25.2	2.8	1.5	2.3
q.	Time spent waiting for an ambulance after a 999 call	8.9	22.0	47.7	16.2	2.4	2.9

n = 660

n = 660

A2.22 In the last two years, have you or a close family member ....

PLEASE TICK ONE BOX ON EACH LINE

		Yes %	No %	(NA) %
a.	... visited an NHS GP? [NHSDOC]	92.3	5.0	2.8
b.	... been an out-patient in an NHS hospital? [NHSOUTP]	70.4	25.2	4.4
c.	... been an in-patient in an NHS hospital? [NHSINP]	49.8	45.7	4.4
d.	... visited a patient in an NHS hospital? [NHSVISIT]	82.2	14.2	3.6
e.	... had any medical treatment as a private patient? [PRIVPAT]	10.6	85.5	3.9

A2.23 [LEGCAN] Please tick one box to show how much you agree or disagree with this statement.

"Smoking cannabis (marijuana) should be legalised"

PLEASE TICK ONE BOX ONLY %

	%
Strongly agree	6.9
Just agree	10.9
Neither agree nor disagree	5.5
Just disagree	12.3
Strongly disagree	61.3
(DK)	0.2
(NA)	2.1

A2.24 And now some questions about the environment.

How much do you agree or disagree with each of these statements?

PLEASE TICK ONE BOX ON EACH LINE

		Strongly agree	Agree	Neither agree nor disagree	Disagree	Strongly disagree	Can't choose	(NA)
a.	[ENVIRDIF] It is just too difficult for someone like me to do much about the environment %	11.7	27.6	16.7	27.6	7.3	5.3	3.9
b.	[ENVIRRGT] I do what is right for the environment, even when it costs more money or takes more time %	9.3	42.9	23.7	9.4	1.3	9.5	4.0

A2.25 [PROTENVP] If you had to choose, which one of the following would be closest to your views?

PLEASE TICK ONE BOX ONLY %

	%
Government should let ordinary people decide for themselves how to protect the environment, even if it means they don't always do the right thing	18.8
OR	
Government should pass laws to make ordinary people protect the environment, even if it interferes with people's rights to make their own decisions	53.3
Can't choose	25.9
(NA)	2.0

n = 660

A2.26 [PROTENVB]
And which one of the following would be closest to your views?
*PLEASE TICK **ONE** BOX ONLY*

%

Government should let <u>businesses</u> decide for themselves how to protect the environment, even if it means they don't always do the right thing — 6.2

OR

Government should pass laws to make <u>businesses</u> protect the environment, even if it interferes with businesses' rights to make their own decisions — 75.1

Can't choose — 15.8

(NA) — 2.9

A2.27 [SHORTOIL]
How true do you think the following statement is?
"Within the next twenty years or so, shortages of oil and gas will be one of the most serious problems for the UK."
*PLEASE TICK **ONE** BOX ONLY*

%

Definitely true — 10.5

Probably true — 48.5

Probably not true — 17.6

Definitely not true — 2.6

Can't choose — 18.0

(NA) — 2.8

A2.28 [RISETEMP]
How true do you think the following statement is?
"Within the next twenty years or so, a rise in the world's temperature caused by the 'greenhouse effect' will be one of the most serious problems for the UK."
*PLEASE TICK **ONE** BOX ONLY*

%

Definitely true — 16.2

Probably true — 46.5

Probably not true — 17.8

Definitely not true — 2.1

Can't choose — 14.6

(NA) — 2.8

---

n = 660

A2.29 [TRAFNOIS]
How true do you think the following statement is?
"Within the next twenty years or so, traffic noise will be one of the most serious problems for the UK."
*PLEASE TICK **ONE** BOX ONLY*

%

Definitely true — 21.2

Probably true — 48.5

Probably not true — 18.3

Definitely not true — 2.5

Can't choose — 6.7

(NA) — 2.8

A2.30 [TRAFCONG]
How true do you think the following statement is?
"Within the next twenty years or so, traffic congestion will be one of the most serious problems for the UK."
*PLEASE TICK **ONE** BOX ONLY*

%

Definitely true — 37.7

Probably true — 49.2

Probably not true — 6.6

Definitely not true — 0.4

Can't choose — 3.3

(NA) — 2.8

A2.31 [DAMAGE]
Which one of these two statements comes <u>closest</u> to your own views?
*PLEASE TICK **ONE** BOX ONLY*

%

Industry should be prevented from causing damage to the countryside, even if this sometimes leads to higher prices — 88.1

OR

Industry should keep prices down, even if this sometimes causes damage to the countryside — 7.7

(DK) — 1.1

(NA) — 3.1

A2.32 [CTRYJOBS]
And which one of these two statements comes <u>closest</u> to your own views?
*PLEASE TICK **ONE** BOX ONLY*

%

The countryside should be protected from development, even if this sometimes leads to fewer new jobs — 68.8

OR

New jobs should be created, even if this sometimes causes damage to the countryside — 26.3

(DK) — 1.4

(NA) — 3.6

A2.33 Please tick one box for each statement below to show how much you agree or disagree with it.

PLEASE TICK ONE BOX ON EACH LINE

n = 660

		Strongly agree	Agree	Neither agree nor disagree	Disagree	Strongly disagree	(DK)	(NA)
	[GOVENVIR]							
a.	The government should do more to protect the environment, even if it leads to higher taxes	11.1	44.0	28.4	11.8	1.8	-	2.9
	[INDENVIR]	%						
b.	Industry should do more to protect the environment, even if it leads to lower profits and fewer jobs	11.4	45.7	28.6	9.8	1.3	0.1	3.1
	[PLENVIR]	%						
c.	Ordinary people should do more to protect the environment, even if it means paying higher prices	11.9	50.7	23.5	9.9	1.1	-	3.0
	[CARALLOW]	%						
d.	People should be allowed to use their cars as much as they like, even if it causes damage to the environment	2.9	11.8	38.1	36.8	7.7	0.1	2.7

A2.34 [RESPRES]
Would you describe the place where you live as ...

PLEASE TICK ONE BOX ONLY

	%
... a big city,	7.8
the suburbs or outskirts of a big city,	16.8
a small city or town,	36.4
a country village,	17.9
or, a farm or home in the country?	18.9
(NA)	2.2

A2.35 Please tick one box for each of these statements below to show how much you agree or disagree with it.

PLEASE TICK ONE BOX ON EACH LINE

n = 660

		Strongly agree	Agree	Neither agree nor disagree	Disagree	Strongly disagree	Can't choose	(NA)
	[RAILSHUT]							
a.	Local rail services that do not pay for themselves should be closed down	4.4	19.4	23.8	35.9	5.1	8.7	2.7
	[BUSPRIOR]	%						
b.	Buses should be given more priority in towns and cities, even if this makes things more difficult for car drivers	10.9	42.4	19.4	19.8	1.1	4.0	2.4
	[CARCNTRY]	%						
c.	A visitor to the countryside these days really needs a car to get around	12.5	60.2	11.6	10.0	1.4	1.2	3.2
	[CAREASY]	%						
d.	Car drivers still are given too easy a time in the UK's towns and cities	4.4	19.4	30.9	34.5	1.8	6.2	2.8
	[BUSSHUT]	%						
e.	Local bus services that do not pay for themselves should be closed down	3.8	15.2	19.7	46.9	8.3	3.8	2.3
	[IMPTRP]	%						
f.	The UK should do more to improve its public transport system even if its road system suffers	11.8	36.1	22.7	18.2	2.0	6.7	2.5
	[CYCPEDPR]	%						
g.	Cyclists and pedestrians should be given more priority in towns and cities even if this makes things more difficult for other road users	17.8	45.6	17.7	11.6	1.5	3.4	2.4

A2.36 Here are some things that might be done about the UK's traffic problems. Please tick one box for each to say how strongly you would be in favour of or against it.

PLEASE TICK ONE BOX ON EACH LINE

		Strongly in favour	In favour	Neither in favour nor against	Against	Strongly against	Can't choose	(NA)
	[TOLLDRIV]							
a.	Drivers charged tolls on all motorways	3.4	18.4	18.9	38.9	11.9	5.7	2.8
	[VEHPERM]	%						
b.	Only vehicles with permits for essential business allowed in city centres in working hours	10.5	40.5	11.7	23.8	5.5	5.7	2.3
	[MOTCHAR1]	%						
c.	Motorists charged for driving in city centres in working hours	4.7	18.1	16.7	43.4	9.4	5.0	2.6
	[PARKCHAR]	%						
d.	Much higher parking charges in towns and cities	3.1	10.5	12.6	48.2	19.4	3.3	3.0
	[COMPCARS]	%						
e.	Shops and offices encouraged to move out of town and city centres	2.4	19.4	19.0	41.3	10.8	4.8	2.4
	[PEDESTR]	%						
f.	Banning company cars except where they are essential for employees in their work	10.5	35.9	22.1	19.3	4.2	5.7	2.4
g.	Many more streets in cities and towns reserved for pedestrians only	17.9	55.7	15.7	3.8	1.0	3.7	2.1

n = 660

A2.37 Please tick one box on each line to show whether you would like to see more or less government spending on each of these.
Remember that if you say "more", everyone's taxes may have to go up to pay for it.
PLEASE TICK ONE BOX ON EACH LINE

[TRPSPND1]	Spend much more	Spend more	Spend the same as now	Spend less	Spend much less	Can't choose	(NA)
a. Improving local bus [TRPSPND1]	9.8	32.9	44.9	3.8	0.4	5.4	2.9
b. Building more roads [TRPSPND2]	6.7	22.8	42.3	15.7	3.7	4.8	4.1
c. Improving local rail services [TRPSPND3]	8.5	31.1	40.7	6.4	1.1	8.4	3.8
d. Improving and widening the roads we already have [TRPSPND4]	10.8	40.7	35.7	5.1	1.5	2.6	3.6
e. Improving long distance rail services [TRPSPND5]	10.4	27.6	41.7	7.0	1.0	8.6	3.7
f. Improving facilities for cyclists and pedestrians [TRPSPND6]	20.0	43.1	27.7	1.8	1.2	3.3	2.8

A2.38a [SINGMUM1] Thinking about a single mother with a child under school age. Which one of these statements comes closest to your own view?

PLEASE TICK ONE BOX ONLY

%
She has a special duty to go out to work to support her child 8.4
She has a special duty to stay at home to look after her child 25.9
She should do as she chooses, like everyone else 58.3
Can't choose 4.9
(NA) 2.5

b. [SINGMUM2] Suppose this single mother did get a part-time job. How much do you agree or disagree that the government should provide money to help with child-care?

PLEASE TICK ONE BOX ONLY

%
Strongly agree 30.1
Agree 43.9
Neither agree nor disagree 11.9
Disagree 6.3
Strongly disagree 1.4
Can't choose 3.9
(NA) 2.5

n = 660

A2.39a [SMUMSCH1] And what about when the child reaches school age? Which one of these statements comes closest to your view about what the single mother should do?

PLEASE TICK ONE BOX ONLY

%
She has a special duty to go out to work to support her child 25.3
She has a special duty to stay at home to look after her child 9.6
She should do as she chooses, like everyone else 57.9
Can't choose 4.5
(NA) 2.6

b. [SMUMSCH2] Suppose this single mother did go out to work. How much do you agree or disagree that the government should provide money to help with child-care outside school?

PLEASE TICK ONE BOX ONLY

%
Strongly agree 20.7
Agree 43.8
Neither agree nor disagree 14.0
Disagree 11.4
Strongly disagree 1.6
Can't choose 5.5
(NA) 3.0

A2.40 Please say how much you agree or disagree that ...
PLEASE TICK ONE BOX ON EACH LINE

	Strongly agree	Agree	Neither agree nor disagree	Disagree	Strongly disagree	Can't choose	(NA)
a. [SMARMUM1] ... unmarried mothers who find it hard to cope have only themselves to blame	8.0	17.8	21.1	30.0	12.0	4.4	6.6
b. [SMARMUM2] ... unmarried mothers get too little sympathy from society	7.7	26.4	29.0	21.1	4.7	4.7	6.5

A2.41 Here are some statements about illegal drugs, such as cannabis, cocaine and heroin.
PLEASE TICK ONE BOX ON EACH LINE

	Strongly agree	Agree	Neither agree nor disagree	Disagree	Strongly disagree	Can't choose	(NA)
[DRUGSC1] a. Doctors must be allowed to prescribe drugs for those who are addicted to them	% 2.1	19.8	16.8	35.1	18.1	5.4	2.8
[DRUGSC2] b. The UK should aim to become a drug-free society	% 38.4	43.6	8.1	3.8	1.8	1.4	3.0
[DRUGSC3] c. Adults should be free to take any drug they wish	% 1.1	5.7	8.9	43.7	35.9	2.1	2.6
[DRUGSC3] d. All adults have a duty to prevent young people from using illegal drugs	% 55.4	33.9	3.4	1.8	1.7	1.2	2.7
[DRUGSC5] e. The use of 'soft' drugs leads to the use of 'hard' drugs	% 33.2	40.3	9.0	7.4	1.7	4.8	3.7
[DRUGSC6] f. All illegal drugs should be made legal	% 2.9	4.1	3.3	34.5	51.3	1.2	2.7
[DRUGSC7] g. The best way to treat people who are addicted to drugs is to stop them from using drugs altogether	% 22.1	29.7	16.8	15.7	3.5	9.3	2.9
[DRUGSC8] h. Taking illegal drugs can sometimes be beneficial	% 1.9	12.3	14.5	32.8	28.4	6.6	3.5
[DRUGSC9] i. The use of illegal drugs always leads to addiction	% 22.6	32.2	16.5	16.8	5.8	6.6	3.2
[DRUGSC10] j. You can never trust someone who is addicted to drugs	% 26.1	33.3	19.0	10.3	1.6	6.9	2.8
[DRUGSC11] k. People who are addicted to drugs should decide for themselves whether they have treatment	% 4.7	23.7	14.1	33.0	15.5	5.7	3.3
[DRUGSC12] l. Taking drugs is always morally wrong	% 25.4	34.2	16.9	12.7	2.5	4.5	3.7
[DRUGSC13] m. All use of illegal drugs is misuse	% 30.3	40.6	10.6	9.4	1.9	4.1	3.0
[DRUGSC14] n. We need to accept that using illegal drugs is a normal part of some people's lives	% 2.5	21.3	13.6	36.2	19.9	3.2	3.3
[DRUGSC15] o. The legalisation of drugs would lead to a considerable increase in misuse	% 29.6	39.7	10.8	9.2	3.4	4.4	3.0
[DRUGSC16] p. The only way to help addicts is to make them have treatment	% 21.4	34.7	17.8	14.6	2.8	5.6	3.1

[PROTRCMX]

A2.42 Some people think that better relations between Protestants and Catholics in Northern Ireland will only come about through more mixing of the two communities. Others think that better relations will only come about through more separation. Which comes closest to your views?

PLEASE TICK ONE BOX ONLY %

Better relations will come about through more mixing	93.2
Better relations will come about through more separation	3.6
(DK)	0.3
(NA)	2.9

A2.43 And are you in favour of more mixing or more separation in...
PLEASE TICK ONE BOX ON EACH LINE

	Much more mixing	Bit more mixing	Keep things as they are	Bit more separation	Much more separation	(DK)	(NA)
a. ...primary schools? [MIXDPRIM]	% 46.9	28.5	20.9	0.9	0.8	0.1	1.9
b. ...secondary and grammar schools? [MIXDGRAM]	% 46.1	32.4	18.0	0.6	0.7	0.1	2.1
c. ...where people live? [MIXDLIV]	% 43.7	36.9	16.4	0.7	0.2	0.1	2.0
d. ...where people work? [MIXDWORK]	% 48.2	37.5	11.5	0.4	0.2	0.1	2.1
e. ...people's leisure or sports activities? [MIXDLEIS]	% 53.4	34.2	9.9	0.5	0.0	0.1	1.9
f. ...people's marriages? [MIXDMARR]	% 26.2	25.2	39.0	2.1	5.0	0.3	2.2

A2.44 People feel closer to some groups than to others. For you personally, how close would you say you feel towards...
PLEASE TICK ONE BOX ON EACH LINE

	Very close	Fairly close	A little close	Not very close	Not at all close	(DK)	(NA)
a. ...people born in the same area as you? [CLSEBORN]	% 13.3	40.0	23.8	15.4	5.5	0.1	2.0
b. ...people who have the same social class background as yours? [CLSECLAS]	% 11.6	45.8	27.5	10.7	2.2	0.1	2.1
c. ...people who have the same religious background as yours? [CLSERELG]	% 12.1	43.1	25.6	13.2	3.3	0.1	2.6
d. ...people of the same race as you? [CLSERACE]	% 12.3	41.9	27.5	11.9	3.6	0.3	2.6
e. ...people who live in the same area as you do now? [CLSELIVE]	% 10.3	40.4	28.5	15.3	3.6	0.1	2.0
f. ...people who have the same political beliefs as you? [CLSEPOL]	% 8.4	32.8	31.4	16.7	7.9	0.1	2.7

[PEACFLNI]

A2.45 How much do you agree or disagree with the following statement?
"Northern Ireland is a much more peaceful place than
people living in Britain think"

*PLEASE TICK **ONE** BOX ONLY*

	%
Strongly agree	45.9
Agree	43.6
Neither agree nor disagree	5.3
Disagree	2.9
Strongly disagree	0.6
(NA)	1.8

[NIGOVPRF]

A2.46 Here are a number of different ways in which Northern Ireland
might be governed in the future. Please tick one box to show
which way you would prefer.

*PLEASE TICK **ONE** BOX ONLY*

Should Northern Ireland ...

	%
... remain part of **the UK** without a separate parliament in Belfast,	22.2
remain part of **the UK** but with a separate parliament in Belfast,	34.1
become part of **the Irish Republic** without a separate parliament in Belfast,	7.0
become part of **the Irish Republic** with a separate parliament in Belfast,	6.1
be governed jointly by **the UK and the Irish Republic** without its own parliament in Belfast,	4.2
be governed jointly by **the UK and the Irish Republic** with its own parliament in Belfast,	10.3
become an **independent state** with its own parliament, separate from both the UK and the Irish Republic?	5.1
Can't choose	9.0
(NA)	1.9

n = 1281

[NIGOVFUT]

A2.47 Now from the same list of possibilities please tick
one box to show which you think Northern Ireland will
in fact have in, say, ten years' time.

*PLEASE TICK **ONE** BOX ONLY*

In ten years' time
Northern Ireland will ...

	%
... still be part of **the UK** without a separate parliament in Belfast,	26.4
be part of **the UK** with a separate parliament in Belfast,	24.3
have become part of **the Irish Republic** without a separate parliament in Belfast,	5.3
have become part of **the Irish Republic** with a separate parliament in Belfast,	6.6
be governed jointly by **the UK and the Irish Republic** without its own parliament in Belfast,	8.2
be governed jointly by **the UK and the Irish Republic** with its own parliament in Belfast,	10.5
have become an **independent state** with its own parliament, separate from both the UK and the Irish Republic?	2.1
Can't choose	14.5
(NA)	2.2

[GBGOVNI]

A2.48a How much say do you think a Westminster government of
any party should have in the way Northern Ireland
is run? Do you think it should have ...

*PLEASE TICK **ONE** BOX ONLY*

	%
... a great deal of say,	19.4
some say,	40.0
a little say,	18.0
or - no say at all?	10.4
Can't choose	10.3
(NA)	1.9

[IRGOVNI]

b. And how much say do you think an Irish government of
any party should have in the way Northern Ireland is
run? Do you think it should have ...

*PLEASE TICK **ONE** BOX ONLY*

	%
... a great deal of say	9.0
some say,	20.0
a little say,	19.8
or - no say at all?	40.2
Can't choose	9.3
(NA)	1.9

n = 1281

270

A2.49 Please tick one box for each statement to show how much you agree or disagree with it.

PLEASE TICK ONE BOX ON EACH LINE   n = 1281

	Agree strongly	Agree	Neither agree nor disagree	Disagree	Disagree strongly	(DK)	(NA)
a. [WELFRESP] The welfare state makes people nowadays less willing to look after themselves %	10.3	29.6	25.4	29.1	3.9	0.0	1.6
b. [WELFSTIG] People receiving social security are made to feel like second class citizens %	10.8	37.1	22.6	26.1	2.1	0.0	1.3
c. [WELFHELP] The welfare state encourages people to stop helping each other %	5.2	24.4	29.7	36.1	2.8	0.0	1.7
d. [MOREWELF] The government should spend more money on welfare benefits for the poor, even if it leads to higher taxes %	12.9	41.3	25.0	17.5	1.8	0.1	1.3
e. [UNEMPJOB] Around here, most unemployed people could find a job if they really wanted one %	8.7	29.3	19.8	34.3	6.0	0.2	1.7
f. [SOCHELP] Many people who get social security don't really deserve any help %	3.8	22.4	25.3	38.7	7.8	0.0	2.1
g. [DOLEFIDL] Most people on the dole are fiddling in one way or another %	10.3	26.2	29.0	27.9	4.7	0.1	1.7
h. [WELFFEET] If welfare benefits weren't so generous, people would learn to stand on their own two feet %	6.9	22.8	22.5	36.7	9.3	0.0	1.7

A2.50 Please tick one box for each statement below to show how much you agree or disagree with it.

PLEASE TICK ONE BOX ON EACH LINE   n = 1281

	Agree strongly	Agree	Neither agree nor disagree	Disagree	Disagree strongly	(DK)	(NA)
a. [REDISTRB] Government should redistribute income from the better-off to those who are less well off %	14.4	37.4	22.6	21.0	3.2	0.1	1.3
b. [BIGBUSNN] Big business benefits owners at the expense of workers %	17.3	44.8	23.9	11.4	1.2	-	1.5
c. [WEALTH] Ordinary working people do not get their fair share of the nation's wealth %	20.0	52.0	17.7	8.4	0.7	-	1.3
d. [RICHLAW] There is one law for the rich and one for the poor %	24.7	42.4	18.7	11.8	1.2	-	1.3
e. [INDUST4] Management will always try to get the better of employees if it gets the chance %	22.2	43.7	21.9	10.3	0.9	0.1	0.9

A2.51 Please tick one box for each statement below to show how much you agree or disagree with it.

PLEASE TICK ONE BOX ON EACH LINE   n = 1281

	Agree strongly	Agree	Neither agree nor disagree	Disagree	Disagree strongly	(DK)	(NA)
a. [TRADVALS] Young people today don't have enough respect for traditional values %	22.8	50.2	17.0	8.3	0.5	-	1.1
b. [STIFSENT] People who break the law should be given stiffer sentences %	31.2	49.0	16.0	2.8	0.2	-	0.9
c. [DEATHAPP] For some crimes, the death penalty is the most appropriate sentence %	24.8	25.1	15.5	22.6	10.8	-	1.1
d. [OBEY] Schools should teach children to obey authority %	35.0	50.7	10.1	3.0	0.1	-	1.0
e. [WRONGLAW] The law should always be obeyed, even if a particular law is wrong %	8.6	29.8	29.3	26.4	4.7	-	1.1
f. [CENSOR] Censorship of films and magazines is necessary to uphold moral standards %	28.9	40.3	18.1	8.8	2.9	0.0	0.9

A2.52a. [QTIME] To help us plan better in future, please tell us about how long it took you to complete this questionnaire.

PLEASE TICK ONE BOX ONLY   n = 660

	%
Less than 15 minutes	4.0
Between 15 and 20 minutes	20.4
Between 21 and 30 minutes	37.3
Between 31 and 45 minutes	25.2
Between 46 and 60 minutes	7.9
Over one hour	4.0
(NA)	1.2

b. And on what date did you fill in the questionnaire?

PLEASE WRITE IN: DATE [ ] MONTH [0] 1995

Thank you very much for your help

Head Office: 35 NORTHAMPTON SQUARE,
LONDON EC1V 0AX
Tel: 0171-250 1866 Fax: 0171-250 1524

Field and DP Office: 100 KINGS ROAD,
BRENTWOOD, ESSEX CM14 4LX
Tel: 01277 200600 Fax: 01277 214117

SCPR *SOCIAL & COMMUNITY PLANNING RESEARCH*

B

P.1430

NORTHERN IRELAND SOCIAL ATTITUDES 1995   Spring 1995

SELF-COMPLETION QUESTIONNAIRE

OFFICE USE ONLY	INTERVIEWER TO ENTER
	1-5 [7] Serial number
6-8 Cluster number	
9-13 Spare	23-26 [0] Interviewer number
14-15 [5][0] Card no.	
16-18 Spare	
19-22 Batch no.	
28-30 Spare	

To the selected respondent:

Thank you very much for agreeing to take part in this important study - the sixth in this annual series. The study consists of this self-completion questionnaire, and the interview you have already completed. The results of the survey are published in a book each autumn; some of the questions are also being asked in twenty-two other countries, as part of an international survey.

Completing the questionnaire:

The questions inside cover a wide range of subjects, but each one can be answered simply by placing a tick (✓) or a number in one or more of the boxes. No special knowledge is required: we are confident that everyone will be able to take part, not just those with strong views or particular viewpoints. The questionnaire should not take very long to complete, and we hope you will find it interesting and enjoyable. **Only you should fill it in, and not anyone else at your address. The answers you give will be treated as confidential and anonymous.**

Returning the questionnaire:

Your interviewer will arrange with you the most convenient way of returning the questionnaire. If the interviewer has arranged to call back for it, please fill it in and keep it safely until then. If not, please complete it and post it back in the pre-paid, addressed envelope, AS SOON AS YOU POSSIBLY CAN.

THANK YOU AGAIN FOR YOUR HELP.

Social and Community Planning Research is an independent social research institute registered as a charitable trust. Its projects are funded by government departments, local authorities, universities and foundations to provide information on social issues in the UK. This survey series is funded mainly by one of the Sainsbury Family Charitable Trusts, with contributions also from other grant-giving bodies and government departments. Please contact us if you would like further information.

n = 621

B2.01 Listed below are various areas of government spending. Please show whether you would like to see <u>more</u> or <u>less</u> government spending in each area.

If you want more spending, this is likely to mean that you will have to pay more taxes. If you want less spending, this is likely to make it possible to cut taxes.

PLEASE TICK ONE BOX ON EACH LINE

		Spend much more	Spend more	Spend the same as now	Spend less	Spend much less	Can't choose	(NA)
a.	Benefits for unemployed people [NEWSPND1]	% 9.3	31.0	37.3	12.0	4.2	4.7	1.5
b.	Benefits for disabled people who cannot work [NEWSPND2]	% 21.6	53.3	21.3	0.9	-	1.0	1.9
c.	Benefits for parents who work on very low incomes [NEWSPND3]	% 17.8	57.3	20.5	0.8	-	1.2	2.4
d.	Benefits for single parents [NEWSPND4]	% 8.5	31.2	41.3	10.4	4.7	1.5	2.4
e.	Benefits for retired people [NEWSPND5]	% 26.0	50.6	18.3	2.3	0.2	1.3	1.3

B2.02 From what you know or have heard, please tick one box on each line to show how well you think <u>state secondary schools nowadays</u> ...

PLEASE TICK ONE BOX ON EACH LINE

		Very well	Quite well	Not very well	Not at all well	(DK)	(NA)
a.	... prepare young people for work? [STATSEC1]	% 9.2	53.0	33.4	3.0	0.3	1.1
b.	... teach young people basic skills such as reading, writing and maths? [STATSEC2]	% 22.9	60.7	13.1	1.4	0.1	1.8
c.	... bring out young people's natural abilities? [STATSEC3]	% 9.4	46.6	36.4	6.1	0.1	1.5

B2.03 From what you know or have heard, please tick one box for each statement about <u>state secondary schools</u> now compared with 10 years ago.

PLEASE TICK ONE BOX ON EACH LINE

		Much better now than 10 years ago	A little better	About the same	A little worse	Much worse now than 10 years ago	(DK)	(NA)
a.	On the whole, do you think school-leavers are <u>better</u> qualified or <u>worse</u> qualified nowadays than they were 10 years ago? [SCHLLEAV]	% 26.1	40.4	19.4	9.1	3.6	-	1.4
b.	Do you think teachers are <u>better</u> paid or <u>worse</u> paid nowadays than they were 10 years ago? [TEACHPAY]	% 19.9	37.1	26.6	11.6	3.1	0.2	1.4
c.	And do you think classroom behaviour is <u>better</u> or <u>worse</u> nowadays than it was 10 years ago? [CLASSBEH]	% 1.5	4.8	13.2	35.6	43.3	0.2	1.5
d.	And do you think the standard of teaching is <u>better</u> or <u>worse</u> nowadays than it was 10 years ago? [TEACHBET]	% 11.4	25.5	40.1	17.8	3.7	0.2	1.4

B2.07 Here are some qualities that students may have developed
by the time they leave university.
a. In your view which is the most important quality
universities should aim to develop in their students?
b. And which is the next most important quality that
universities should aim to develop?

PLEASE TICK ONE BOX ONLY
IN EACH COLUMN

n = 621

	[UNISHLD1] Most important %	[UNISHLD2] Next most important %
Self-confidence	12.0	14.6
How to live among people from different backgrounds	7.6	8.0
Skills and knowledge which will get them a good job	40.2	15.9
A readiness to challenge other people's ideas	2.1	5.1
An ability to speak and write clearly	1.1	5.5
Knowledge that equips people for life in general	17.9	30.3
(NA)	19.1	20.6

B2.08a And which one of these qualities do you think universities
actually do develop most in their students?
b. And which next?

PLEASE TICK ONE BOX ONLY
IN EACH COLUMN

	[UNIDOES1] Most developed %	[UNIDOES2] Next most developed %
Self-confidence	14.7	12.4
How to live among people from different backgrounds	5.9	10.6
Skills and knowledge which will get them a good job	35.0	14.2
A readiness to challenge other people's ideas	12.3	13.8
An ability to speak and write clearly	7.2	10.6
Knowledge that equips people for life in general	6.7	17.0
(NA)	18.3	21.4

n = 621

B2.04 And from what you know or have heard, please tick one
box for each statement about universities and colleges
now compared with 10 years ago.

PLEASE TICK ONE BOX
ON EACH LINE

	Much better now than 10 years ago	A little better	About the same	A little worse	Much worse than 10 years ago	(DK)	(NA)
[UNIQUAL] a. On the whole, do you think that students leaving university are better qualified or worse qualified nowadays than they were 10 years ago? %	20.8	33.4	38.4	3.7	2.3	0.5	0.9
[UNITEACH] b. And do you think that the standard of teaching in universities is better or worse nowadays than it was 10 years ago? %	15.4	26.2	48.3	6.0	2.0	0.9	1.2
[UNIJOBS] c. And do you think that students leaving university have better or worse job prospects nowadays than they had 10 years ago? %	3.8	10.7	14.2	41.7	28.1	0.5	1.1

B2.05 Please tick one box to show how much you agree or
disagree that ...

PLEASE TICK ONE BOX
ON EACH LINE

	Strongly agree	Agree	Neither agree nor disagree	Disagree	Strongly disagree	Can't choose	(NA)
[SKILLIMP] a. ... when recruiting school-leavers, employers pay too much attention to practical skills and training, and too little to exam results %	5.2	19.9	24.7	35.4	7.3	6.3	1.1
[EXAMIMP] b. ... when choosing students, universities pay too much attention to exam results, and too little to practical skills and training %	12.6	45.3	20.3	10.9	2.0	8.0	1.0

B2.06 Here are some things that universities might make public, so
that people can see how well they are doing. In your view
how important is it that they should publish details of ...

PLEASE TICK ONE BOX
ON EACH LINE

	Essential	Very important	Fairly important	Not very important	Not at all important	Can't choose	(NA)
[UNIVPUB1] a. ... how many students complete their degree? %	15.0	32.7	30.3	13.4	2.0	4.9	1.6
[UNIVPUB2] b. ... how many students get a first class degree? %	9.1	25.1	36.6	20.7	1.1	5.4	1.9
[UNIVPUB3] c. ... how many students get a job when they finish? %	30.2	45.2	13.1	4.1	1.3	4.6	1.5

273

B2.09 Please tick one box for each of these statements about the European Union (EU) to show how much you agree or disagree.

PLEASE TICK ONE BOX ON EACH LINE

		Strongly agree	Agree	Neither agree nor disagree	Disagree	Strongly disagree	Can't choose	(NA)
	[EECBRIT1]							
a.	If we stay in the European Union, Britain will lose control over decisions that affect Britain	% 13.2	27.6	22.8	21.6	2.0	9.8	3.0
	[EECBRIT2]							
b.	The competition from other EU countries is making Britain more modern and efficient	% 5.9	41.3	25.1	12.8	1.7	10.1	3.1
	[EECBRIT3]							
c.	Lots of good traditions will have to be given up if we stay in the EU	% 7.8	24.1	18.6	31.3	5.9	9.2	3.1

B2.10 Some say that more decisions should be made by the European Union. Others say that more decisions should be made by individual governments. Do you think decisions about taxes should mostly be made by the European Union or mostly by individual governments?

PLEASE TICK ONE BOX ON EACH LINE

		Mostly made by the EU	Mostly made by individual governments	Made by both equally	Can't choose	(NA)
a.	Decisions about taxes?	% 8.0	66.6	14.3	8.0	3.2
	[ECDEC1]					
b.	And what about decisions about controlling pollution?	% 28.4	30.3	30.0	7.4	3.8
	[ECDEC2]					
	[ECDEC3]					
c.	Decisions about defence?	% 13.6	49.3	23.7	9.2	4.2
	[ECDEC4]					
d.	Decisions about the rights of people at work?	% 20.4	43.5	24.9	7.7	3.5
	[ECDEC5]					
e.	Decisions about immigration?	% 17.2	44.3	23.9	10.8	3.8

We would like to ask you about your family and friends. For example, about how often you see or visit them, and when you turn to them for help and advice.

MOTHER

[MUMVISIT2]

B2.11a First, your mother. How often do you see or visit her?

PLEASE TICK ONE BOX ONLY %

She is no longer alive	43.5
She lives in the same household	15.9
Daily	9.0
At least several times a week	9.5
At least once a week	10.6
At least once a fortnight	3.8
At least once a month	1.5
Several times a year	2.3
Less often	1.5
Never	0.3
(NA)	1.9

NOW PLEASE GO TO B2.12a ON PAGE 3

[MUMJURNY]

b. About how long would it take you to get to where your mother lives? Think of the time it usually takes door to door.

PLEASE TICK ONE BOX ONLY %

Less than 15 minutes	19.8
Between 15 and 30 minutes	9.5
Between 30 minutes and 1 hour	3.3
Between 1 and 2 hours	2.1
Between 2 and 3 hours	0.9
Between 3 and 5 hours	1.0
Between 5 and 12 hours	1.0
Over 12 hours	0.7
(NA)	2.2

n = 621

B2.11c *[MUMPHONE]*
How often do you have any contact with your mother by telephone?

PLEASE TICK ONE BOX ONLY

	%
Daily	7.1
At least several times a week	12.9
At least once a week	8.5
At least once a fortnight	1.0
At least once a month	0.7
Several times a year	1.9
Less often	1.2
Never	4.2
(NA)	2.9

d. *[MUMWRITE]*
And how often do you have any contact with your mother by writing?

PLEASE TICK ONE BOX ONLY

	%
Daily	0.2
At least several times a week	-
At least once a week	-
At least once a fortnight	0.2
At least once a month	0.3
Several times a year	2.1
Less often	5.5
Never	29.3
(NA)	2.9

FATHER

B2.12a *[DADVIST2]*
How often do you see or visit your father?

PLEASE TICK ONE BOX ONLY

	%
He is no longer alive	54.5
Lives in same household	13.1
Daily	6.8
At least several times a week	5.5
At least once a week	5.4
At least once a fortnight	3.6
At least once a month	2.0
Several times a year	2.5
Less often	1.8
Never	2.2
(NA)	2.6

b. *[DADJURNY]*
About how long would it take you to get to where your father lives? Think of the time it usually takes door to door.

PLEASE TICK ONE BOX ONLY

	%
Less than 15 minutes	12.8
Between 15 and 30 minutes	7.3
Between 30 minutes and 1 hour	3.3
Between 1 and 2 hours	2.0
Between 2 and 3 hours	0.7
Between 3 and 5 hours	0.7
Between 5 and 12 hours	1.1
Over 12 hours	1.1
(NA)	3.4

NOW PLEASE GO TO B2.13a ON PAGE 5

n = 621

B2.12c *[DADPHONE]*
How often do you have any contact with your father **by telephone**?

PLEASE TICK ONE BOX ONLY

	%
Daily	3.5
At least several times a week	6.3
At least once a week	7.2
At least once a fortnight	2.7
At least once a month	1.5
Several times a year	1.5
Less often	1.0
Never	5.9
(NA)	2.8

d. *[DADWRITE]*
And how often do you have any contact with your father **by writing**?

PLEASE TICK ONE BOX ONLY

	%
Daily	-
At least several times a week	-
At least once a week	-
At least once a fortnight	-
At least once a month	0.5
Several times a year	1.5
Less often	4.3
Never	23.5
(NA)	2.6

BROTHERS AND SISTERS

B2.13a *[SIBLINGS]*
How many brothers and sisters <u>aged 18 or older</u> do you have?
(We mean brothers/sisters who are still alive; please include step-brothers/sisters, half brothers/sisters and adopted brothers/sisters).

PLEASE TICK ONE BOX ONLY

	%	
None	9.4	**NOW PLEASE GO TO B2.14a ON PAGE 11**
One	21.8	
Two	18.0	
Three	16.0	
Four	11.6	
Five or more	21.6	
(DK)	0.9	
(NA)	0.6	

The questions on this, and the next, page are about your brother/sister. If you have more than one adult brother/sister, please think about the one you have <u>most contact</u> with.

b. *[BROSIS]*
Firstly, please tick a box to show whether this person is your <u>brother</u> or your <u>sister</u>.

PLEASE TICK ONE BOX ONLY

	%
Brother	40.0
Sister	47.9
(Brother and sister)	0.7
(NA)	2.0

c. *[SIBVISIT]*
How often do you see or visit this <u>brother/sister</u>?

PLEASE TICK ONE BOX ONLY

	%	
He/she lives in the same household	9.2	**NOW PLEASE GO TO B2.14a ON PAGE 11**
Daily	9.4	
At least several times a week	11.1	
At least once a week	20.8	
At least once a fortnight	8.0	
At least once a month	10.2	
Several times a year	11.6	
Less often	7.1	
Never	1.6	
(NA)	1.5	

B2.13d [SIBJURNY]
About how long would it take you to get to where this brother/sister lives? Think of the time it usually takes door to door.

PLEASE TICK ONE BOX ONLY

	%
Less than 15 minutes	28.5
Between 15 and 30 minutes	18.6
Between 30 minutes and 1 hour	14.2
Between 1 and 2 hours	5.8
Between 2 and 3 hours	2.8
Between 3 and 5 hours	2.8
Between 5 and 12 hours	2.3
Over 12 hours	3.7
(NA)	2.9

e. [SIBPHONE]
How often do you have any contact with this brother/sister by telephone?

PLEASE TICK ONE BOX ONLY

	%
Daily	4.5
At least several times a week	13.0
At least once a week	22.0
At least once a fortnight	10.9
At least once a month	8.0
Several times a year	10.0
Less often	4.3
Never	5.8

f. [SIBWRITE]
And how often do you have any contact with this brother/sister by writing?

PLEASE TICK ONE BOX ONLY

	%
Daily	0.1
At least several times a week	0.9
At least once a week	0.3
At least once a fortnight	0.2
At least once a month	0.6
Several times a year	8.0
Less often	11.4
Never	56.4
(NA)	3.4

SONS AND DAUGHTERS

B2.14a [CHILDREN]
How many sons and daughters aged 18 or older do you have? (We mean sons/daughters who are still alive; please include step-sons/daughters and adopted sons/daughters).

PLEASE TICK ONE BOX ONLY

	%
None	53.7
One	9.3
Two	12.9
Three	9.8
Four	7.0
Five or more	6.0
(NA)	1.3

NOW PLEASE GO TO B2.15e ON PAGE 13

The questions on this, and the next, page are about your son/daughter. If you have more than one adult son/daughter, please think about the one you have most contact with.

b. [CHDSEX]
Firstly, please tick a box to show whether this person is your son or your daughter.

PLEASE TICK ONE BOX ONLY

	%
Son	19.6
Daughter	22.5
(Son and daughter)	1.2
(NA)	2.9

c. [CHDVISIT]
How often do you see or visit this son/daughter?

PLEASE TICK ONE BOX ONLY

	%
He/she lives in the same household	21.0
Daily	5.4
At least several times a week	5.7
At least once a week	5.2
At least once a fortnight	1.6
At least once a month	1.1
Several times a year	2.9
Less often	0.5
Never	0.2
(NA)	2.7

NOW PLEASE GO TO B2.15a ON PAGE 13

B-12

[CHDJURNY]

B2.14d About how long would it take you to get where your son/daughter lives? Think of the time it usually takes door to door.

PLEASE TICK ONE BOX ONLY

	%
Less than 15 minutes	8.7
Between 15 and 30 minutes	5.8
Between 30 minutes and 1 hour	1.7
Between 1 and 2 hours	1.5
Between 2 and 3 hours	0.4
Between 3 and 5 hours	1.2
Between 5 and 12 hours	1.6
Over 12 hours	0.6
(NA)	3.7

[CHDPHONE]

e. How often do you have any contact with this son/daughter by telephone?

PLEASE TICK ONE BOX ONLY

	%
Daily	5.0
At least several times a week	7.2
At least once a week	5.0
At least once a fortnight	1.2
At least once a month	0.7
Several times a year	0.7
Less often	0.4
Never	1.2
(NA)	3.8

[CHDWRITE]

f. And how often do you have any contact with this son/daughter by writing?

PLEASE TICK ONE BOX ONLY

	%
Daily	0.4
At least several times a week	0.1
At least once a week	0.1
At least once a fortnight	0.3
At least once a month	0.9
Several times a year	2.8
Less often	2.8
Never	13.6
(NA)	4.3

n = 621

B-13

OTHER RELATIVES

[GRANDPTS]

B2.15a Now think of all your other adult relatives - those still living and aged 18 or older. How many of each do you have?

(Begin with your grandparents. Please write in a number to show how many grandparents you have.

If you have none, tick 'NONE', and then go on to the next relative.)

	Median NUMBER	OR	NONE %
Grandmother, grandfather	0	OR	66.3
Adult grandchildren	0	OR	71.8
Aunts, uncles	5	OR	16.0
Parents-in-law and adult brothers-in-law and sisters-in-law	4	OR	19.8
Adult nieces, nephews, cousins and other relatives (AN APPROXIMATE NUMBER WILL DO)	14	OR	6.2

[MOSTCNTC]

b. Thinking of all these adult relatives, which one do you have most contact with?

PLEASE TICK ONE BOX ONLY

	%
Grandmother	6.8
Grandfather	0.7
(Grandmother and Grandfather)	0.6
Granddaughter	3.0
Grandson	1.5
(Granddaughter and Grandson)	0.3
Aunt	13.9
Uncle	4.2
(Aunt and Uncle)	0.7
Mother-in-law	16.4
Father-in-law	3.0
Sister-in-law	16.4
Brother-in-law	10.4
(Sister-in-law and brother-in-law)	0.5
Other adult female relative	8.1
Other adult male relative	2.4
(Other male and female relative)	0.1
None of these	5.0
(No adult relative)	1.3
(NA)	5.0

n = 621

The questions on this page are about the adult relative you have just ticked, that is, the one you have most contact with.

n = 621

[RTVVISIT]
B2.15c How often do you see or visit this relative?

PLEASE TICK ONE BOX ONLY % **NOW PLEASE GO TO B2.16a ON PAGE 16**

	%
He/she lives in the same household	2.8
Daily	8.0
At least several times a week	17.6
At least once a week	24.7
At least once a fortnight	10.4
At least once a month	10.3
Several times a year	10.1
Less often	3.3
Never	0.6
(No adult relative)	1.3
(Do not contact any adult relatives)	5.0
(NA)	5.9

[RTVJURNY]
d. About how long would it take you to get to where this relative lives? Think of the time it usually takes door to door.

PLEASE TICK ONE BOX ONLY %

	%
Less than 15 minutes	39.9
Between 15 and 30 minutes	19.6
Between 30 minutes and 1 hour	13.5
Between 1 and 2 hours	5.1
Between 2 and 3 hours	3.1
Between 3 and 5 hours	1.7
Between 5 and 12 hours	1.0
Over 12 hours	1.1
(No adult relative)	1.3
(Do not contact any adult relative)	5.0
(NA)	5.9

n = 621

[RTVPHONE]
B2.15e How often do you have any contact with this relative by telephone?

PLEASE TICK ONE BOX ONLY %

	%
Daily	5.2
At least several times a week	12.7
At least once a week	19.7
At least once a fortnight	12.4
At least once a month	9.5
Several times a year	9.0
Less often	5.7
Never	10.7
(No adult relative)	1.3
(Do no contact anay adult relative)	5.0
(NA)	5.9

[RTVWRITE]
f. And how often do you have any contact with this relative by writing?

PLEASE TICK ONE BOX ONLY %

	%
Daily	-
At least several times a week	-
At least once a week	-
At least once a fortnight	0.2
At least once a month	0.2
Several times a year	6.0
Less often	10.6
Never	-
(No adult relative)	1.3
(Do not contact any adult relative)	5.0
(DK)	68.0
(NA)	5.9

| | | n = 621 |

FRIENDS

Thinking now of close friends - not your husband or wife or partner or family members - but people you feel fairly close to.

[PALS]
B2.16a How many close friends would you say you have?

NONE	11.9%	**NOW PLEASE GO TO B2.17 ON PAGE 18**
Median (including 0):	**4**	
(NA)	1.2%	

[SEXPAL]
b. Now thinking of your best friend, or the friend you feel closest to. Is this friend a man or a woman?

		%
PLEASE TICK **ONE**	Man	33.0
BOX ONLY	Woman	52.2
	(Man and woman)	0.9
	(NA)	2.0

[PALVISIT]
c. How often do you see or visit this friend?

		%	
PLEASE TICK **ONE**	He/she lives in the same household	2.2	**NOW PLEASE GO TO B2.17 ON PAGE 18**
BOX ONLY	Daily	13.4	
	At least several times a week	20.7	
	At least once a week	24.4	
	At least once a fortnight	10.1	
	At least once a month	8.2	
	Several times a year	5.5	
	Less often	1.9	
	Never	0.3	
	(NA)	1.5	

[PALJURNY]
d. About how long would it take you to get to where your friend lives? Think of the time it *usually* takes door to door.

		%
PLEASE TICK **ONE**	Less than 15 minutes	42.6
BOX ONLY	Between 15 and 30 minutes	22.5
	Between 30 minutes and 1 hour	12.6
	Between 1 and 2 hours	3.1
	Between 2 and 3 hours	1.1
	Between 3 and 5 hours	1.5
	Between 5 and 12 hours	0.7
	Over 12 hours	0.5
	(NA)	1.5

| | | n = 621 |

[PALPHONE]
B2.16e How often do you have any contact with this friend by telephone?

		%
PLEASE TICK **ONE** BOX ONLY	Daily	4.9
	At least several times a week	15.9
	At least once a week	25.7
	At least once a fortnight	9.5
	At least once a month	9.1
	Several times a year	6.6
	Less often	2.7
	Never	9.6
	(NA)	1.9

[PALWRITE]
f. And how often do you have any contact with this friend by writing?

		%
PLEASE TICK **ONE** BOX ONLY	Daily	-
	At least several times a week	0.1
	At least once a week	0.2
	At least once a fortnight	0.7
	At least once a month	1.2
	Several times a year	8.5
	Less often	9.9
	Never	63.4
	(NA)	1.9

B2.17 Now we'd like to ask you about some problems that can happen to anyone.
First, there are some household and garden jobs you may really can't do alone - for example, you may need someone to hold a ladder, or to help you move some furniture.

a. Who would you turn to first for help?

b. And who would you turn to second?
PLEASE TICK ONLY ONE AS YOUR FIRST CHOICE AND ONE AS YOUR SECOND CHOICE

n = 621

	[HELPJOB1] a. FIRST CHOICE %	[HELPJOB2] b. SECOND CHOICE %
Husband/wife/partner	53.5	3.3
Mother	4.6	6.4
Father	7.6	7.4
(Mother and Father)	0.2	0.3
Daughter	2.8	8.5
Son	8.9	17.8
Sister	2.7	4.6
Brother	5.3	9.0
(Sister and Brother)	0.3	-
Other relative, including in-laws	1.8	9.1
Closest friend	3.1	7.1
Other friend	0.2	5.0
Neighbour	3.7	11.0
Someone you work with	0.2	0.6
Social service, or home help	0.2	0.9
Someone you pay to help	1.5	3.1
(Other)	0.2	-
No-one	1.2	2.1
(NA)	2.0	3.7

BEFORE GOING ON TO THE NEXT QUESTION, PLEASE CHECK TO SEE THAT YOU HAVE ONLY TICKED ONE FIRST CHOICE AND ONE SECOND CHOICE

B2.18 Suppose you had an illness and had to stay in bed for several weeks, and needed help around the home with shopping and so on?

a. Who would you turn to first for help?

b. And who would you turn to second?
PLEASE TICK ONLY ONE AS YOUR FIRST CHOICE AND ONE AS YOUR SECOND CHOICE

n = 621

	[HELPBED1] a. FIRST CHOICE %	[HELPBED2] b. SECOND CHOICE %
Husband/wife/partner	53.9	3.9
Mother	16.1	12.0
Father	0.6	9.0
(Mother and Father)	0.3	0.3
Daughter	9.4	17.4
Son	3.3	11.1
Sister	5.5	10.2
Brother	0.8	3.3
(Sister and Brother)	0.3	-
Other relative, including in-laws	1.6	10.5
Closest friend	2.7	6.5
Other friend	0.3	2.0
Neighbour	1.1	5.3
Someone you work with	0.1	0.2
Health visitor	0.2	0.3
Church, clergy or priest	-	0.7
Someone you pay to help	0.7	1.7
(Other)	0.4	0.7
No-one	0.9	1.5
(NA)	1.7	3.5

BEFORE GOING ON TO THE NEXT QUESTION, PLEASE CHECK TO SEE THAT YOU HAVE ONLY TICKED ONE FIRST CHOICE AND ONE SECOND CHOICE

n = 621

B2.19 Suppose you needed to borrow a large sum of money.

a. Who would you turn to first for help?

b. And who would you turn to second?
PLEASE TICK ONLY ONE AS YOUR FIRST CHOICE AND ONE AS YOUR SECOND CHOICE

	[HELPMNY1] a. FIRST CHOICE %	[HELPMNY2] b. SECOND CHOICE %
Husband/wife/partner	20.1	3.4
Mother	9.4	7.8
Father	10.9	8.0
(Mother and Father)	0.1	0.2
Daughter	3.4	5.5
Son	3.3	5.1
Sister	2.8	6.3
Brother	3.1	7.1
Other relative, including in-laws	2.9	10.7
Closest friend	0.8	3.7
Other friend	0.1	0.4
Neighbour	0.1	0.2
Someone you work with	-	1.0
Bank, Building Society or other financial institution	31.0	15.1
Employer	-	2.4
Government or social services	1.6	4.2
(Other)	0.3	0.2
No-one	7.0	14.1
(DK)	0.2	0.2
(NA)	2.9	4.5

BEFORE GOING ON TO THE NEXT QUESTION, PLEASE CHECK TO SEE THAT YOU HAVE ONLY TICKED ONE FIRST CHOICE AND ONE SECOND CHOICE

n = 621

B2.20 Suppose you were very upset about a problem with your husband, wife or partner, and haven't been able to sort it out with them. Even if you are not married or have no partner, what would you do if you were?

a. Who would you turn to first for help?

b. And who would you turn to second?
PLEASE TICK ONLY ONE AS YOUR FIRST CHOICE AND ONE AS YOUR SECOND CHOICE

	[HELPPRB1] a. FIRST CHOICE %	[HELPPRB2] b. SECOND CHOICE %
Husband/wife/partner	10.3	0.4
Mother	15.1	6.1
Father	1.6	2.3
(Mother and Father)	0.5	-
Daughter	9.8	5.5
Son	3.7	6.0
Sister	10.8	9.4
Brother	4.1	5.7
Other relative, including in-laws	2.5	8.7
Closest friend	18.6	17.8
Other friend	1.2	6.4
Neighbour	0.5	1.5
Someone you work with	1.0	2.2
Church, clergy or priest	6.5	7.1
Family doctor (GP)	2.6	4.3
Psychologist, psychiatrist, marriage guidance or other professional counsellor	1.5	2.8
(Other)	0.2	0.1
No-one	7.4	10.2
(DK)	0.2	0.4
(NA)	1.8	3.2

BEFORE GOING ON TO THE NEXT QUESTION, PLEASE CHECK TO SEE THAT YOU HAVE ONLY TICKED ONE FIRST CHOICE AND ONE SECOND CHOICE

B2.21 Now suppose you felt just a bit down or depressed, and you wanted to talk about it.

a. Who would you turn to first for help?

b. And who would you turn to second?

PLEASE TICK ONLY ONE AS YOUR FIRST CHOICE AND ONE AS YOUR SECOND CHOICE

n = 621

	[HELPDPR1] a. FIRST CHOICE %	[HELPDPR2] b. SECOND CHOICE %
Husband/wife/partner	47.8	4.2
Mother	5.8	11.4
Father	0.4	2.8
(Mother and Father)	0.1	0.2
Daughter	5.1	9.1
Son	1.8	5.2
Sister	6.3	10.4
Brother	2.2	4.5
Other relative, including in-laws	0.7	3.7
Closest friend	16.9	18.5
Other friend	0.3	5.8
Neighbour	0.7	1.6
Someone you work with	0.1	1.8
Church, clergy or priest	1.7	5.2
Family doctor (GP)	5.0	6.6
Psychologist, psychiatrist, marriage guidance or other professional counsellor	0.5	1.5
(Other)	0.2	-
No-one	2.5	4.6
(NA)	1.7	2.9

BEFORE GOING ON TO THE NEXT QUESTION, PLEASE CHECK TO SEE THAT YOU HAVE ONLY TICKED ONE FIRST CHOICE AND ONE SECOND CHOICE

n = 621

[PROVCARE]
And now some questions about things you may have done for other people.

B2.22a Firstly, in the past five years have you yourself provided regular help or care for an adult relative, friend, neighbour or colleague because of pregnancy, an illness, disability or other problem?

PLEASE TICK ONE BOX ONLY

	%	
Yes	47.9	→ ANSWER b.
No	50.3	→ NOW PLEASE GO TO B2.23
(NA)	1.8	

b. [CAREWHO]
Please tick a box to show who you provided with regular care because of pregnancy, an illness, disability or other problem.
If you have provided regular help or care more than once, please tell us about the most recent time.

PLEASE TICK ONE BOX ONLY

	%		%
Husband/wife/partner	9.8	Grandmother	0.8
Mother	9.3	Grandfather	0.6
Father	4.2	Grandmother-in-law	0.2
(Mother and Father)	0.2	Grandfather-in-law	-
Mother-in-law	2.8	Aunt	0.8
Father-in-law	0.9	Uncle	1.1
Daughter	2.4	Other female relative	0.2
Son	1.1	Other male relative	0.6
Daughter-in-law	0.2	Closest friend	2.0
Son-in-law	-	Other friend	1.6
Sister	3.3	Neighbour	2.0
Brother	0.5	Someone you work with	0.9
Sister-in-law	1.6	Other person	0.1
Brother-in-law	0.6	(NA)	2.1

n = 621

[RECCARE]

B2.23a And in the past five years have you received regular help or care from an adult relative, friend, neighbour or colleague because of pregnancy, an illness, disability or other problem?

*PLEASE TICK **ONE** BOX ONLY*

	%	
Yes	24.3	→ **ANSWER b.**
No	72.7	→ **NOW PLEASE GO TO B2.24**
(NA)	2.9	

[CAREFRM]

b. Please tick a box to show from whom you received regular care because of pregnancy, an illness, disability or other problem.
If you have received regular help or care more than once, please tell us about the most recent time.

*PLEASE TICK **ONE** BOX ONLY*

	%		%
Husband/wife/partner	10.5	Grandmother	-
Mother	4.7	Grandfather	-
Father	0.3	Grandmother-in-law	-
(Mother and Father)	0.1	Grandfather-in-law	-
Mother-in-law	0.5	Aunt	-
Father-in-law	-	Uncle	-
Daughter	3.2	Other female relative	0.4
Son	0.2	Other male relative	-
Daughter-in-law	0.1	Closest friend	0.5
Son-in-law	0.1	Other friend	-
Sister	2.3	Neighbour	0.5
Brother	0.2	Someone you work with	-
Sister-in-law	0.3	Other person	0.4
Brother-in-law	-	(NA)	2.9

n = 621

[LENDMONY]

B2.24a Have you in the past five years helped out an adult relative, friend, neighbour or colleague with a loan or gift of money of £100 or more, to help with some special emergency or problem?

*PLEASE TICK **ONE** BOX ONLY*

	%	
Yes	28.6	→ **ANSWER b.**
No	69.4	→ **NOW PLEASE GO TO B2.25**
(NA)	2.0	

[MONEYWHO]

b. Please tick a box to show who you helped out with a loan or gift of money of £100 or more, for some special emergency or problem.
If you have helped out someone more than once, please tell us about the most recent time.

*PLEASE TICK **ONE** BOX ONLY*

	%		%
Husband/wife/partner	1.4	Grandmother	-
Mother	2.5	Grandfather	-
Father	0.4	Grandmother-in-law	-
Mother-in-law	0.8	Grandfather-in-law	-
Father-in-law	0.2	Aunt	0.2
Daughter	4.5	Uncle	-
Son	5.2	Other female relative	0.7
(Daughter and Son)	0.2	Other male relative	0.9
Daughter-in-law	-	Closest friend	1.3
Son-in-law	0.4	Other friend	1.8
Sister	2.5	Neighbour	0.5
Brother	2.4	Someone you work with	0.7
Sister-in-law	0.7	Other person	-
Brother-in-law	1.2	(NA)	2.0

[n = 621]

B2.25a *[BORWMONY]*
And in the past five years have you personally received a loan or gift of money of £100 or more from an adult relative, friend, neighbour or colleague to help with some special emergency or problem?
PLEASE DO NOT INCLUDE MONEY LEFT TO YOU IN A WILL

%

Yes   22.1 → **ANSWER b.**

No   76.4 → **NOW PLEASE GO TO B2.26**

(NA)   1.5

b. *[MONEYFRM]*
Please tick a box to show from whom you received a loan or gift of money of £100 or more, for some special emergency or problem.
If you have received such a loan or gift more than once, please tell us about the most recent time.

PLEASE TICK ONE BOX ONLY

%

Husband/wife/partner	1.7
Mother	5.5
Father	4.7
Mother-in-law	0.7
Father-in-law	1.3
Daughter	0.5
Son	1.0
Grandmother	1.1
Grandfather	0.1
Grandmother-in-law	0.2
Grandfather-in-law	-
Aunt	0.7
Uncle	-
Other female relative	-
Other male relative	0.1
Closest friend	0.5
Other friend	0.7
Neighbour	0.1
Someone you work with	0.1
Other person	0.2
(NA)	1.5

B2.26 How much do you agree or disagree with each of these statements?
PLEASE TICK ONE BOX ON EACH LINE

		Strongly agree	Agree	Neither agree nor disagree	Disagree	Strongly disagree	Can't choose	(NA)
a.	*[INTOUCH1]* People should keep in touch with relatives like aunts, uncles and cousins even if they don't have much in common	18.2	50.0	21.4	7.6	0.6	0.5	1.6
b.	*[KIDSGO]* Once children have left home, they should no longer expect help from their parents	3.7	11.5	11.4	51.9	17.7	1.5	2.4
c.	*[FAMHELP]* People should always turn to their family before asking the state for help	10.9	40.5	17.2	20.9	5.0	2.8	2.7
d.	*[FRIENDS1]* On the whole, my friends are more important to me than members of my family	2.4	3.3	10.7	52.2	28.2	0.7	2.4
e.	*[INTOUCH2]* People should keep in touch with close family members even if they don't have much in common	15.5	63.1	13.0	5.5	0.2	0.8	1.9
f.	*[BLAMEFAM]* People are too quick to blame the family for social problems	9.7	39.4	25.5	17.3	2.8	2.2	3.0
g.	*[ALLRELAT]* I try to stay in touch with all my relatives, not just my close family	8.1	45.6	20.5	20.6	2.0	1.8	1.5
h.	*[FRIENDS2]* I'd rather spend time with my friends than with my family	3.2	7.6	17.8	47.8	19.4	2.4	1.9

The % symbol appears at the start of rows a, b, c, d, e, f, g, h.

B2.27 *[IMISSMOST]*
Apart from people who live in your household, who would you miss most if you could no longer have any contact?
PLEASE TICK ONE BOX ONLY

%

A family member not living in my household	62.4
A member of my spouse/partner's family not living in my household	4.6
A childhood friend	5.5
Another friend	10.2
Someone else	1.5
Can't choose	14.2
(NA)	1.7

Note: questions B2.28 - B.37 are the same as questions A2.42 - A2.51 of Version A of this questionnaire.

B-28

[Q7TIME]
B2.38a. To help us plan better in future, please tell us about
how long it took you to complete this questionnaire.
PLEASE TICK ONE BOX ONLY

%

Less than 15 minutes   6.6

Between 15 and 20 minutes   25.5

Between 21 and 30 minutes   33.8

Between 31 and 45 minutes   21.6

Between 46 and 60 minutes   7.7

Over one hour   3.5

(NA)   1.3

b.   And on what date did you fill in the questionnaire?

PLEASE WRITE IN:

				O		1995

DATE   MONTH

Thank you very much for your help

Subject Index

Queen's University, Belfast, 115

reform measures, 4–6
religious divisions, 48–9
religious integration, 119–22
Republic of Ireland
  birth rate, 194
  domestic division of labour, 187–90
  gender roles, 177–82
  labour market, 176–7
  marriage and children, 190–8
  NI trust in, 130–1
  role of Irish government, 52–3
  women and work, 175–6, 182–7
Republican Labour Party, 164
'Roads to Prosperity' (White Paper), 138
Robinson, Mary, 199
role reversal, 181–2
Royal Ulster Constabulary (RUC)
  community perceptions of, 117–19
  drug seizures, 70

school children
  illicit drug use, 71–3
school leavers, 9–10
school performance, 11–12
schools information, 5–6
Scotland, 159
Scottish Highers, 8
secondary schools, 2–12, 5–6, 9
sectarianism, 153–4
  young people, 48
selective schools, 1
self-employment, 162
share ownership, 160, 162
Singapore, 199
single parent benefits, 27–30, 43
  evaluation of, 31–4
single-sex schools, 1
Sinn Fein
  child benefit, 40
  economic beliefs, 165, 168
  health spending, 26–7
  social benefits, 23–4, 28, 45

support for, 57, 124, 129
social class, 102–34
  Catholic middle class, 102–3
  class consciousness, 110–15
  class profiles, 106–10
  community relations, 115–22
  and economic beliefs, 159–64
  ideology scores, 112–13
  loyalist working class, 103, 104
  politics, 122–31
Social Democratic and Labour Party (SDLP)
  child benefit, 40
  economic beliefs, 164, 168
  health spending, 26–7
  social benefits, 23–4, 28, 45
  support for, 57, 124, 156
social support
  family and friends, 91–4
social system
  evaluating benefits and beneficiaries, 30–4
social welfare. *see* welfare system
  welfare dependency, 34–7
socialism, 164
Speed, 71, 72
spending priorities, 2–3
spouse, role of, 93–4
student loans, 16–17
support networks, 87–100

taxation
  and social benefits, 21–4, 29–30, 44–5
  and transport, 141–2
teachers, 5, 6, 10
teaching standards, 9–10
tests, 6
Thatcher, Margaret, 160
trade unions, 162
transport, 138–49
  future use of car, 145–9
  gap between attitudes and behaviour, 149
  government policy, 138–9
  improving public transport, 142–4
  pedestrians and cyclists, 144
  protecting environment, 139–42, 148–9

Ulster Democratic Party (UDP), 103
'Ulster' identity, 127
Ulster Unionist Party
    child benefit, 40
    cross-class support, 124
    economic beliefs, 164, 165, 168
    health spending, 27
    support for, 48, 55–6
    welfare dependency, 35
    welfare system, 24, 45
unemployment, 21, 43–4
    percentages, 108–9
unemployment benefits, 27–30
    evaluation of, 31
    welfare dependency, 35–6
unionism, 49–50
United States of America, 98, 155, 190
    social relationships, 87–8
universities. *see* higher education

value systems, 175–6
Vanguard, 164
VAT, 44
vocational education, 8–9
voting, decline in, 64–5

Wales, 159
'Way Forward, The', 139
welfare system, 20–45
    scope of, 37–43, 43
    social benefits, 27–30

spending on, 21–4
spending priorities, 24–7
women
    class profiles, 107–9
    domestic division of labour, 187–90
    family life cycle, 182–7
    gender roles, 177–82
    marriage and children, 190–8
    moderate mindset model, 64
    and nationalism, 133
    part-time work, 177, 184–5, 189–90, 198–9
    politics, 124, 133–4
    religious integration, 122
    work and family life, 175–200
Women's Coalition, 105
working class, 132
    Catholic percentage, 108
    Protestant percentage, 108

young people
    apathy, 60
    cluster analysis, 58–9
    community relations, 47–66
    constitutional preferences, 50–3
    electoral behaviour, 64–5
    identity of, 49–53
    illicit drug use, 72, 83
    moderate mindset model, 61–4
    moderation of, 57–9
    perceptions of prejudice, 53–5, 58
    politics, 55–7, 60–1